PITT SERIES IN
POLICY AND
INSTITUTIONAL
STUDIES

National Elections

AND THE

AUTONOMY OF

AMERICAN STATE

PARTY SYSTEMS

James Gimpel

UNIVERSITY OF PITTSBURGH PRESS

Published by the University of Pittsburgh Press, Pittsburgh, Pa., 15260
Copyright © 1996, University of Pittsburgh Press
Manufactured in the United States of America
Printed on acid-free paper

LIBRARY OF CONGRESS CATALOGING-IN-PUBLICATION DATA

Gimpel, James G.
    National elections and the autonomy of the American state party
  systems / James Gimpel.
        p.   .cm. — (Pitt series in policy and institutional studies)
    Includes bibliographical references and index.
    ISBN 0-8229-3940-1 (cloth : alk. paperp). — ISBN 0-8229-5597-0
  (pbk. : alk. paper)
      1. Political parties—United States—States.   2. State
  governments—United States.   I. Title.   II. Series.
JK2261.G56   1996
324.273—dc20   95-53044
                                                                           CIP

A CIP catalogue record for this book is available from the British Library.
Eurospan, London

For Veronica

Contents

Preface

This book seeks to understand political behavior in important region of the country that has often been overlooked in the literature on state politics. At one time, the far western states could be considered a politically unimportant stepchild of the East and South, a trend follower with little to add to our understanding of American politics. Now, it is possible to consider the West a trend leader. Other parts of the country have found their populations moving to this once peripheral region. In the wake of this migration, older, more established states have found themselves looking westward in an effort to understand the future. To paraphrase Idaho Democrat Larry Echohawk, the nation's first American Indian attorney general, the West "is what the rest of America wants to be." My argument here is that the West is the pattern for understanding what the rest of America is becoming.

I owe my interest in this region to my upbringing on the Great Plains, more West than Midwest. As a child, I remember, on every family vacation we traveled westward, often to Wyoming, Colorado, New Mexico, Arizona, and California. My mother, who grew up in California and Oregon, told wonderfully interesting stories about midcentury life in the West. This westward orientation was apparently shared by others I grew up with. Of the one hundred students in my high school graduating class, seventy-five of them migrated to the West. This westward orientation was so imprinted in my consciousness I had a difficult time imagining the East. It seemed distant, foreign, and inaccessible. Ironically, I have found myself living a short distance from the Atlantic Ocean for some time. But to this day, an unnatural feeling comes over me when I'm traveling in an eastbound direction on a highway.

My interest in state politics was first sparked by my reading of Sarah McCally Morehouse's state politics textbook as a second-year undergraduate. Morehouse raised many of the questions I address and introduced me to the works of V. O. Key.

As my familiarity with the West and my curiosity about state politics mingled, Mark Hansen, my graduate school mentor, made me realize that the western states and their politics can be best understood in contrast to their more established, eastern counterparts. In a field dominated by some landmark North-South contrasts, it is uncommon to find many East-West contrasts. But my goal here is not to establish some new paradigm. As odd as it may sound to say this about a work in political science, my principal aim has been to gain a little self-understanding.

Along the way, I have sought the guidance of Mark Hansen more than any other person. I am very privileged to have studied under him at the University of Chicago. Others who gave generously of their time to make this a better book include Henry Brady, the late J. David Greenstone, Gary Orfield, Eric Uslaner, Paul Herrnson, Frank Sorauf, Mark Graber, Robin M. Wolpert, Patricia Conley, and Robert Eisinger. I also acknowledge the contributions made by Darrell M. West and the other anonymous reviewers who read the manuscript.

The chairman of my department, Jon Wilkenfeld, provided two summers of indispensable financial support. In later stages of the project, I received encouragement, assistance, and advice from many established scholars, including Thad Brown, Mark Westlye, Richard Winters, Paul Brace, Maureen Moakley, Jeffrey Stonecash, Merle Black, Mark Peffley, Helen Ingram, John Bibby, John Francis, Peter Galderisi, Robert Stein, David Berman, Gilbert St. Clair, F. Chris Garcia, Florence Heffron, Thad Beyle, and Clyde Wilcox. Two undergraduate mentors, William Collins and Francis Wilhoit, have cheered me on as I have tried to follow in their footsteps.

Steve Boyenger, David Cantor, Kathryn Doherty, and Michael Wright labored diligently as my research assistants. Cantor and Boyenger, in particular, read the project in its entirety and helped smooth out the prose. Holly Harle and Mike Boisvenue, two Capitol Hill friends, kindly provided research assistance before and after I left the U.S. Senate. Marie Gates and Chris Nagel helped me to locate, order, and prepare the polls I use in the analysis. Jane Flanders, Peter Oresick, Kathy McLaughlin, and the editorial staff at the University of Pittsburgh Press patiently coached me through the crucial final stages of the publication process.

I owe sincere thanks to the politicians and their aides, both active and retired, who were able to bear with my sometimes naive questions and return rich and interesting accounts of developments in their states' politics: John Miller (Wash.), Sid Morrison (Wash.), Gretchen White (Wash.), Mark O. Hatfield (Oreg.), David Henderson (Oreg.), Alan Cranston (Calif.), Vic Fazio (Calif.), Richard Stallings (Idaho), Bob Stump (Ariz.), Lisa Jackson (Ariz.),

Steve Schiff (N.M.), Joe Skeen (N.M.), Suzanne Eisold (N.M.), John LaFalce (N.Y.), Sherwood Boehlert (N.Y.), Ray McGrath (N.Y.), George Hochbrueckner (N.Y.), William Hughes (N.J.), Bob Borski (Pa.), Bob Walker (Pa.), Louis Stokes (Ohio) and Howard Metzenbaum (Ohio).

While this long list of intellectual creditors greatly advanced my work, that does not mean they agree with what I have said or even liked what they read of the manuscript. More than a few pointed out flaws and mistakes that have since been corrected. Errors that remain, of course, are my own.

Finally, and most important, there are the special and emotional thanks I owe to the precious people in my life who stand outside the academic and political circles in which I professionally travel. Many personal friends and family members hoped and prayed this book would come to completion. God graciously listened. Veronica, your unconditional support has meant everything. Because you stand so far out front, this book is dedicated to you.

PART I

Introduction

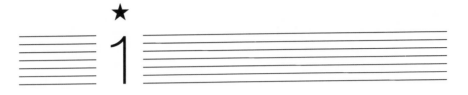

National Elections
and the Autonomy of
American State Party Systems

The Possibility of an Autonomous State Politics

IN THE American federal system, must state party systems exist as shadows of their national counterpart or can state systems operate and survive as distinct and autonomous political entities? If state parties are distinct, their uniqueness lies in the local conditions that shape electoral alignment and movement. State history is not merely a carbon copy of national history, nor are state elections simply second-rate versions of national elections.[1] In what follows, I show that it is difficult, but possible, to maintain a state politics organized differently from national politics. Major upheavals in the two-party balance of presidential voting may leave lower offices untouched. At certain times and places state parties even shift opposite of the national tide.

My argument proceeds in two steps. I begin by studying electoral behavior in state politics. In a representative democracy, government is thought to be responsive to electoral interests. The federal structure of our government leaves open the possibility that the distribution of these interests in statewide elections could differ from their distribution in national elections. So the first step is to understand the association of state and national party electorates. While the issues of national politics may drive basic cleavages through state electorates, there are times and places where there have not been complete alignment. The second step is to evaluate the implications of the alignment, or lack of it, for state politics. Here the task is to explore how differences between state and national politics exert influence on the political behavior of voters, candidates, and state party organizations.

Autonomous state party systems are those where the local party coalitions are consistently different from national party coalitions. An important recent work by Robert Erikson, Gerald C. Wright, and John P. McIver has clearly shown that the national party labels do a poor job explaining local gubernatorial and U.S. Senate election outcomes.[2] It is appropriate to wonder why this is so. Perhaps state party alignments have formed around local issues independent of national party positions. Alternatively, many voting blocs comprising the national party constituency are simply absent in a particular state. For some reason, the local constituency of the party differs from that party's national constituency, undermining our capacity to explain local politics in national terms.

This independence of state from national politics affects the cohesion of the party system because it weakens linkages between officeholders, candidates, and party organizations. A local candidate, possessing a coalition quite unlike the national party, will have different priorities from a presidential contestant. In this manner, the independent movements of state and national politics stand as an obstacle to the cooperation of candidates and officeholders at different levels of the federal system.[3] When candidates do not cooperate, party-building efforts are inhibited.

What I am describing as disruptive of party organization can be captured by the term *electoral incongruence,* meaning that local electoral coalitions are constituted differently from national coalitions. Nineteenth-century party systems provide ample evidence of the presence of an incongruent state politics in many areas of the country. Voting allegiances emanated from local orientations rather than from the rhetoric of national political leaders.[4] In the West, states entering late into the Union, some as late as 1912, missed the polarization of North and South. The issues of the slavery party system failed to cue voting in these areas because party loyalties emerged out of the local conflicts of territorial governance.[5] Thus, state party systems may be electorally incongruent because local conditions create party constituencies that are imperfectly reflective of national coalitions.

A more contemporary cause of electoral incongruence is the shift of presidential politics away from state politics. The surge of conservative presidential Republicanism beginning in the early 1980s posed a threat and a challenge to liberal Republican leaders in eastern states. Divisions arose within the local Republican parties of New York, Massachusetts, and other places that had previously been dominated by liberals.[6] Conservatives were on the march and primaries that were once controlled or controllable burst open with right wing forces capturing nominations against the standing liberal order. Usually, these conservative candidates did not compete nearly as well locally as they did in the most prominent national races. Where they did win, their victories were often only temporary. State politics, in the Northeast, resisted the national tide and was dragged along very reluctantly.

Still, over time, it is possible to observe regions and states where national and local politics are congruent. In these areas, national and local alignments neatly match, and state-level voting behavior is influenced mostly by issues of national importance. The state electorate and national electorate of a given party consist of the same people. State elites take positions very much like their national counterparts. Much of the campaign battle in presidential years is waged by the national party and the presidential candidates. The same electoral coalition groups voting for the presidential candidates can be expected to show up and vote for the gubernatorial, House, and Senate candidates. Partisan attachments in the electorate are predictable and voters generally lean toward one of the two major parties.

The relative congruence of state with national politics is an important foundation for cohesive party organizations, that is, those organizations where there are few factional divisions and candidates find it easy to work together. There are, to be sure, prerequisites for vigorous political party organizations other than the absence of factionalism: control over nominations, patronage, hierarchical structure, autonomy, and institutionalization. However, if party unity is also fundamental, the congruence of state and national coalitions should not be ignored. This logic is straightforward: party regulars can organize states at lower cost when voter alignments exhibit consistency. In this sense, the reliability of the electorate releases party elites from the chore of having to mobilize a full majority of the voters in every campaign.[7] State party elites in congruent states can "piggyback" their mobilization efforts on the national parties. Unsavory national-level candidates need not be differentiated from the more attractive local-level candidates. The congruence of electoral alignments allows local party officials to nominate candidates who think and act like their national counterparts. In addition, when electoral coalitions are congruent, there are few alternatives to existing partisan groupings. Nothing ensures the capacity to control nominations like the absence of alternative electoral coalitions upon which to base a primary challenge.[8]

When state political alignments are sufficiently different from national ones, party elites cannot assume that identifiable social groups will behave so predictably on election day. In an electorally incongruent state, individual candidates must concern themselves with finding, then mobilizing, *their* electorate. The need to differentiate one's candidacy from the local electorate's perception of the national party is more of an imperative. Because state elites and voters are different from national elites and voters, there is much more room for conflict within party organizations. Some incumbent and aspiring officeholders will associate with the national party candidates and issues; others will not. This has been the source of much of the intraparty strife in northeastern states in the last fifteen years. The national party moved out of alignment with local party tradition as presidents Ronald Reagan and George Bush pushed national institutions in a conservative direction. Earlier in this century, presidential nominees came mostly from this region. Recent national party leaders, however, have originated from the booming and conservative South and West. New intraparty squabbles emerged in the early 1980s about whether voters should be presented with conservative state candidates to match the conservative national candidates for whom they were voting. Political mavericks like Lewis Lehrman arose in this setting to capture the New York gubernatorial primary. Lehrman was opposed by Republican party regulars and was ultimately defeated in the general election by Mario Cuomo. Republican party activists, figuring that presidential conservatism would trickle-down-the-ticket, discovered that liberal themes were still popular in statewide general elections.

The more general point, however, is that voters in state politics often have a different electoral world to consider—one separate from the trends of presidential politics. Some states, such as Oregon and Idaho, have always presented very different electoral choices in local contests. Local cleavages have consistently crosscut national party cleavages virtually since statehood. Split-ticket voting is a historical commonplace, if not a norm. Other states, like Pennsylvania and Ohio, have been very much tied to national trends until recently. Here, partisan voting remains strong, but split-ticket voting is an emerging phenomenon as local candidates are increasingly out of step with the national scene. This independent behavior was seldom observed in earlier times when local cleavages were unambiguously congruent with national party alignments.

The Role of Crosscutting Electoral Cleavages

A state's autonomy from national party alignments may have its roots in one or more of several sources in the electoral foundations of state politics. Schematically, the possible types of electoral incongruence are illustrated in the diagrams that follow. There are three fundamental ways in which local alignments can differ from national ones:

Issue Incongruent: Partisanship the Same, Cleavages Differ

Diagram A of figure 1.1 depicts a national alignment where the national electorate is evenly divided between the two parties on some dominant dimension. Diagram B represents a state where the partisan proportions of the parties are similar to the national proportions but there is an orthogonal line of cleavage that bisects the national cleavage. The horizontal line represents a local crosscutting theme that is determining certain partisan groups independent of the dominant national alignment. Here, the division of the party system is defined in one way at the national level and in another at the state level. Not all the partisans of parties R (Republican) and D (Democratic) at the presidential level are partisans of the same party at the state level. Since the national party themes are not driven all the way through the federal system, the incongruent constituencies split their ballots. These ticket-splitters are would-be Republicans and would-be Democrats because they "would be" voting straight Republican and straight Democratic if it were not for the crosscutting local cleavage.

Partisan Incongruent: Partisanship Differs, Cleavages the Same

A more typical form of incongruence is the one represented in figure 1.2. In Diagram A the national party system is lopsided in favor of Democrats. Diagram B exemplifies a state party system that does not literally crosscut the national party system. The themes that define partisanship are the same at both levels, but there is simply a different proportion of these partisans at the state level. So, for example, Diagram B of figure 1.2 suggests a situation in which a state's elections would be lopsided in favor of the Democrats if the state electorate was composed of the same proportion of partisans as the

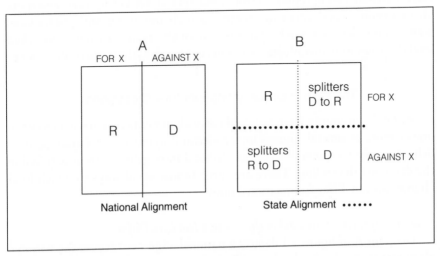

Figure 1.1   The Issue Incongruent State Party System

national electorate. However, as the bold vertical line suggests, this state's elections are more competitive because those proportions are different. Republicans are far more competitive in state elections than in national ones.

Issue-Partisan Incongruent: Partisanship Differs, Cleavages Differ

Finally, the most lopsided form of incongruence is the one in which the state's party system is comprised of different coalitions and the party division is dissimilar to the national party system. In Diagram A of figure 1.3, the national electorate is aligned in favor of Democrats. However, in the state (Diagram B), not only are the partisan groupings proportioned differently as in figure 1.2, but also there is a crosscutting cleavage as in figure 1.1. The state party's electorate is skewed away from the national electorate in both ways.

The Sources of Electoral Incongruence

V. O. Key first used the term *electoral differentiation* to refer to the fact that local electors are mobilized by "campaign emphases" other than those that are mobilizing the rest of the country.[9] The electorate is *differentiated* from its national counterpart and from the electorates in other states. Incongruent two-party states (fig. 1.1) are those where a state's electorate is quantitatively similar in its partisan composition to its national counterpart, but is mobilized to vote on different issues. Somehow the dominant national coalitions have little presence and have been recast by the voters' local or

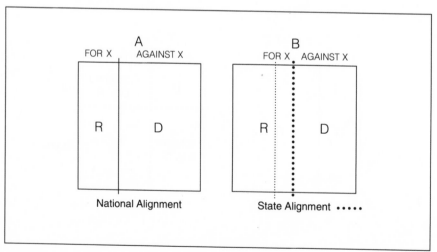

Figure 1.2   The Partisan Incongruent State Party System

regional concerns. Party competition may persist at the same level of intensity, but it is located on a different dimension from that on which the national parties compete. Figure 1.2 represents an electorate that is quantitatively different from the national electorate in its partisan composition, but is mobilized on the same issues. The national issues are salient, but there are different proportions of partisans. In this situation, party competition may be more or less intense than that occurring at the national level. Figure 1.3 symbolizes an electorate that is both quantitatively different from the national electorate and one that is mobilized by different issues. Not only are there different proportions of partisans at the local level, partisanship itself is being defined differently. Here, party competition may persist, but with a different level of intensity and on a different dimension.

What Are the Effects of Electoral Incongruence?

The persistent autonomy of state from national politics adversely affects the capacity of state political parties to control nominations, organize slates of candidates, and win elections. In other words, when state and national cleavages are askew, party organizations may find it difficult to avoid factionalism. V. O. Key first suggested this in *American State Politics: An Introduction.* The state party, he alleged, could not maintain its position against the national tide if its leadership and candidates were different from the national parties and presidential nominees. Local party leadership can create tempo-

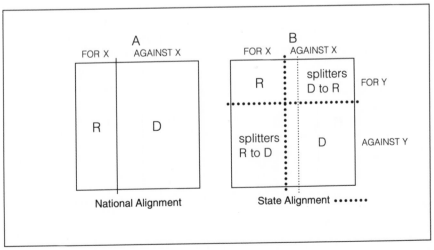

Figure 1.3   The Issue-Partisan Incongruent State Party System

rary groupings of partisans that differ from the national groupings, but this differentiation can be only momentary. For organizations to thrive, state cleavages must be congruent with national cleavages. Key not only recognized that the crisscrossing of state and national cleavages is a recipe for disunity, but also questioned whether crosscutting cleavages could persist.[10] Strife among party leaders over the proper direction of the party stood as the single greatest barrier to the endurance of an autonomous state politics. For Key, then, there was some doubt whether a state party system could be autonomous from the national party system. Echoing this sentiment, Duane Lockard argued that "autonomy" was too strong a word to describe the separateness of state politics.[11] All states are eventually pressured to come into line with national partisanship.

At the electoral level, James L. Sundquist argues that the strength of national partisan attachments in the electorate eventually overtakes the state with a differentiated party system. Apparently borrowing from social psychology, Sundquist even suggests that the voter feels psychological pressure to resolve the contradiction inherent in split-ticket voting.[12] Others are not so sure. Several have pointed out the persistence of dealignment and electoral incongruence in the post–New Deal period.[13] According to this body of work, realignments are often, if not usually, partial. The American party system is based on an accumulation of cleavages, both national and local. The concept of realignment need not be thought of as a single crosscutting issue that affects all states or all segments of the electorate.[14]

If Key and Sundquist are correct, the prospects of a lasting autonomy for a state's party system have never been very bright. A dealigned state will eventually become realigned; national realignments will be total realignments. Similarly, Sundquist argues that the New Deal realignment was extended to every state although it took longer for some states to realign than for others. In Oregon, for example, the Democratic party did not register convincing gains in statewide elections until the mid- to late 1950s.[15] Following critical elections, we should eventually expect the dominant national line of cleavage to be driven through the federal system, profoundly affecting elections at all levels, but it may take some time.

I intend to test this notion of the totality of realignments in this book. While it may be true that in most regions of the country it is difficult to maintain a state politics organized differently from national politics, there are some regions where it is less difficult than others. In some places, independence from national party politics not only persists, but its persistence has important consequences for political party cohesion.

Party Cohesion, Competitiveness, and the
Causes of Candidate-Centered Politics

There is a rough and approximate political geography to political party cohesion in the twentieth century. Political party organizations in the West and South have been factionalized and candidate-centered, while the bastions of unity appear in the Midwest and Northeast.[16] David R. Mayhew suggests that the key components of formal party organization strength are autonomy, longevity, hierarchy, control over the nomination process, and reliance on material incentives.[17] The weak party organizations in the South and West have generally lacked these defining elements of the unified party.

Competition between the parties has often been considered instrumental to building party organization. In his landmark work, *Southern Politics,* Key made it abundantly clear that one-partyism was responsible for the absence of effective party organizations. The absence of competition in the South facilitated the control over governmental policy by the "haves" in the society as opposed to the "have-nots." One-partyism bred a lazy form of southern factionalism that provided no institutional mechanism for the expression of lower-class viewpoints. He observed that "a loose factionalism gives great negative power to those with a few dollars to invest in legislative candidates. A party system provides at least a semblance of joint responsibility between governor and legislature . . . [but] the independence of candidacies in an atomized politics makes it possible to elect a fire-eating governor who promises great accomplishments and simultaneously to elect a legislature a majority of whose members are committed to inaction."[18] Because there was no party competition for any major office, there was no party leadership, no party discipline, and no incentive for legislators to uphold their governor's program to generate a good record for the next election.[19] The absence of competition led to a corresponding absence of party cohesion.

In the South, then, the multifactionalism of the one-party system ultimately led to bad governance. There was no incentive to organize and cooperate to elect a candidate who was genuinely able to translate election promises into policy. Why? Because there was no fear of retribution at the polls. An overwhelming Democratic majority in the electorate ensured victory by whomever was capable of capturing the primary nomination. Consequently, competition occurred only within the primary. When the Republicans finally began to make advances in Tennessee, North Carolina, and Virginia, the Democratic parties began to organize, proving that even a minimal amount of competition was enough to generate a corresponding degree of discipline.[20]

12

INTRODUCTION

As Sarah Morehouse summarily states, when Key turned to the Northeast and upper Midwest, he found that states with unified parties were also the states in which the balance of electoral strength between the parties tended to be even. Moreover, it was in these two-party states where the partisan cleavages dividing the two parties on the national level projected themselves into the politics of the state.[21]

According to Key, the differences between the one-party factional and bipartisan competitive states basically boiled down to proportions of "liberals" and "conservatives."[22] Where the proportions are equal, we should expect close party competition. Where the proportions are unequal, a single party always dominates and one-party factionalism ensues. Furthermore, in the competitive states, the party organizations seriously attempted to play a positive and controlling role in the nominating process. Good candidates with good programs are essential to avoid losing the party's hard won gains. In the one-party situation, however, there is little responsibility, because the factions are seldom permanent and are based on personalities rather than enduring institutions. Logically then, the states with equal proportions of partisans would have strong, disciplined parties, whereas the one-party states

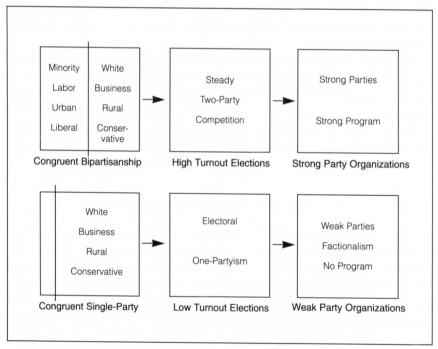

Figure 1.4 The Traditional Model of Party Unity: The Competition/Cohesion Thesis

might have weak, factionalized parties. In its basic form, Key's theory of what causes party strength and weakness appears something like the diagrams in figure 1.4.

For the South and for old-party states in the upper Midwest and Northeast, Key's argument works. The far western states, however, pose a particular problem for the competition/cohesion thesis. The West, like the South, is a region in which formal state and local organizations have been fragmented; but, unlike the South, two-party competition has been steady much as it has been in midwestern and northeastern states.[23] This raises the question of how a state's political system can lack party unity in the presence of two-party competition. In the South, there is no such puzzle. For years, election turnout was one-sided and there was only one real party. Oddly enough, however, the political battles in the West are frequently competitive for most major offices. On the basis of the competition/cohesion theory (see fig. 1.4), one would expect to see unified parties in two geographic regions, the West and the Midwest/Northeast. Instead, elections are candidate-centered in the former. One would think that the elites in the western states would have an incentive to coordinate their election efforts, since the opposition party is a real threat. For some reason, however, the model seems to break down. Something else is at work. Bipartisan electoral competition has not provided the level of party discipline and party unity to be found in the competitive states in the upper Midwest and Northeast.

A popular alternative explanation—that party weakness in the North is a direct result of progressive institutions like the direct primary system of nomination and civil service reform—ignores the widespread use of the primary and the adoption of civil service reform in states with and without unified parties.[24] In the Midwest and Northeast, intense two-party competition and machinelike organizations exist alongside states with many progressive institutions. Why isn't this the case in the West?

A Modified Theory of Party Disunity

The argument here is that the far western states are different from states in other regions. The electorate, while divided nearly equally between the parties, is not composed of the same coalitions that prevail in other parts of the country. From one election to the next, cleavages are not always consistent. In a recent survey of western voting behavior, Paul Kleppner has noted that the electorate's collective response "is not securely anchored in ongoing partisan attachments."[25] There may be some limited basis for class conflict, racial conflict, ethnoreligious conflict, or urban-rural conflict, but these major national cleavages have not had the salience in the West that they have had in older areas. These dominant national cleavages have been crosscut by one or more regional cleavages that elites and electors see as more important in campaigns for major offices.

An alternative model of candidate-centered politics might suggest that the parties are dividing the electorate nearly equally in most state elections, but the cleavages along which the states are dividing are unclear (see fig. 1.5). This makes it difficult to identify a consistent coalitional profile that all candidates must represent in order to win office.

Not only do the local issues divide the electorate in unpredictable ways, the transiency of the local populations complicates the task of organizing and mobilizing the electorate. Party disunity follows from an uncrystallized political setting. Elites have an incentive *not to cooperate* with national party leadership and may even lack the incentive necessary to cooperate with each other. In the old South, there was no incentive to cooperate with other candidates and with the national party, but also no incentive to avoid cooperating. It made no difference since the South was monolithically one-party. In the Northeast and upper Midwest, the incentive to cooperate is strong because state and national cleavages are well defined and congruent. Blessed with a stable population, a candidate easily distinguishes friendly from enemy territory. In the competitive West, however, elites have an incentive to be uncooperative with the national party, since the issues mobilizing voters often cut across national party cleavages. In addition, the mobility of the western population makes it more difficult to locate and organize predictable electoral pockets of support from one race to the next. Migrants who find themselves in a completely foreign political setting often go through a significant psycho-

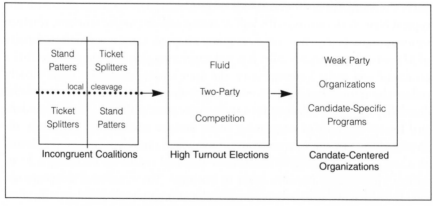

Figure 1.5   An Alternative Model of Party Disunity

logical reorientation in their political thinking. They have weaker commitments and tend to be more individualistic in making political calculations. Candidates confronted with sea changes in an area's population must be very cautious. A once friendly area might be inundated with hostile partisans a few years later. New voters lack established patterns of behavior and might be completely unaware of the well-entrenched patterns of their neighbors.[26] For these reasons, local elites might fare better in state elections by differentiating themselves from national party candidates and positions.

If the voting electorate exhibits stability even around a local cleavage, then elites might have an incentive to cooperate with each other in setting the local party apart from national party leadership. Party unity is possible under this condition. If crosscutting cleavages are plural and electoral groupings are subject to subtle changes from election to election, however, local elites might stray away from associations with other local elites that may identify them as having a particular ideology or as being a wing of a party. Elites must avoid being typecast or pigeonholed because flexibility and independence are the keys to political survival in a transient electoral setting.

What is the source of this electoral differentiation between the local and the national electorate? Aside from the party-weakening impact of a migrant population, the western states—as political jurisdictions—rely on an economy based on a large self-employment sector, a narrower industrial base, and a dispersed, nonethnic labor force. A typical Oregon county is 1 percent black and 2.5 percent Hispanic; has 20 percent of its work force employed in manufacturing, with 9 percent self-employed; and has a population density of only twenty-seven people per square mile. Also, Oregon has always had a narrow income distribution.[27] In settings such as these, national cleavages on redistributive and racial themes make rural populations homogeneous. Local party divisions form around issues of local concern. Contrast this with the typical New York county, with half as many self-employed workers, thirteen times as many blacks, four times as many Hispanics, and a population density of 371 persons per square mile. It is not surprising that because of New York's economic and social heterogeneity, the state's party coalitions more closely reflect the national parties. Moreover, population stability has ensured the durability of these coalitions for much of the state's history. Population density lowers the cost of organizing these various groups into politically effective blocs.[28] In the western states, however, a candidate cannot get elected as often by serving readily identifiable national coalitions such as blacks or whites, rich or poor persons, labor or business. These national cleavages appear in the East where there is considerable economic and social stratification by city, county, and region, but settlement patterns in the West are mixed and less stratified by region, city, and neighborhood. Politically relevant population groups are dispersed—that is, homogenized—and economies have been less stratified.

The Practical Result of Crosscutting Electoral Cleavages

To summarize, I am arguing that when a state's political party coalitions are dissimilar to that of the national parties, there are consequences for party unity. In the western states, the practical consequences are visible in wide-open primaries where each candidate is searching for a distinctive electoral pocket of support. These pockets may not be very visible, and even if they are, they may be numerous enough to draw multiple primary challengers. One can commonly find five, six, or seven candidates fighting within one party for an elusive electoral base (see table 1.1). Relatively few of the gubernatorial contests since 1960 have had only one candidate per primary. Only four primary contests of the eighty-two (excluding Utah's convention nominated candidates in 1988 and 1980) in the nine states listed in table 1.1 were uncontested in both parties—a minuscule 5 percent. In these states, primaries have always been crowded.

By contrast, in old-party states such as Ohio, Illinois, Connecticut, Rhode Island, New York, New Jersey, and Pennsylvania, contested primaries are much rarer and a very recent phenomenon. In the 1960s, for instance, the coalitional profiles of presidential and gubernatorial electorates were closely related and primaries usually had far fewer candidates. This is changing. While New York, Rhode Island, and Connecticut continue to have limited primary competition, New Jersey had seen an overall increase in the number of primary contestants due to the extension of public financing to would-be nominees. Other eastern states with a traditional party past have seen new forms of competition emerge because electoral patterns have changed. Even in these once congruent states, New Deal cleavages have faded, party organizations have splintered, and their influence over the nomination process has withered. New forms of party competition at the presidential level continue to isolate conservative presidential voting from voting further down the ticket. This has presented new conflicts for candidates and organizations. What is to be made of the presidential patterns? Are they to be followed? Or can state level candidates and organizations chart an independent course? None of these conflicts existed in these states in earlier times, when both presidential candidates and a larger plurality of the nation's voters lived in the Frost Belt—or at least more closely reflected the mainstream values and economic interests of this once dominant region.

Table 1.1   Number of Primary Contestants in Gubernatorial Elections in Nine Western States, by Party, 1960–1992

	Ariz.		N.Mex.		Calif.		Idaho		Ore.		Wash.		Mont.		Utah		Nev.	
	R	D	R	D	R	D	R	D	R	D	R	D	R	D	R	D	Rᵃ	D
1960	1	1	2	3	–	–	–	–	–	–	2	3	2	6	2	2	–	–
1962	1	3	1	4	3	4	3	6	2	4	–	–	–	–	–	–	2	4
1964	2	4	1	1	–	–	–	–	–	–	3	5	1	2	2	2	–	–
1966	3	3	2	2	5	6	2	3	2	4	–	–	–	–	–	–	2	6
1968	1	3	2	6	–	–	–	–	–	–	5	3	4	6	2	1	–	–
1970	1	3	6	3	1	10	2	3	3	3	–	–	–	–	–	–	2	4
1972	–	–	–	–	–	–	–	–	–	–	4	5	4	5	1	1	–	–
1974	5	4	4	6	6	18	1	1	5	10	–	–	–	–	–	–	4	6
1976	–	–	–	–	–	–	–	–	–	–	5	4	2	1	2	2	–	–
1978	3	2	2	2	7	9	6	1	7	7	–	–	–	–	–	–	4	8
1980	–	–	–	–	–	–	–	–	–	–	6	7	3	4	1ᵇ	1ᵇ	–	–
1982	2	2	3	4	5	13	2	1	5	9	–	–	–	–	–	–	3	6
1984	–	–	–	–	–	–	–	–	–	–	2	3	1	2	2	2	–	–
1986	2	3	6	1	2	5	1	1	7	7	–	–	–	–	–	–	5	2
1988	–	–	–	–	–	–	–	–	–	–	3	4	3	6	1ᵇ	1ᵇ	–	–
1990	5	2	4	4	4	11	3	1	7	1	–	–	–	–	–	–	8	6
1992	–	–	–	–	–	–	–	–	–	–	4	5	2	7	2	2	–	–

Source: Richard M. Scammon and Alice McGillivray, eds., *America Votes* (Washington, D.C.: Elections Research Center, various years).

a. In Nevada's elections from 1978 to 1988, the Republican primary ballot had a "none of these" category also included in this count.

b. Utah nominated by convention in 1980 and 1988.

Plan of the Book

The chapters that follow examine structures of party competition in states with and without a strong party tradition. In chapter 2, I evaluate competition and electoral incongruence in nineteen states between 1914 and 1990. I then look specifically at the contemporary period, roughly from 1952 to 1990. The task will be to show that in states with a history of party unity, patterns of party competition reflect basic stability, consistency, and predictability. By contrast, weak-organization states are typified by considerable electoral volatility. Voting for one office is not at all like voting for another. The next step is to show that the unreliability of these electorates has promoted candidate-centeredness and party factionalism.

Taking up several exemplary states exhibiting substantial party strength, chapters 3 and 4 will identify the political cleavages prevailing in older, more stable regions of the country. These are states with a durable partisan tradition, where local voting habits are similar to national voting habits. Using a variety of evidence, I show that these states have exhibited party influence over candidates and campaigns for some time. This influence is made possible by the durability of partisan attachments in the electorate. Strong personalities do emerge (Rockefeller, Cuomo), but electoral patterns are relatively stable. I use both aggregate and individual-level data to show that the congruence of state electoral coalitions with national coalitions is evident in gubernatorial elections drawn from recent history. An examination of these elections illustrates some departure, however, from national orientations in the later contests, along with a diminished role for party organizations.

The candidate-centered political traditions of the far western United States will be examined in chapters 5 through 8. Beginning with New Mexico and Arizona and continuing through California, Washington, Oregon, and Idaho, I present the case for an autonomous state politics. With a variety of evidence, I argue that in these states electoral coalitions rarely match those at the national level. In turn, this distinctiveness has generated party factionalism and candidate-centeredness. Economic and racial cleavages are often present but do not divide the community to the same extent. In addition, groups mobilized around persistent redistributive New Deal themes find it difficult to coalesce in states that are sparsely settled. Aggregate data suggest that these states are usually not geographically segmented by race and class. Examinations of selected gubernatorial races provide ground-level evidence that campaigns, issues, and electoral coalitions in this region *are* different.

Finally, in chapter 9, I discuss what the detailed state-level studies mean in the context of the theory presented in chapter 1. Older industrial states are changing. Their political behavior is increasingly separate and separable from their national politics. Thus, the far western states have become a model for understanding changes coming to the rest of the nation. Cohesive state and local organizations are largely a thing of the past, even in the industrial East and Midwest. This is because the electoral foundations for traditional party politics have given way to a less reliable, more candidate-centered, locally autonomous system.

2

The Variants of Two-Party Competition

I N THE first chapter, I argue that the competition/cohesion thesis fails—two-party competition is not a sufficient condition for the maintenance of unified parties. Even in competitive settings, cooperation among party elites is threatened when local cleavages undermine the significance of the prevailing national party labels. This statement of the problem defines the cases of interest: (1) competitive two-party states with a history of centralized, unified party organizations—grouped, as they are, primarily in the Northeast and upper Midwest; (2) the states of the Mountain region and Far West, with competitive traditions but lacking developed party organizations.[1]

The theory and expectations have been stated, but theories are often false. Two preliminary questions need to be answered: Do we really find steady party competition in states with intensely candidate-centered elections? And are independent voters and candidates to be found in competitive, two-party, factionalized states, or are voters and candidates in all states equally free of party attachments?

The first task is to evaluate the congruence of aggregate electoral margins in the two groups of states. My theoretical expectation is that there will be more noticeable differences between presidential voting and voting further down the ticket in the candidate-centered states. The competitiveness and dispersion in the vote for these states is indicated by the figures in table 2.1 for four levels of office: president, U.S. Senate, U.S. House, and governor from 1914 to 1990.[2]

Party Competition and Party Organization Weakness

Table 2.1 presents the mean Republican percentage of the total vote for each of the four offices in each of nineteen states. Data for House seats are aggregate and do not address competition in individual districts, except, of course, in those states where there is a single at-large district. The standard deviations, designated S, provide a convenient measure of dispersion from the mean. The coefficient of variation, designated V, is a straightforward indicator of dispersion that is also easily interpreted.[3] Like the standard deviation, low scores on the V indicate a tight clustering around the mean and therefore a fairly consistent pattern. High values indicate a wide variation around the mean. The coefficient of variation is interpreted as a percentage of the mean. So, for example, in Nevada, Republican presidential election returns typically vary within 23 percent of their mean, whereas in Illinois the typical variation is within 13.7 percent of the mean.

Among the traditional party states, New Jersey, Delaware, and Pennsylvania are the most Republican in presidential elections and Rhode Island the least. In all the old-party states except Rhode Island, the elections at each level of office are closely competitive, falling within three to four points of 50 percent.[4] The smaller standard deviations among the eastern and midwestern states also suggest a consistently tight pattern of two-party competition, especially for U.S. Senate seats and the governorships.

Among the eleven western states, elections for president are equally competitive. However, the pattern of competition for lesser offices is different from the old-party states. The uniformity in electoral results disappears. Still, one can argue from the means reported in table 2.1 that presidential contests in all nineteen states are competitive and gubernatorial contests are competitive in all but a few states. Using the means as the sole measure of competition, however, obscures the critical difference between forms of party competition in the two regions. The difference is not to be found in Republican and Democratic percentages of the two-party or total vote. Rather, following David Brady's method of analyzing the history of U.S. House elections, it the measures of dispersion that reveal the structure of party competition.[5] Competition figures for the four offices uniformly show more dispersion and less consistency in the competitive western states. In gubernatorial contests, California, Oregon, and Washington have very unstable patterns of party competition with standard deviations averaging thirteen percentage points. None of the traditional organization states displays this level of volatility. In U.S. Senate elections, Washington, Oregon, California, Arizona, and Idaho vary widely and, again, no eastern state is comparable.

Table 2.1 Average Percentage and Swing in the Republican Vote for President, Governor, U.S. House, and U.S. Senate in Nineteen States, 1914–1990

	President			Governor			House			Senate		
	Mean	S.D.	V	Mean	S.D.	V	Mean	S.D.	V	Mean	S.D.	V
Traditional Party States												
Illinois	51.7	7.1	13.7	51.1	8.4	16.5	50.3	6.4	12.7	48.6	8.6	17.5
Pennsylvania	51.9	8.1	15.6	51.7	8.1	15.6	52.3	7.5	14.4	52.6	6.2	11.8
New Jersey	53.1	8.6	16.2	48.6	8.2	16.9	51.0	5.3	10.3	50.8	7.7	15.2
Ohio	51.7	7.8	15.0	49.3	5.6	11.4	52.1	4.9	9.5	48.5	7.0	14.4
New York	49.3	7.9	15.6	45.6	7.6	16.6	46.6	4.5	9.6	47.4	9.1	19.2
Connecticut	51.2	6.1	12.2	49.6	7.6	15.3	49.8	6.1	12.2	48.4	6.6	13.6
Delaware	51.8	6.7	12.9	54.1	7.4	13.8	50.9	7.6	14.9	51.0	7.0	13.7
Rhode Island	45.8	10.1	22.0	46.4	11.0	23.8	44.4	9.5	21.5	43.7	11.2	25.7
Mean	50.8	7.8		49.6	8.0		49.7	6.4		48.8	7.9	
Weak Party States												
Nevada	49.6	11.4	23.1	42.9	9.9	23.2	42.4	10.7	23.2	44.2	7.0	15.9
California	49.4	8.8	17.9	55.7	13.1	23.5	49.8	12.7	25.4	53.8	15.2	28.2
New Mexico	49.4	7.8	15.8	48.5	3.7	7.7	46.7	5.8	12.4	48.2	9.3	19.3
Colorado	52.5	9.1	17.3	47.1	8.0	16.9	50.0	6.3	12.6	49.7	7.6	15.2
Arizona	50.2	11.8	23.6	45.0	10.0	22.3	41.3	15.5	37.5	41.7	11.3	27.2
Idaho	54.9	11.1	20.2	46.7	8.1	17.4	53.0	7.2	13.6	54.5	11.1	20.4
Oregon	49.5	8.5	17.2	52.2	12.4	23.8	50.2	10.3	20.5	55.0	9.6	17.4
Washington	48.1	9.1	18.9	50.9	13.7	26.8	48.7	10.1	20.1	40.9	10.2	24.9
Montana	49.0	9.8	19.9	46.9	7.7	16.4	46.6	6.6	14.2	41.4	7.9	19.0
Wyoming	54.9	9.8	17.8	48.9	9.8	13.9	55.7	8.1	14.6	52.3	8.1	14.6
Utah	53.2	13.0	24.3	45.7	8.1	17.7	49.9	7.9	15.9	51.0	10.1	19.9
Mean	51.0	10.0		48.2	9.5		48.6	9.2		48.4	9.8	

Source: Richard M. Scammon and Alice McGillivray, eds., *America Votes* (Washington, D.C.: Elections Research Center, various years), and author's calculations.

Differences between mean presidential voting and mean voting for the other offices, as reported in table 2.2, show that the two groups of states are unique.[6] These figures compare presidential voting to voting for U.S. House, Senate, and governor from 1914 to 1990 and compare the paired arrays for significant differences using the standard t-statistic. Among the states with a tradition of strong parties, there are few differences between the paired offices. U.S. Senate voting does not differ from presidential balloting in any of these states. More important, gubernatorial voting usually does not differ significantly from presidential voting. However, in most western states there are considerable differences between presidential voting and voting for the other three offices.

Differences in the patterns of competition are reflected not so much by the

Table 2.2   T-test of Difference in Means Between Presidential Voting and Voting for U.S. House, Governor, and U.S. Senate, 1914–1992

	House		Governor		Senate	
	Mean	T	Mean	T	Mean	T
Traditional Party States						
Illinois	.44	.35	.70	.73	2.63	1.68
Pennsylvania	−1.07	.85	−1.56	.97	−2.01	1.42
New Jersey	1.16	.76	3.95	2.11*	.13	.07
Ohio	−1.20	.88	2.15	1.10	2.57	1.52
New York	2.31	1.92*	1.44	.85	1.45	.79
Connecticut	1.10	.98	2.92	1.98*	2.23	1.71
Delaware	−.18	.11	−2.26	1.76	−.38	.29
Rhode Island	1.25	.75	−1.28	.54	1.78	1.04
Weak Party States						
Nevada	6.15	2.92**	5.29	2.10**	4.86	2.62**
California[a]	−1.83	.91	−6.82	3.13**	−6.24	2.32**
New Mexico	3.04	2.38**	.72	.63	1.81	1.28
Colorado	1.65	1.30	5.13	2.25**	2.25	1.38
Arizona	8.27	4.63**	4.63	2.37**	7.16	5.53**
Idaho	.75	.47	6.80	2.90**	1.33	.58
Oregon	−1.71	.88	−3.06	1.26	−5.36	2.65**
Washington	−1.41	.88	−3.36	1.59	6.85	3.00**
Montana	1.70	1.06	2.01	.96	6.48	3.97**
Wyoming	−1.44	.92	4.46	2.24**	.89	.61
Utah	2.51	1.51	7.53	3.17**	3.24	1.90*
**p < .05 *p < .10						

Source: Richard M. Scammon and Alice McGillivray, eds., *America Votes* (Washington, D.C.: Elections Research
   Center, various years), and author's calculations.
Note: Values reported are average differences and t-statistics on the differences between presidential-gubernatorial,
   presidential-U.S. House, and presidential-U.S. Senate voting. Negative signs indicate offices that are more
   Republican than presidential contests. Significance tests are 2-tailed.
   a. California's near-unanimous victories by Earl Warren (1946, governor) and Hiram Johnson (1934, U.S.
   Senate) have been eliminated from these calculations because of their cross-filed candidacies.

difference in average vote share as in the dispersion of electoral margins around those averages. At one extreme is New York, with its very competitive and consistent two-partyism, and at the other extreme are California, Arizona, Oregon, and Washington, with competition but no cohesion. Close two-party competition alone is insufficient to bring about a corresponding degree of consistency in electoral margins from one office to the next. Competition is not a sufficient condition for a predictable two-party division in the electorate.

Party voting at the local level in the Mountain and Far West regions is not congruent with voting at the very top of the ticket. Elections to high offices in the East and Midwest are occasionally independent of presidential partisanship while similar elections in the West are *usually* independent. This can be disadvantageous for western party leaders because they are unable to depend upon a predictable share of the electorate from election to election. A party organization cannot provide issue leadership by slating a full set of candidates who think and act the same if no one can be confident of the party's underlying electoral support.

Individual candidates, on the other hand, may not be at a disadvantage if they are able to differentiate themselves from unsavory partisans at other levels of office. The weak partisan ties of the western electorate proved to be a tool of political survival for the likes of Earl Warren and Hiram Johnson in California and Earl Snell, Wayne Morse, and Charles McNary in Oregon, in an era of generally dim Republican prospects. The progressive independence of candidates and voters in the Pacific West, in particular, explains the success of those states' independence from national electoral forces during the 1930s and 1940s (see appendix table A.1).

The Imperfect Trickle-Down of Presidential Republicanism (1952–1990)

Thirty years ago, V. O. Key claimed that party was a solvent of *federalism,* arguing that "while the governmental system may be federal the voter in the polling booth usually is not."[7] Since the incongruent margins in the aggregate level findings from table 2.2 cannot be entirely the result of mobilization surge and decline (drop-off), the data begin to cast serious doubt on this generalization for the present time and for Key's era as well. While Key may have been correct if his remarks were aimed at describing politics in the traditional and competitive two-party states of the Northeast and upper Midwest, the West did not fit this description at the time he wrote.

What about the time since Key wrote? Has recent presidential Republicanism overcome federalism to determine state-level political support? The period from 1952 to the present is generally recognized as a period of Republican presidential ascendancy. Since 1952, and including the 1992 election, Republicans have won seven of the eleven presidential elections—six of which were by landslide margins. Only one of the three Democratic victors won by a landslide margin—Lyndon Johnson in 1964. Locally, however, the West has charted a course of its own.

Clearly, the extent to which U.S. state politics is nationalized has been overblown. While the western states have voted strongly Republican in recent presidential elections, Democrats have overwhelmingly dominated the

Table 2.3   The Imperfect Trickle-Down of Presidential Republicanism: Party Control of the Western Governorships, 1964–1990

	Nev.	Calif.	N.Mex.	Colo.	Ariz.	Idaho	Ore.	Wash.	Mont.	Wyo.	Utah
1964	D	D	D	R	D	R	R	R	R	R	D
1965	D	D	D	R	D	R	R	R	R	R	D
1966	R	R	R	R	R	R	R	R	R	R	D
1967	R	R	R	R	R	R	R	R	R	R	D
1968	R	R	R	R	R	R	R	R	D	R	D
1969	R	R	R	R	R	R	R	R	D	R	D
1970	D	R	D	R	R	D	R	R	D	R	D
1971	D	R	D	R	R	D	R	R	D	R	D
1972	D	R	D	R	R	D	R	R	D	R	D
1973	D	R	D	R	R	D	R	R	D	R	D
1974	D	D	D	D	D	D	D	R	D	D	D
1975	D	D	D	D	D	D	D	R	D	D	D
1976	D	D	D	D	D	D	R	R	D	D	D
1977	D	D	D	D	D	D	R	R	D	D	D
1978	R	D	D	D	D	D	R	R	D	D	D
1979	R	D	D	D	D	D	R	R	D	D	D
1980	R	D	D	D	D	D	R	R	D	D	D
1981	R	D	D	D	D	D	R	R	D	D	D
1982	D	R	D	D	D	D	R	R	D	D	D
1983	D	R	D	D	D	D	R	R	D	D	D
1984	D	R	D	D	D	D	R	D	D	D	R
1985	D	R	D	D	D	D	R	D	D	D	R
1986	D	R	R	D	R	D	D	D	D	D	R
1987	D	R	R	D	D	D	D	D	D	D	R
1988	D	R	R	D	D	D	D	D	R	D	R
1989	D	R	R	D	D	D	D	D	R	D	R
1990	D	R	R	D	D	D	D	D	R	D	R
%Rep.	30	63	33	37	33	32	74	74	26	37	26

Source: Richard M. Scammon and Alice McGillivray, eds., *America Votes* (Washington, D.C.: Elections Research Center, various years).

western governorships (table 2.3).[8] This is not merely a fluke or an accident of the off-year election calendar. Even Montana and Utah, holding gubernatorial elections simultaneously with presidential elections, have been dominated by Democratic governors. A two-stage realignment process fails to work because local Democrats can field candidates that refuse to carry the baggage of a George McGovern, Jimmy Carter, Walter Mondale, Michael Dukakis, or an unpopular national party label. In many western states, then, it appears that independence from national partisanship has helped astute Democratic governors and members of Congress combat Republican presidential ascendancy, just as Republicans were often able to resist the New Deal

Table 2.4   T-test of Difference in Means Between Presidential Voting and Voting for U.S. House, Governor, and U.S. Senate, 1952–1990

	House		Governor		Senate	
	Mean	*T*	*Mean*	*T*	*Mean*	*T*
Traditional Party States						
Illinois	2.86	1.63	.80	.48	4.41	1.91*
Pennsylvania	1.57	.94	.57	.26	−2.27	1.11
New Jersey	4.22	2.01*	6.42	2.32**	1.23	.52
Ohio	.05	.02	4.34	1.39	6.38	2.69**
New York	3.81	2.15**	1.83	.82	.92	.30
Connecticut	3.41	1.85*	6.65	2.70**	5.07	2.41**
Delaware	1.57	.61	−2.67	.84	−1.03	.47
Rhode Island	3.33	1.13	−1.43	.32	2.12	.70
Weak Party States						
Nevada	15.71	8.49**	14.14	4.00**	10.01	5.24**
California[a]	5.43	2.24**	−2.31	1.05	−.22	.06
New Mexico	5.93	3.18**	3.83	2.77**	4.08	1.85*
Colorado	4.67	3.12**	9.18	3.10**	3.05	1.26
Arizona	5.29	3.58**	10.46	4.05**	8.97	4.54**
Idaho	6.57	4.10**	15.40	5.92**	10.34	4.64**
Oregon	6.41	3.24**	−3.06	1.64	−3.45	1.68
Washington	4.22	1.85*	−5.03	1.27	14.48	5.49**
Montana	4.51	2.06*	6.72	2.57**	8.05	3.99**
Wyoming	2.00	.88	10.08	3.60**	2.40	1.39
Utah	8.31	3.36**	18.23	6.53**	9.75	4.77**

   **p < .05   *p < .10

Source: Richard M. Scammon and Alice McGillivray, eds., *America Votes* (Washington, D.C.: Elections Research Center, various years), and author's calculations.

Note: Values reported are average differences and t-statistics on the differences between presidential-gubernatorial, presidential-U.S. House, and presidential-U.S. Senate voting. Negative signs indicate offices that are more Republican than presidential contests. Significance tests are 2-tailed.

tide in the 1930s and 1940s. The governorships have remained "electorally disaggregated" in the western United States.[9]

This trend toward an autonomous state politics is visible in only two states with a traditional party past. Table 2.4 presents the t-statistics for the difference between mean presidential voting and voting for U.S. House, U.S. Senate, and governor for each of the nineteen states for the 1952–1990 period. Among the eastern industrial states, only the gubernatorial vote in New Jersey and Connecticut is distinct from presidential voting in the post–New Deal period. Pennsylvania's vote margins remain the most consistent with its presidential balloting. Generally, the magnitude and incidence of incongruence remain smaller in the old-party states than in the West.

Presidential-Gubernatorial Incongruence Since the 1950s

Overwhelming presidential Republicanism has done nothing to swing western governorships in the same direction. Table 2.4 presents the actual average percentage difference between presidential voting and gubernatorial voting from 1952 to 1990 (third column). Negative signs indicate that gubernatorial voting is more Republican than presidential voting. There is only a slight absolute difference (2.6 percent) between presidential voting and gubernatorial voting in states with traditional organizations. However, in weak-party states, large discrepancies persist, exceeding ten points, on average, in the Mountain states.

In the East, recent presidential Republicanism has not translated into local Republican gains. In U.S. House and U.S. Senate elections, individual candidates resist landslide presidential tides more often and in more places than earlier in this century. In this sense, the old-party states of the East are less different from the rest of the country than they were in the years immediately following the New Deal realignment. Even the eastern states have watched federalism eat away at party cohesion.

The source of the persistent autonomy of state from national politics in recent years is the dissociation of presidential voting behavior from behavior in state elections. Perhaps the victory of Bill Clinton will keep the top of the ticket from becoming permanently out of harmony with voting lower down. Recent presidential results in these states show that competitors in presidential elections have been mismatched, while Democrats in local races fare well. These persistently split results may have little to do with the rise of independent voters. As Key pointed out and Burnham reminds us, an independent voter is not necessarily the same thing as a ticket-splitter.[10] More ticket-splitting does not necessarily entail more independent party identification. Lifelong, committed Democrats voted for Ronald Reagan—they do not claim to be independents. However, if one combines the independent identifiers with those who are partisan identifiers but split their ballots anyway, this group is likely to be a plurality of the electorate in future elections. The consequence is that all states may eventually develop an autonomy from presidential politics. This autonomy has been a persistent fact of political life in the western United States and is quickly becoming a fact in the East as well.

What Are the Causes of Incongruence?

The kind of candidate-centered voting represented by the inconsistent electoral results in the competitive weak-party states does not occur merely by chance. Western voters have had weaker partisan attachments for some time.[11] The causes of nonparty voting can be traced to the electoral differentiation of a state's electoral party from the national electorate. Three basic types of incongruent state politics arise when: (1) state and national electoral parties are proportionally similar in size, but the cleavages that define party coalitions are different; (2) state and national electorates are proportionally different, but the cleavages that define party coalitions are the same; (3) state and national electorates are proportioned differently and cleavages also differ. These three types of incongruence suggest how national cleavages can lose their salience as one moves from one jurisdiction to another.

Which socioeconomic cleavages divide the electorates of the western states and which do not? In the process of answering these questions, we may begin to understand the electorates themselves. Of course, if state-representing survey data were available, this task of understanding political cleavages could be undertaken with more precision. Individual-level data do not exist on a state basis for all states, nor for all election years stretching back to 1914. National polls, after all, do not represent states. For purposes of historical comparison, ecological data, by county, are perhaps the most adequate source. As Walter Dean Burnham shows, demographic data can be correlated with county-level voting returns to expose voting behavior at an aggregate level.[12] I will develop this more general level of analysis in coming chapters to establish whether the state-level patterns of voting behavior are traceable to different social and economic characteristics of counties and populations.[13] My goal, however, is not to predict candidate choice with a comprehensive and elaborate model of voting behavior. The point of the data analysis is to present an approximate picture of state-level cleavages and the distance between groups with distinct, politically relevant traits. For these purposes, I do not require a precise model of the vote.

If the theory presented in the opening chapter is correct, the fundamental difference between the party states exhibiting a tradition of party unity and the West will be that certain foundations for national party conflict are present in the former and absent in the latter. The following generalizations about national alignments should hold true for the post–New Deal party system in gubernatorial voting in traditional organization states.

Urban-Rural Cleavages[14]

In states where House, U.S. Senate, and gubernatorial elections look very much like presidential elections, we are likely to find urban-suburban or upstate-downstate conflict. Suburban and rural areas, especially from the 1960s onward, should vote predominantly Republican in gubernatorial elec-

tions. One would expect urban areas to vote Democratic. The areas of traditional and predictable regional partisan alignments within states should be
the areas of traditional party organization where the competition/cohesion
thesis works best. I measure urbanization by the percentage of the county
living in an urban area.

Racial Cleavages

Areas with large minority populations (outside the South) are likely to
have a larger Democratic vote than those with small minority populations,
especially after the 1950s when minorities became politically active in both
national and state politics. This generalization may not hold when evaluating
ecological data for earlier times. The measure for race is the percentage of the
county that is nonwhite.

Class and Economic Cleavages[15]

The post–New Deal period has taught us to expect that areas where the
economy is fueled by manufacturing and heavy industry would not vote
Republican. We would expect areas with higher family incomes and higher
levels of education to be associated with strong gubernatorial Republicanism.
Median income is the measure for the class standing of the county; the
percentage of people employed in manufacturing is the measure for the size
of the blue-collar electorate.

If the theory is correct, these generalizations about the divisions between
groups will not hold for the western, candidate-centered states. Tables A.2
and A.3 in the appendix illustrate the impact of four socioeconomic variables
on the county-level voting behavior in ten factionalized, western states and
five of the traditional organization states of the Midwest and Northeast
in 1980 and 1982 and 1960 and 1962.[16] Although they are weighted for
population, these data should be evaluated with caution for states like Nevada
and Arizona, since such large percentages of these states' populations reside
in one or two counties. Because of the uneven population distribution, much
of the relevant electoral variation occurs within two jurisdictions. Nevertheless, several noteworthy patterns are evident. Most generally, one can see that
these four variables explain much more of the county-level vote in the eastern industrial states than in the western region. In addition, as the figures for
the average slope for the 1960 and 1962 races show, the national New Deal
cleavages between urban and rural and industrial and nonindustrial areas
have more of a divisive presence in the old-party states than in the western
region. Even in states like Utah and Washington, with on-year gubernatorial
elections, there is some discrepancy between state and presidential politics. In

several western states, the cleavages separating counties work *opposite* to the way I have hypothesized for traditional party states. For instance, manufacturing employment brightens Republican prospects in California, Utah, Wyoming, and New Mexico in the 1980 and 1982 contests. Higher incomes drop the Republican voting in Idaho, Utah, and California in the same races. The one demographic variable that does consistently divide western counties is race (percentage nonwhite). Racial divisions, however, are only statistically significant in sporadic instances, whereas they are more consistently significant in midwestern and eastern states. The major difference between the western and old-party states is that the cleavages are much more divisive in the latter (see appendix tables A.2 and A.3).

Comparing elections of the 1960s to those of the 1980s shows that the traditional New Deal divisions are not as evident as they once were, even in states with old party organizations. By 1980, the proportion of workers employed in manufacturing had political implications in only a few places. In several contests, as in New York in 1982, manufacturing employment *increased* the county-level Republican vote. This weakening of New Deal patterns corresponds to a decline in party unity in once strong-party states, as both Republican and Democratic organizations have lost control over nominations.

In states that once formed the core of the New Deal party system, economic and social forces have gradually steered the electorate away from predictable alignments, making it difficult for party elites to form strategy around a stable electoral base. An example of a change of this type is the decline in organized labor over the twenty-year period. Labor had much less power in the 1980s due to deindustrialization and the diminished influence of organizations that once politicized manufacturing. Only in Pennsylvania and New York has the size of the unionized labor force remained unchanged from the 1960s to the 1980s (table 2.5). New York remains the most unionized state in the nation, but the kinds of workplaces in which unions successfully organize have changed. Heavy industry—once the heart of the most Democratic and activist unions—has declined even in New York State. Public-sector unions (teachers, government employees) are now among the most loyal and active constituencies of the Democratic party. Nevertheless, the figures in table 2.5 are a striking contrast to figures for the western states, where only Washington has a similar proportion of union members. Only one-fifth of California's work force was unionized by the mid-1980s, and only 12.8 percent of the Arizona and New Mexico work forces were influenced by organized labor.[17] These figures underscore a simple point: the absence of certain cleavages is often the result of the absence of or small size of certain constituencies. There can be no division between union and nonunion voters where

Table 2.5   Percentage of the Labor Force Belonging to Labor Unions in Six States with a
Strong Party Tradition, 1960–1982

	1960	1970	1980	1982
Connecticut	23.7	24.2	18.7	18.9
New Jersey	37.9	29.4	22.3	19.9
New York	31.9	35.7	36.5	35.8
Ohio	34.1	36.4	30.0	27.4
Pennsylvania	26.1	37.2	28.8	27.0
Illinois	43.2	35.8	29.5	27.5

Source: Leo Troy and Neil Sheflin, *Union Sourcebook* (West Orange, N.J.: Industrial Relations Data Information
Service, 1985).

there are no labor organizations or where labor organizations are not highly
politicized.

Evidence for Incongruent Cleavages Among Voters

County-level analysis reveals clear differences in the extent to which state
electorates are divided by national themes. My suggestion is that these differences are responsible for the party factionalism and candidate centeredness
observable in the western states. Are county-level differences in state electoral cleavages traceable to the voters? The lack of comprehensive state polling data extending back to the 1960s and earlier has made it difficult to verify
that ecological patterns have their roots in actual voter-level differences. At
the same time, much of the polling data presented in run-of-the-mill newspaper coverage of elections is not sufficiently detailed to determine whether
party coalitions in one state differ from those in another.

A cumulative data file containing pooled responses to questions commonly appearing in the ICPSR's *American National Election Studies* (ANES)
from 1952 to 1992 is available to evaluate the extent to which these states are
truly distinct. These data yield interesting information on split-ticket voting.
Since some states are not well represented even with the pooled data, I have
grouped the states into two categories following David R. Mayhew's scheme:
traditional organization states and states lacking any semblance of party
organization (see table A.4).[18] The differences between the two groups of
states have remained fairly constant from the 1950s to the present. The
eleven western states led all other states, and groups of states, in split-ticket
voting in state elections in each of the last four decades for which ANES data

are available. However, these states have not always led the nation in split-ticket voting from president to U.S. House or president to U.S. Senate races. Over the last thirty years, the southern electorate has been more likely than westerners to split the ballot between presidential and congressional races, although the South is much less likely to split the ballot in state races. Even so, weak-party states in the West still outdo regular organization states in the degree of split-ticket voting between president and Congress. Incongruent cleavages, then, are traceable to the voters themselves. The differences visible in the aggregate data are not solely due to roll-off and drop-off.

In the next several chapters, I will determine how state elections divide voter coalitions in ways different from presidential elections. Unfortunately, the ANES cumulative data file is inappropriate for state-level analyses because individual states are not properly represented. Exit polling data are limited primarily to elections in the 1980s and 1990s and will not allow in-depth comparisons over time. But the theory does not necessarily require individual-level data analysis for its validation. A state electorate can be incongruent with the national party coalitions because voters split their ballots or because different voters are voting from one office to the next (roll-off), or one election to the next (drop-off). Conversion and differential mobilization can both be sources of party-weakening crosscutting cleavage. Furthermore, even if similar voters behave alike in Toledo, Ohio, and Phoenix, Arizona, they may not be *organized* to vote their interests in the same way in both places. In the western states, the traditional New Deal coalition groups are dispersed and not located in easily organized pockets of interest. Even if there are few individual-level differences in voting behavior, the aggregate differences indicated by the county-level analysis (tables A.2 and A.3) suggest the presence of enough disruption to frustrate efforts to maintain party unity.

Conclusions

This chapter has suggested that incongruent cleavages in state electoral systems may have roots at the individual level. At the very least, the county-level data indicate that gross gubernatorial voting patterns do not regularly follow presidential patterns in the western states. These discrepant patterns persist because the issues that shape national party conflict have less salience in western state politics than in the East and Midwest. Because the economic and social composition of the electorate does not divide voters on prominent national issues, incumbency and personal appeals to voters by western gubernatorial candidates become all the more powerful. Responding to an independent electorate, candidates choose issues that will best fit an unorthodox political environment. It is not surprising, therefore, that fragmented party organizations have been the norm in these states. The battle to mobilize voters in this region is much more complicated than elsewhere. In many cases, those mobilized for a given party in state-level elections are not the same people that are activated for that party in a presidential election. By contrast, differences between the locus of party conflict in state elections and the locus of party conflict in national electorates have not been as pronounced in the industrial East and Midwest.

PART II

The Eroding
Foundation
of Party Unity
in Eastern
Industrial States

Introduction

THE influence of strong, unified political parties on candidates, elections, and public policy has been of enduring interest to political scientists. I am inverting the question by asking about the influence of candidates, electorates, and elections on party unity. According to well-established generalizations about American politics, cohesive party organization is important for at least four reasons: (1) the strong party is able to control the nomination of candidates; (2) because it can control the nomination process, the strong party organization can discipline party elites; (3) in a competitive environment, organizationally strong parties are more responsible and responsive to the electorate; and (4) organizationally strong parties in a two-party setting are programmatic, policy-making parties.[1]

Suppose, however, that a party's control over the nomination process, its responsiveness to the electorate, and its capacity to exercise discipline over elites, are possible because the organization wins from time to time. Parties are held together by a paramount end, to win elections. There may be subordinate reasons for maintaining party unity, such as good government, sustaining patronage, attaining better management of party finances, and performing community service. For these goals to be consequential, however, an organization must win at least some elections.[2] In this manner, a political party's ability to field electable candidates is instrumental to all other goals.

The cause of party unity is advanced by electoral inertia. Conflicts emerge within the organization when the electorate has undergone or is experiencing significant social change. Electoral instability is likely to generate intraparty strife, which will break down party discipline; there will be quarrels over the nomination process and over who should be endorsed. By contrast, when partisanship is institutionalized, party habits solidify with substantial agreement among elites on the goals, purposes, issues, and policies of the party. Party unity is possible when electoral conditions are stable, cleavages divide the community predictably, and the same participants turn out year after year. The *loyalty* of the electorate provides a firm foundation for party building.[3]

If this theory of party organization politics is accurate, then party organization, per se, is not the cause of party responsibility and discipline. Because the strength of an organization depends upon the ability to define the interests of the party masses, organizational cohesion is an intervening variable between electoral environment and party responsiveness. Maverick candidacies and candidate-centered elections are not *causes* of party weakness. They are effects—signs that the party system is in disarray at its electoral roots.

To show that stable coalitions of constituent interests lie behind unified party structure, this study must go beyond the aggregate vote proportions presented in the opening pages of chapter 2. If one relies only on vote proportions, one misses the possibility that different offices have distinctive electoral bases. If gubernatorial and presidential electoral bases are similar, it makes sense to conduct coattail studies and to simply stop there.[4] However, if the presumption that gubernatorial and presidential electoral bases are linked is wrong, then indices constructed from state-wide figures will not detect the varying electoral bases and the variation in electoral concerns. Electoral divisions measured by state-level election returns could exhibit stability, while the constituencies of the gubernatorial and presidential parties differ. So, unless the analysis extends beyond aggregate data, there is no way to ensure that the discrepant percentages are capturing differences in the constituencies of the state and national parties, differences in voter participation and mobilization at one of the two levels, or some combination of the two.

The Project of the State Studies

Beginning with an analysis of political coalitions in New York, New Jersey, Ohio, and Pennsylvania, the next several chapters assess the congruence of cleavages in electorally competitive states that exhibit unified and factional party patterns. New York, Pennsylvania, Ohio, and New Jersey are examples of states with a history of influential parties. These states have been chosen because each has a history of competitive parties that wage serious organization-influenced campaigns.[5] State and national electoral bases are not very different, or at least not so different as in the weak-party states. Historically, in these states counties that vote in presidential elections also vote Republican and Democratic in state elections and in about the same proportions over time.

Data Sources on Political Cleavages in State Politics

Two types of data are available for describing divisions between coalitions of voters.[6] I present both ecological and individual-level data wherever possible. For the 1980–1992 period, political cleavages are assessed using exit polls for most of the states discussed. Polls are the best source, but exit polls sampled by state, perhaps the most precise measure, have existed only since the late 1970s. National polls go back to the 1940s, but they fail to represent states. Aggregate, county-level data are available back to the nineteenth century, giving adequate historical scope, but county-level behavior may not reflect actual individual voting tendencies. County boundaries are arbitrarily drawn and frequently do not present a precise picture of individual interests.

Reliance on ecological data may be useful to those who seek to understand *elite* behavior. Elites generalize about their electorates. For instance, they typically find them to be much more issue-oriented and informed than they really are.[7] Politicians also tend to think in terms of groups and aggregates, not individuals. When interviewed, elites do not make statements like "I have lost Ann Smith's vote in three out of the last four elections." Instead, they say something like "Multnomah County has always been a difficult county for Republicans to win," or "The labor vote in western Washington is generally Democratic." Aggregates are not necessarily counties or regions, but party leaders rarely think in terms of specific individuals. It would be strange and unnatural for them to have such detailed knowledge about who votes for whom. While the imperfect knowledge of politicians does nothing to resolve the statistical problems of ecological inference, it may indicate that there is a rationale for using county-level data that extends beyond mere convenience.

To understand elite behavior—including the behavior of party organizations and candidates—county-level data, although imperfect for individual-level purposes, may be an adequate second-best strategy for another reason. County-level figures capture the relative concentration of particular constituencies within states. This is important, since groups compete for influence. Blue-collar workers may vote the same in Los Angeles as they do in Toledo, but there may be competing interests in the Los Angeles area that keep blue-collar interests from being a dominant influence. In northern Ohio in the 1960s, the labor bloc was monolithic and not in competition with any groups of similar size. In southern California, Seattle, Phoenix, and Portland, the labor bloc may have found itself competing with other groups for influence. The aggregate data, then, provide an accurate picture of the relative size and strength of groups that may seek to influence the political system in a given state, county, or region.

To make comparisons across states, I contrast selected gubernatorial races in each state with adjacent presidential elections. In the state of Washington, which holds gubernatorial elections in presidential election years, comparisons are particularly easy when data are available. For the other states, gubernatorial races are compared to the previous presidential contest. Cross-sectional snapshots of races in the same election periods ensure that certain conditions remain constant. That all states encountered the choice between Nixon and Kennedy, Carter and Reagan, is important for comparison purposes. The 1960 presidential election is important because it was the closest contest in recent history. No one has claimed that 1960 was a realigning election; it is the one presidential race one would least likely expect to have an impact on partisanship, issues, and gubernatorial voting in the following years. The 1980 presidential race is compared to 1982 (1981 in New Jersey, 1980 in Washington State) gubernatorial voting. This presidential contest, one of the most lopsided in recent history, was hailed by Republicans and conservatives as a realigning election.[8] The gubernatorial contests following the 1980 presidential race provide insight into whether presidential results influence state-level balloting in an election period where one might suspect a strong relationship. Conversion is more likely to result from a landslide presidential election than from a closely fought contest. Models for other races from 1960 to 1992 are also presented to evaluate the congruence of presidential and gubernatorial voting.

Following the pattern of results presented at the end of chapter 2 (appendix tables A.2, A.3), I do not include party identification in any model, ecological or individual, to predict the vote. The reasoning for this goes beyond the unavailability of county-level party registration data for many states. Party identification has always been a highly variable construct from state to state. Including party identification in the regression models would almost certainly boost the predictive power of any vote-explaining equation. It would obscure, however, what is of basic importance in this project: the more fundamental coalitional divisions that divide (or fail to divide) partisans in the state elections of interest. Inasmuch as the goal is to describe the coalitions that constitute the parties, it makes little sense to include party identification as an explanatory variable.

Hypotheses and Theoretical Expectations

As long as the political alignments of the old-party states are stable, the electorate in those states is not as likely to be swayed by personalities as in the western states, meaning that individual races will be more politically competitive in spite of the presence of incumbents with widespread name recognition.[9] Durable electoral divisions will appear over time: specifically, Republican voting should increase markedly as the percentage of blue-collar workers, urban residents, and minority voters declines. Republican voting should decrease as the proportion of poor households rises. When these relationships are flat, changes in such traits do not produce significant differences in political behavior. Finally, one must assess the extent to which partisan voting in gubernatorial elections follows partisan voting in presidential contests. In a state like New Jersey, where political party activity has been very strong, gubernatorial voting may be expected to mimic presidential voting except in unusual presidential landslide years (1972) where national candidates are mismatched. Gubernatorial voting in states like New York, Ohio, Pennsylvania, New Jersey, and Illinois would most likely be impervious to short-term presidential forces due to the basic stability of partisan attachments.

By contrast, in states with a long history of candidate-centered rather than party-oriented electioneering, not only will the political alignments differ from the dominant national system, but also partisan voting for gubernatorial candidates will shift back and forth with individual elections often being quite lopsided (see chapter 2). The cleavages dividing the community will vary, generating individualistic candidacies.

The differences between candidate-centered and party-centered states can be partly attributed to the presence or absence of certain constituencies. Until the 1970s, for example, economies in the western region were based on one, two, or three principal business sectors. The infrastructure necessary to support heavy urbanization and industrialization did not emerge until the mid-twentieth century. As late as 1960, the most industrialized western state, California, had only 22 percent of its labor force employed in manufacturing, with a much smaller fraction employed in heavy industry (nondurables). About 30 percent of New York and New Jersey's work forces were employed in manufacturing. By 1980, California had pulled even only with New York in the percentage of the work force employed in industry. This economic history suggests an electoral foundation that has been ill suited to supporting a conventionally divided partisan politics.

The lack of readily identifiable national coalition groups in western-state politics has allowed party leaders much more flexibility in mobilizing local coalitions of their own making. Second, the sparse settlement patterns in western cities and states has made them unsuitable for the traditional party machinery that benefits from concentrated populations. Candidates are forced to search far and wide for votes rather than relying on one urban area such as Chicago, Philadelphia, Cleveland, or New York City for control of the election. Where populations are concentrated, such as Phoenix and Las Vegas, they are politically divided in a way that Cleveland and Chicago are not. Even when a state could be controlled from one population base, that area must be carefully sifted to identify politically sympathetic voters.

Divisions in the community in the western states do not clearly reflect national cleavages, even if elites work to connect the two. When electoral interests are not divided by the major national cleavages, elites may talk about the national issues but must find and represent the issues and interests that are of local consequence. There is much discussion by candidates of valence issues, such as the economy. Position issues, however, determine cleavages, and this is where the West is different. Since electors are homogeneous, the successful party candidate will win often by landslide proportions. The problem, however, is that today's position issues may not be tomorrow's. That same party's candidate may lose by just as wide a margin when the tide turns and new themes emerge. This is the unstable nature of party disunity in the western United States.

The Once Firm Foundation: New York and New Jersey

New York: Electoral Background

FROM THE 1930s through the 1970s, there was a nice symmetry between New York's state politics and the national New Deal party system. There is a straightforward explanation for this correspondence. New York was the most politically dominant state in the country until the 1970s when it was replaced by California as the most populous. Not only were many nationally recognized candidates from New York (Smith, Roosevelt, Dewey, Harriman, Willkie), but New York also had the largest congressional delegation. The electoral coalitions in New York State even predate the major national cleavages of the New Deal and post–New Deal eras. Throughout the thirties and forties, New York State—its voters and politicians—was the central player in determining the New Deal alignment.[1]

Just as national politics took on a redistributive tone following the Great Depression, New York politics divided along similar lines. As national politics was dividing between city and countryside, and by race and class, these same sources of conflict separated New Yorkers. Regionally, Democrats drew much of their support from New York City. Republicans drew their support from upstate rural and suburban areas around New York City. Ray McGrath, a Long Island Republican and veteran of the state legislature, indicated that substate regionalism was especially visible in the annual state budget battle:

> As a function of budgeting, more money goes to the City than to the suburbs. The suburbs have managed to carve out school aid as their major plum from state government. The rural areas resent this.

There is also conflict over hydroelectric power. Downstate would like
to tap into upstate's hydroelectric resources. This hasn't happened
yet.[2]

George Hochbrueckner, a Democratic politician and former state legislator
representing heavily Republican Suffolk County agreed: "The budget battle
is where the regionalism emerges. The determination of school aid is probably the biggest regional issue for the suburbs."[3]

The regional division in New York politics has not been economic in any
definite occupational sense. Manufacturing was the largest single employment source for heavily Democratic New York City in 1960.[4] But it was also
the largest single sector of employment for many of the Republican counties
upstate. Upstate areas had agriculture which New York City does not. Agriculture, however, was not sufficient enough to make farming the dominant
interest in all but the most rural counties.

Rather, regionalism in New York was built on the liberal-conservative
differences discussed by V. O. Key. "City voters are most likely to take the
'liberal' position, favoring government action to solve problems, while non-
City voters are likely to take the opposite, 'conservative' position."[5] The
conflict was really a split between that facet of the New Deal that concerned
government's proper role in the economic sphere. The regional division was
over taxation and government spending on social programs and schools and
bond issues to cover debt, much of which was perceived to go to New York
City. Upstate voters have generally perceived New York City politicians as
seeking liberal, big-spending policies, and the upstate areas have produced
conservative candidates to oppose New York and to defend low taxes and their
own interests, such as hydroelectric power.[6] This geographic division is illustrated in maps 3.1 and 3.2 where the darkly shaded areas representing counties in the most Republican quintile are all located upstate.

The division between upstate and New York City is not always a partisan
one. John LaFalce, a Democratic politician from Tonawanda, near Buffalo, said
that when he first entered New York politics in the early 1970s, a major issue
for his upstate constituency was Republican Governor Nelson Rockefeller's
spending. Rockefeller was so closely associated with high taxes that LaFalce
ran his 1972 state legislative race on the motto "Chipping Away at the Rock."
The need for New York City votes has restrained Republican governors like
Rockefeller from adopting the fiscally conservative positions of the national
party.[7] The trade-off is such that Republican governors have often found
themselves opposed by state legislators from upstate in both parties.

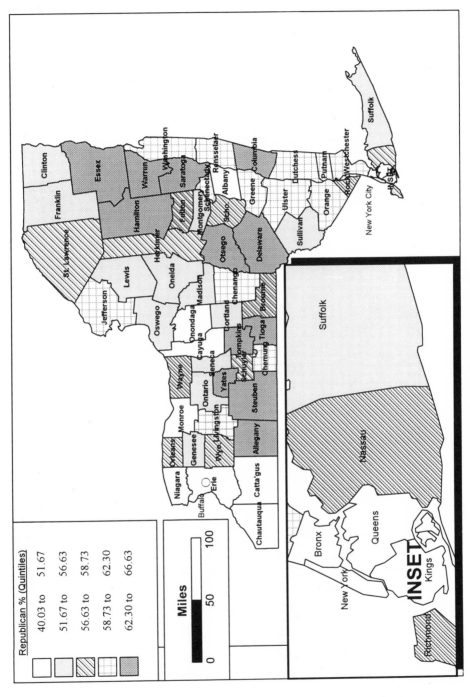

Republican % (Quintiles)

	40.03 to 51.67
	51.67 to 56.63
	56.63 to 58.73
	58.73 to 62.30
	62.30 to 66.63

Miles

0   50   100

Map 3.1   Average Republican Gubernatorial Vote in New York State, 1962–1970

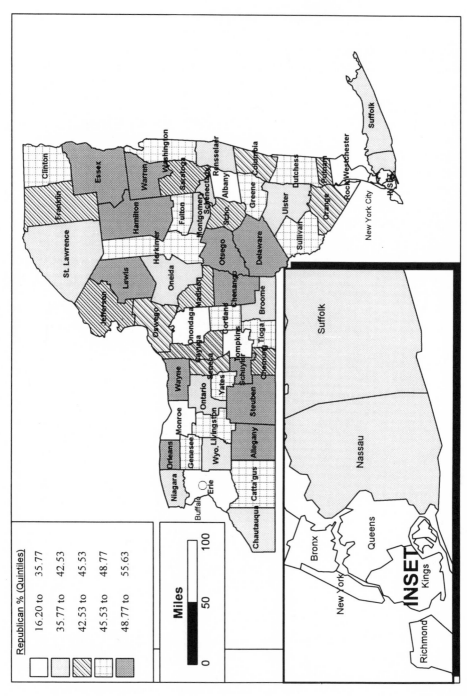

Republican % (Quintiles)

- 16.20 to 35.77
- 35.77 to 42.53
- 42.53 to 45.53
- 45.53 to 48.77
- 48.77 to 55.63

Miles

0   50   100

Map 3.2   Average Republican Gubernatorial Vote in New York State, 1982–1990

Party Organizations in New York State

New York has long been one of the strongest organization states in the country. When typologized by county, the areas of high population density tend to produce the strongest parties while those of low density produce comparatively weak ones.[8] Some regional variation, then, occurs in the process of leadership and recruitment for these organizations. Some of this variation can be attributed to the constituency characteristics of an area. In New York City, there are more people who want positions than there are positions to fill. Organizations screen potential candidates, and there is substantial intraparty competition for both elected office and patronage. Preprimary recruitment is dominated by party leaders, and selected candidates are affirmed or ratified by party activists and, ultimately, party voters. The limited opportunity offered by the traditional parties in New York City may explain the appeal of the minor parties there. Outside the City and its closest suburbs, the minor parties have almost no organization.[9]

In the suburban areas, Republican leadership is as strong as Democratic leadership is in New York City. Nassau County has a vigorous Republican machine and a weaker Democratic organization. The Nassau Republican machine is noteworthy for its role in controlling the recruitment and nomination of candidates. Ray McGrath was recruited to run for state legislature by the Nassau Republican organization, and he gave it generous credit for launching many political careers:

> The party was very instrumental in recruiting me. When I got out of graduate school, I had no political interests. Then, they asked me to help in a campaign. Later, they helped me secure financing to run.
>
> Nassau County is one of the few places where you can still run without being independently wealthy. The organization will help you finance your campaign and get out the voters. Every committeeman in the 1096 precincts in Nassau county is responsible for gathering support for each candidate.
>
> The Nassau organization may be weaker now than it was before but it is still light years ahead of everywhere else. We get voters out for free, whereas most other places it requires fortunes.[10]

In Suffolk County, parties are organized on a village or area basis and party leaders are less involved in the recruitment process. George Hochbrueckner said that he ran his own campaigns in Suffolk because the Democratic organization could not deliver a county with a two to one Republican edge.[11] Primaries have been rare in both Suffolk and Nassau Counties. Westchester

County is controlled by solid Republican leadership, where well-developed municipal organizations and the county leadership exercise firm control over nominations.

An earlier analysis maintained that party control over the nomination process varied widely by region—strongest in the urban areas, of middling strength in the suburban areas, and weakest in rural areas. In rural areas, the organizations must go out of their way to find candidates for the many low-level, low-paying positions, so there is less competition within the rural organization for party jobs.[12] Upstate, then, the presence of organizations is spotty. John LaFalce indicated that Erie County (Buffalo) had a strong Democratic organization but that the other county organizations (Niagara and Orleans) in his congressional district did not have much influence. Congressman Sherwood Boehlert, from the Utica area, said that Chenango, Ostego, and Delaware counties, in his congressional district in central New York had influential organizations (see maps 3.1 and 3.2, above). He attributed the strength of these organizations to the leadership of the county chairs, "good leaders with solid patronage bases." But, there is a continuum in the constituent service function of the parties: "the New York City parties are more deeply involved in the lives of their communities than the parties upstate."[13]

In New York City, the local party is a "problem-solving institution" and is more likely to flourish because there are problems. Each of these county- and city-based organizations provide a solid hierarchical basis for the statewide organizations. The Democratic state organization is dominated by New York City locals: the Republican organization is dominated by suburban and upstate metropolitan elements. Since 1970, party involvement in the selection of gubernatorial candidates has waned. Until that point, candidates were selected by convention rather than the direct primary, but the party leadership maintained control over nominations until very recently. Would-be primary challengers often find themselves drawn to one of the minor parties. Still, New York primaries for the two major parties have been more crowded as the minor parties have only a small electoral following. As is evident from the 1982 election, however, the candidacy of Lewis Lehrman was not an accident of a direct primary so much as it was a result of an electorate that was less and less influenced by local political organizations.

New York State: Politics in the Post–New Deal Period

Regional, economic, and racial cleavages have divided New York politics for most of this century. Results of a regression analysis of county-level socioeconomic characteristics on several presidential and gubernatorial elec-

Table 3.1 Influences on Republican Presidential and Gubernatorial Voting in New York State, by County, 1960–1992

	Constant	Income	% Urban	Minority	% Mfg.	Adj. R²
President, 1960	39.3	1.57* (.20)	−.48* (.05)	−.01 (.16)	.02 (.10)	.87
Governor, 1962	42.2	1.64* (.20)	−.43* (.05)	.07 (.17)	−.15 (.10)	.82
President, 1968	53.1	.45* (.15)	−.20* (.05)	−.63* (.14)	−.11 (.09)	.85
Governor, 1970	68.0	.30 (.20)	−.14* (.06)	−.44* (.17)	−.43* (.11)	.61
President, 1972	64.5	.33 (.20)	−.11* (.06)	−.77* (.18)	−.03 (.12)	.76
President, 1980	48.9	.44* (.16)	−.04 (.05)	−.33* (.10)	−.29* (.11)	.74
Governor, 1982	57.0	.24 (.13)	−.18* (.04)	−.49* (.09)	.26* (.08)	.93
President, 1988	66.7	−.02 (.02)	.05 (.03)	−.67* (.05)	−.49* (.09)	.83
Governor, 1990	36.4	−.02 (.02)	−.07* (.03)	−.34* (.04)	−.10 (.07)	.75
President, 1992	46.1	−.01 (.02)	.04 (.03)	−.46* (.04)	−.36* (.08)	.76

*p < .05   N=62

Source: Bureau of the Census, *County and City Databook* (Washington, D.C.: GPO, various years); Richard M. Scammon, *America Votes* (Washington, D.C.: Elections Research Center, various years); *County and City Extra* (Lanham, Md.: Bernan Press, 1992).

Note: Multiple linear regression, WLS estimation; unstandardized regression coefficients weighted for population; standard errors in parentheses; income is expressed in thousands of constant 1992 dollars.

tions since 1960 are reported in table 3.1. The standard demographic indicators predictably divide the state, with urban-rural and racial divisions appearing most consistently. In the early 1960s, the patterns of urban, racial, and class voting were especially pronounced. Moreover, there is a strong similarity between the cleavages dividing New Yorkers in the 1960 presidential contest and those dividing the state in the 1962 gubernatorial race. This illustrates the durability of New York's electoral coalitions during that decade.

New York's statewide races have usually been issueless campaigns in which party loyalty and turnout have played the key roles. Robert Morgenthau lost to Nelson Rockefeller in 1962 because his partisans—Jewish, Puerto Rican and black voters in New York City—stayed home and there were no issue appeals with which an urban Democrat could woo upstate and suburban Republicans. Rockefeller won because his base of partisans remained loyal and he was able to attract the votes of some ethnic Democrats.[14] Note in table 3.1 the absence of racial divisions in the 1962 vote. Having lost segments of traditional Democratic support, Morgenthau's candidacy was weakened, proving that the cohesion of party coalitions influences political outcomes. In the 1960 race, with both organizations working at full strength, a ten-point increase in the percentage of the population residing in urban counties led to a 4.8 percent drop in Nixon's vote. But in the 1962 contest, Rockefeller lost 4.3 points for every ten-point increase in urbanization (table 3.1). With his penchant for spending, traditional Democratic constituencies such as construction unions and welfare recipients considered him to be friendly to their cause.[15]

The Rise of Candidate-Centeredness in New York State

In recent years, class has not been as prominent an influence in New York politics as ethnic and racial cleavage have been. In the 1982 Mario Cuomo–Lewis Lehrman race, for instance, voting was only weakly determined by the class status of counties, surprising, given Lehrman's doctrinaire, conservative views.[16] The 1982 contest was different in some important respects from the Rockefeller contests twenty years earlier. In 1982 the country was in a serious economic recession. Gubernatorial voting decisions often reflect the attitudes of voters toward the incumbent president. The 1982 election in New York was viewed widely as a barometer of voters' reaction to the Reagan administration's fiscal policies as well as the lingering unemployment and high interest rates of the late 1970s.[17]

Concern with the economy, however, does not necessarily generate cleavages between groups since the economy is an issue that everyone considers to be important. If economic times are bad enough, traditional party cleavages may be submerged as nearly everyone turns against the party in power. In New York, so clearly part and parcel of the Rust Belt decline, local conditions would ensure an anti-Republican vote. Fully 62 percent of New York voters claimed that Reaganomics had hurt the state's economy, compared to only 42 percent of the voters in California. Republican Lew Lehrman was able to avoid a landslide loss on the basis of his considerable fortune. Considering the eleven million dollars he had invested, three times more than Cuomo, Lehrman should have won.[18] As testimony to the tendency for valence issues to work against the president's party, Cuomo was victorious because he successfully tagged Lehrman as a wealthy father of the economic downturn. He repeatedly called attention to the money Lehrman was spending in the campaign, saying at one point, "This is a contest between experience money can't buy and the exposure money can buy."[19] As dominated as this big-money campaign was by the candidates, persistent aspects of the state's partisanship emerged in this contest, as Lehrman lost every New York City borough. Lehrman had no support among the City's liberal independent blocs that Rockefeller had successfully attracted twenty years earlier. Had Lehrman been able to attract the support of New York City liberals, he would have won. Cuomo, in fact, won with victories only in New York City's five counties and Westchester, where his running mate was the county executive. But Lehrman ran surprisingly well in many of the industrial counties upstate where a ten-point increase in the percentage employed in manufacturing increased his vote by 2.6 percent.

The presence of New York's third-party system has had the effect of encouraging a more candidate-centered politics. In contrast to the highly competitive 1982 contest, the 1990 race between Mario Cuomo and Pierre Rinfret was a complete mismatch. Evidently, Republicans abandoned their candidate as a lost cause early in the contest. The third-party candidacy of Herbert London was hailed as one of Rinfret's biggest obstacles. Polls prior to the election showed that both London and Rinfret were in a dead heat, with Cuomo leading them both by about fifty points. Consistent with the notion that conservative presidential tides have brought about the dissolution of party unity in the northeast, London's challenge was self-described as an attempt to "wake up" the Republican party and bring it up-to-date with the conservative tone of the national party.[20] Had this split not occurred, Cuomo may still have won but the contest would have been much less lopsided. Rinfret and London together polled about 45 percent of the three-party vote. Following the election, in which he finished third, London called for the takeover of the party by conservatives. The challenge for the Republicans for some years to come will be to either shed their liberal tradition or reconcile the emboldened conservatives to that tradition. Such a challenge was never much of a threat to unity when Republicans were winning under Nelson Rockefeller's autocratic rule.

New York is noteworthy for its early development of intensely personal campaigns centering around self-financed candidacies; which is surprising given the heralded strength of New York's political parties. Personality politics is generally thought to be opposite to the politics of strong political party organizations. Yet, even as Rockefeller ran with predictable electoral support from certain Republican areas of the state, it is fair to say that his personality dominated state politics during the 1960s and early 1970s. Both Lehrman and Cuomo also ran campaigns in which they were the central players. Cuomo went around the regular organization and set up separate structures in every county that had endorsed his 1982 primary rival, Mayor Koch.[21] This tendency to run independently of organization support has emerged because the New York party structure remains highly decentralized. While these organizations are still influential locally, they have a more difficult time unifying to conduct and coordinate statewide races. In addition, the local organizations command less and less of the vote. Citizens no longer rely upon the cues of local party machines, making it possible to launch a successful, self-guided candidacy that appeals directly to the unattached masses.

National Divisions in the New York Electorate

Party machinery greatly benefits from a stable electorate with strong party attachments. Candidate-centered races emerge when that electorate is no longer so predictably divided, that is, when traditional coalitions dissolve. Have New York's electoral divisions become less predictable? Polling data from recent elections show that national political divisions are still present in New York politics, although they are less pronounced now than they were in the 1950s and 1960s (see table 3.2).[22] Among voters, race is the most consistently salient cleavage in contemporary New York State. The 1980 and 1984 presidential elections were the most racially polarized due to the especially high turnout levels of minority voters in presidential election years. Racial differences between the parties are obviously heightened with a greater surge in the loyal Democratic voting of African Americans.

Table 3.2 also shows that labor and clan cleavages vary significantly across elections. These fluctuations reflect the electoral instability that has generated lopsided, incumbent-oriented contests. How do New York's political divisions compare to national political divisions? New York follows the nation primarily with respect to the racial component of its politics (compare table 3.2 to appendix table A.5). Otherwise, the state's recent political divisions are only dimly reflective of national party divisions. Today, New York is less integral to the national party system than it has ever been.

Table 3.2 Logit Analysis of the Influence of Race, Income, and Union Membership in New York State Elections, 1980–1992

	Constant	Race	Income	Labor	No. of Cases	Predicted Null (%)
President, 1980	2.78	−1.77*	.03*	−.25	1,809	64
		(.006)	(.001)	(.10)		57
Effect		−41.0	0.7	−6.0		
Governor, 1982	2.03	−1.39*	.09*	−.35*	2,070	57
		(.005)	(.005)	(.003)		53
Effect		−33.0	2.2	−8.6		
Senate, 1982	0.24	−.86*	.08*	−.25*	1,975	75
		(.006)	(.001)	(.003)		74
Effect		−16.0	1.6	−5.2		
President, 1984	2.97	−2.10*	.06	−.27*	1,141	69
		(.21)	(.04)	(.13)		52
Effect		−47.0	1.5	−6.7		
Governor, 1986	0.92	−1.56*	.06*	−.07*	1,203	69
		(.008)	(.002)	(.004)		66
Effect		−26.0	1.2	−1.5		
Senate, 1986	2.37	−1.37*	.05*	−.11*	1,200	65
		(.001)	(.001)	(.004)		59
Effect		−33.0	−1.2	−3.0		
President, 1988	1.52	−1.35*	−.01	−.03	1,571	57
		(.15)	(.04)	(.11)		55
Effect		−30.0	−0.2	−0.7		
Senate, 1988	0.51	−1.09*	−.07	−.01	1,460	74
		(.20)	(.04)	(.12)		73
Effect		−18.0	−1.4	−0.2		
Governor, 1990[a]	1.35	−1.61*	.10*	−.09*	1,587	56
		(.01)	(.002)	(.004)		55
Effect		−33.0	2.5	−2.2		
President, 1992	0.75	−1.11*	.03	−.36*	1,431	64
		(.18)	(.05)	(.12)		64
Effect		−22.1	1.0	−7.1		
Senate, 1992	1.61	−1.33*	−.02	−.20*	1,625	58
		(.16)	(.04)	(.11)		50
Effect		−30.2	−0.5	−5.0		

Source: ICPSR, CBS News/New York Times, *Election Day Surveys*, 1980, 1982, 1986. ABC News/Washington Post, *50 State Poll*, September–November, 1988. Voter Research and Surveys, *General Election Exit Poll*, 1990, 1992.
Note: Dependent variable: 0 = Democrat, 1 = Republican; MLE coefficients; standard errors in parentheses; *p < .05; Effect = change in odds of voting Republican from moving x one unit at the means of the other variables.
a. For the 1990 gubernatorial race, the dependent variable combines both Republican and Conservative party votes.

Electoral Change and the Rise of Candidate-Centered Politics

The decline in party unity in New York is associated with the increasingly variable electoral cleavages from election to election. In 1960, the cracks in New York City's party machinery were just beginning to show, but party machinery had not yet fallen apart.[23] At the same time, in Nassau, Westchester, and Suffolk counties, the Republican machines remained the dominant force in that party's politics. Machines from both parties remained active in the party politics of Albany and Buffalo through the 1960s. Some remain, but they have lost much of their power because they cannot control nominations as they used to. The electorate is not as often cued by deep partisan attachments. In the 1982 gubernatorial race, for instance, only 23 percent of the voters identified party as the primary reason for supporting their candidate.[24]

According to David R. Mayhew, Tammany began to fall when the post war "in-migration" of "white professionals took exceptional interest in issues."[25] The reform-oriented, liberal Democrats initiated a series of slating contests that they ultimately won. This transformation in the electoral base of the Democratic party was enough to cause the eventual demise of the old guard that was based in blue-collar and ethnic neighborhoods. Republican regularity, on the other hand, has been challenged by the animation of conservative themes in large segments of the electorate.

From the perspective of the argument here, it is important that the changing electorate encouraged candidates to work outside traditional machinery, either on their own, or, as in Herbert London's (1990) case, with minor parties. The changing electorate undermined the control of the old guard by challenging its capacity to monopolize the nomination process around the old style of politics. The new and more liberal party leadership that eventually won control was far from the New York Democrats of the days of Al Smith and Franklin D. Roosevelt.

Evidence of the increasingly independent electorate is labor's fickle Democratic allegiance. Reagan won 45 percent of the labor vote in 1980, and even Lew Lehrman won 39 percent in the midst of a recession. Apparently the labor-nonlabor cleavage in New York State has not been strong enough to overpower the regional acculturation of many voters. Upstate labor union members are much more likely to vote Republican than those in New York City. Even in the earlier statewide contests of the 1960s, the differences between manufacturing and nonmanufacturing counties were not statistically significant (see table 3.1, above). Counties in upstate regions are cross-pressured by conflicting cues and when confronted by a Democrat from New

York City, some will vote against her or fail to turn out—independent of their class-based ties to a party or their economic interests.

New York has gradually moved from the old politics of party organizations to the new politics of candidate self-sponsorship. As John Kenneth White has pointed out, Mario Cuomo's 1986 landslide was his alone. Similarly, Daniel Patrick Moynihan swamped his Republican opponent in 1988 while Michael Dukakis barely won the state.[26] This reorientation to a candidate-centered politics was forced on the New York Republican party by Nelson Rockefeller's leadership coupled with the conservative drift of the national Republican party. While Rockefeller's influence generally benefited his party, however, more recent candidate-centered efforts, like Lew Lehrman's, have divided it. As the national Republican party has moved to the right of the state party in New York, the state party has faced an uncomfortable choice: Do we follow the national party with more conservative candidates such as Lew Lehrman? or do we follow the liberal Rockefeller legacy? This dilemma did not exist in 1940, when the Republican party's presidential candidates were very much like New York's state officeholders. The effect of skewed state and national party ideologies has been to split the electoral party and to increase the number of contested primaries.

New Jersey: Electoral Background

Since the 1930s, politics in New Jersey has been intensely competitive by region, race, and class. Regionally, New Jersey, like New York, is virtually two separate states. The north is a mixture of urban and suburban. The south, except Camden, is small-town and rural. South Jersey thinks of itself as so distinct, that its voters have supported ballot measures to secede from the state, the most recent attempt occurring in 1981. William Hughes, a Democratic politician from Ocean City, explained the regional differences in political, economic, and cultural terms:

> The north has the population centers. They get almost everything from state government, transportation dollars, for instance. We're different in the south. We have different attitudes. We're small-town. We know each other and get along with our neighbors. There's none of that big-city suspicion in southern New Jersey.[27]

The rural south and the north suburbs are generally Republican. The industrial, north coastal counties have voted decisively Democratic. Maps 3.3 and 3.4 show the geographic distribution of gubernatorial partisanship, averaged across elections in the 1960s and the 1980s. The state's political subsections are remarkably similar across the twenty-year period.

New Jersey differs from New York because there is a sharp labor-nonlabor division alongside the regional split. In few states has the blue-collar vote been able to exert more influence in the politics of the Democratic party. In addition, class cleavages, as determined by income disparity, have sharply divided the state at least since the 1930s. Racial divisions have not been as visible at the county level, being submerged in the politics of the labor-dominated Democratic party. Atlantic County (Atlantic City), home to the greatest concentration of African Americans, has been a solidly Republican area since the late 1940s—not necessarily because blacks vote Republican

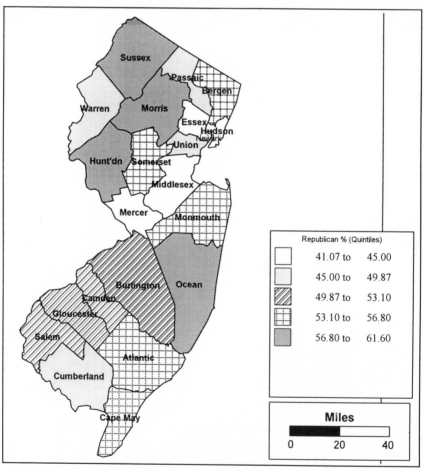

Map 3.3   Average Republican Gubernatorial Vote in New Jersey, 1961–1969

(although many did for Republican Governor Tom Kean in 1981 and 1985) but principally because of low turnout.

The close relationship of gubernatorial to presidential voting is readily apparent in both the 1961 and 1981 races (fig. 3.1). For every ten-point increase in Richard Nixon's percentage of the 1960 presidential vote, there was a 7.3 percent increase in the Republican gubernatorial candidate's vote. The 1981 scatterplot shows that the Republican candidate, Thomas Kean, ran much stronger than Reagan. A ten-point increase in Ronald Reagan's vote from county to county led to a 14.6 percent increase in Tom Kean's winning percentage. The presidential voting behavior of the counties has not changed over time. Voting in the 1960 presidential contest is highly related to vot-

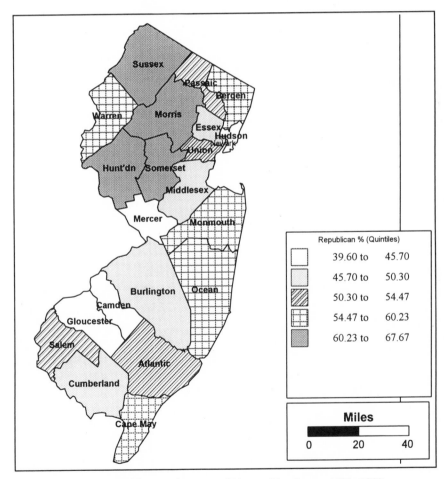

Map 3.4   Average Republican Gubernatorial Vote in New Jersey, 1981–1989

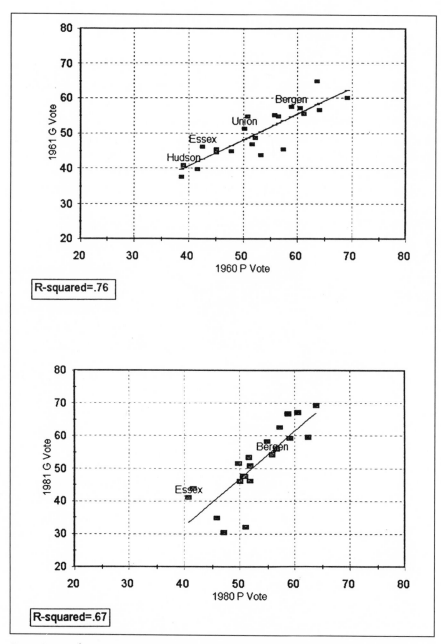

Figure 3.1 Relation Between Republican Percentage of the Vote for President and Governor in New Jersey, by County, 1960–1961 and 1980–1981

Source: Richard M. Scammon and Alice McGillivray, eds., *America Votes* (Washington, D.C.: Elections Research Center).

ing in the Carter-Reagan race twenty years later. Presidential voting patterns in 1960 explain 84.2 percent of the statistical variation in the 1980 presidential vote.

Party Organizations in New Jersey

While New Jersey political organizations have experienced some decline in influence, they have also experienced growth and rejuvenation.[28] In most states, state party organizations are coalitions of county organizations. In New Jersey, gubernatorial nominees have usually relied upon county bosses for endorsement and support. Because the state has fewer counties than New York, party cohesion requires less consensus building. Local party organizations are strongest in the urban counties, although Republicans have been well organized in the southern part of the state. Organizations are strongest for Democrats where there are concentrated national coalition groups, such as blue-collar labor voters.[29] In these areas, partisan loyalties are reinforced by the issues of national politics.

Like New Yorkers, New Jersey politicians are unashamed of their party tradition. The 1961 appeal by gubernatorial candidate James Mitchell to the bossism controlling his opponent would not work to win votes in a state as politically well organized as New Jersey. The party organizations had a strong hold on the electorate pushing out the personal characteristics and issues of the candidates.[30]

One-party municipalities play the dominant role in county organization politics, even in strong two-party counties such as Camden and Passaic. John Blydenburgh provides the following explanation:

> Population distribution within the county apparently is an important factor in explaining strong county organizations. Seven of the twelve counties have one or two large municipalities, the control over which has been used to control the county. Since city government is organized hierarchically, it is possible for one or few persons to control a city. Since one or a very few cities dominate a county, city organization leads to county organization.[31]

Once the two hierarchical factions are established—one urban the other nonurban—the only task that remains is to count votes. Since the urban area has most of the votes, the municipal machine usually controls the county, often propelling would-be underdogs to victory in primaries. A competitive political environment has generally secured a place for party organizations in the state's politics.

New Jersey State Politics in the Post–New Deal Period

Typical of post–New Deal New Jersey elections was the competitive race between Democrat Richard J. Hughes and Republican James Mitchell for the 1961 governorship. Hughes, an obscure judge from Trenton, won the race in an upset of former cabinet official Mitchell by relying entirely on the turnout of traditional Democratic coalition groups.[32] Labor issues and qualifications to govern punctuated the campaign attacks of Hughes. He argued that Mitchell had fought against minimum wage legislation as secretary of labor and claimed that Mitchell was a carpetbagger, having "played no part in New Jersey's affairs for the last twenty-five years."[33] Mitchell campaigned against bossism and the economic decline of the state during the incumbent Democratic administration.

Both candidates campaigned alongside national party leaders. Mitchell had the active support of former President Eisenhower in whose cabinet he had served. Mitchell was also assisted on the stump by Governor Rockefeller of New York and Governor Volpe of Massachusetts. President Kennedy came to Trenton five days before the election to tell voters that he was proud to urge the election of Hughes and that Hughes wanted the same things for the nation that he did. Kennedy had carried the state the year before by a scant 22,000 votes. In response to Kennedy's visit, Mitchell claimed that his state's elections were unrelated to national politics and that Kennedy's presence would not help Hughes.[34] Mitchell's argument about the difference between state and national politics was unconvincing given the durability of party attachments in the New Jersey electorate. In a state where the electorate is divided along national lines, there are few issue voters who would cross over based on state-level concerns. Consequently, Mitchell's strongest campaign attack—that Hughes would be the puppet of political bosses who would rule the state in the background—would not overcome the more fundamental Republican deficit in voter registration.

What unquestionably put Hughes over the top was his strength in pro-union, traditional Democratic areas. In the eight counties with the highest proportion of workers in manufacturing, Mitchell won a majority in only two, one of which was his home turf—the traditionally Republican Union County—which he won by a mere 6,665 votes. Mitchell's main campaign theme of political bossism could not spark many voters in counties tied to the Democratic machines. Hughes, on the other hand, was especially helped by party organizations in the key counties of Essex, Union, Passaic, Mercer, Middlesex, and Camden (see maps 3.3 and 3.4, above).

As for the four national elements of New Deal partisanship: the minority population of New Jersey was small and dispersed, having no decisive impact

Table 3.3 Influences on Republican Presidential and Gubernatorial Voting in New Jersey, by County, 1960–1992

	Constant	Income	% Urban	Minority	% Mfg.	Adj. R²
President, 1960	49.9	1.34* (.30)	−.26* (.07)	−.37 (.20)	−.53* (.15)	.73
Governor, 1961	39.5	1.40* (.35)	−.15* (.07)	−.20 (.20)	−.62* (.16)	.63
President, 1968	36.3	.90* (.20)	−.18* (.06)	−.22 (.11)	−.27 (.14)	.75
Governor, 1969	71.9	.19 (.21)	−.08 (.06)	−.37* (.13)	−.30* (.15)	.55
President, 1972	76.8	.04 (.13)	−.08* (.04)	−.56* (.08)	−.13 (.09)	.85
President, 1980	61.8	.08 (.16)	−.05 (.06)	−.44* (.09)	−.08* (.13)	.74
Governor, 1981	42.1	.91* (.35)	−.27* (.10)	−.10 (.21)	−.12 (.30)	.48
President, 1988	69.2	.10 (.10)	−.10 (.05)	−.51* (.07)	.02 (.12)	.88
Governor, 1989	38.4	.40* (.14)	−.23* (.07)	−.16 (.11)	.10 (.18)	.71
President, 1992	35.9	.21 (.12)	−.04 (.06)	−.25* (.10)	.12 (.16)	.56

*p < .05   N=21

Source: Bureau of the Census, *County and City Databook* (Washington, D.C.: GPO, various years); Richard M. Scammon and Alice McGillivray, eds., *America Votes* (Washington, D.C.: Elections Research Center, various years).

Note: Multiple linear regression, WLS estimation; unstandardized regression coefficients weighted for population; standard errors in parentheses.

on the machine-controlled election. Predictably, though, higher income areas did vote for Mitchell (table 3.3). Gerald Pomper suggests that New Jersey's voting was divided more along urban-rural than class lines. In the 1961 election, urbanization had the expected impact, favoring Hughes by 1.5 points for every ten-point increase in urbanization. Blue-collar populations had much to say about which counties voted against Mitchell. A ten-point increase in the percentage of the population employed in manufacturing generated a drastic 6.2 percent drop in Republican Mitchell's share of the vote.

One measure of effective political organization is high turnout by partisans. The 1961 gubernatorial race was decided by partisan participation backed by the county machines.[35] The Hughes forces were organized in the big urban centers—Jersey City and Newark. While Republicans have solid organizations, they are located in the smaller urban centers—Atlantic City, Monmouth, and Somerset Counties and in suburbs. By controlling the largest cities, Democrats controlled the county machinery and the mobilization effort.[36] This solid base of strength consistently won elections.

The Emerging Candidate-Centeredness in New Jersey

By the early 1980s, the importance of local political organizations in the state's politics had waned considerably. Not coincidental with this development, the tendency for industrial areas to vote Democratic fell drastically from the early 1960s (table 3.3). What appeared to divide the state in the 1981 race between Tom Kean and Jim Florio was not manufacturing from nonmanufacturing areas. Instead, a combination of urban-rural and class cleavages emerged. Florio struggled to bring the blue-collar voters back to the Democratic column after their defection to President Reagan the year before. He made much of his working-class, Italian-American background, but to no avail. Kean's campaign successfully tied Florio to the unpopular retiring governor Brendan Byrne.

The 1981 contest was about as issueless as earlier contests had been, but there was a new element of candidate-centeredness. Much like the race of twenty years earlier, the two candidates were not sharply divided on most state matters.[37] Both were pro-choice, both were strong supporters of environmental causes and the arts. Both believed in cracking down on crime and expanding prisons and favored treating juvenile offenders as adults. Kean had even sponsored gun control legislation when he was in the state legislature.

Issueless races can still be candidate- rather than party-centered, Kean narrowly won the contest—which was surprising, given the Democrats' two to one edge in registration. He won again in 1985, again showing his ability to win crossover voters. Kean's geographic base was similar to that of Mitchell's—winning in the suburban counties and rural areas downstate. Florio won in the urban and industrial counties next to New York City and in his home district around Camden (map 3.4, above).

The 1989 gubernatorial race shows how Republican candidates from states with moderate traditions can often marginalize themselves by following conservative presidential politics. In this contest, Florio ran once again, but won this time by a sizeable margin. Unlike the 1982 contest, the candidates had very distinct issue positions. Republican Jim Courter situated himself to the right of Tom Kean and in the mainstream of Reagan-Bush presidential politics. This left Florio to claim that he represented Kean's moderate legacy. State voters, for their part, didn't buy the Courter message of continued deregulation, tax breaks to businesses, and his conservative antiabortion and environmental records as a member of Congress.[38]

According to press accounts, Florio was able to capitalize on the anxiety created at the end of the state's impressive economic expansion during the Kean years. The race was particularly negative with an unusual amount of press coverage focused on the candidates themselves. Courter was perceived as bumbling and dishonest, a flip-flopper on issues and a candidate without credibility. His main liability appeared to be his overly conservative views. When the votes rolled in, Florio had brought nearly all of the Reagan Democrats back into his party's fold. Independents favored Florio by a two to one margin.

National Divisions in the New Jersey Electorate

In the past, New Jersey's electoral divisions have reflected the strong traditions of the state rooted in its stable population. Labor voters are no longer located in the easily organizable, concentrated geographic pockets of thirty years ago. They remain predominantly Democratic, but there are many exceptions now. In the 1989 gubernatorial contest, around 70 percent of voters in labor union households voted for Florio, compared with just 45 percent for Michael Dukakis the year before. This radical degree of fluctuation is new in the state's postwar history.

In the 1989 gubernatorial contest, racial polarization was at a nine-year low (see table 3.4). Minorities were 18 percent less likely to vote for Courter than white voters. This may reflect the success Tom Kean had in attracting some African-American support in his own gubernatorial bids in 1981 and 1985. As in New York, racial polarization was greatest in the presidential contests of 1980, 1984, and 1988, where the highly publicized national elections exercised substantial influence on turnout and issue content. State-level Republican candidates for U.S. senator and governor did slightly better with minorities—undoubtedly benefiting from their lighter turnout in off years.

Comparing New Jersey's political divisions to those in national elections (see table 3.4 and appendix table A.5) suggests that in presidential elections cleavages between white and nonwhite voters are almost as strong as they are

Table 3.4   Logit Analysis of the Influence of Race, Income, and Union Membership in New Jersey Elections, 1980–1992

	Constant	Race	Income	Labor	No. of Cases	Predicted Null (%)
President, 1980	2.81	−2.06*	.27*	−.38*	1,523	68
		(.009)	(.001)	(.004)		64
Effect		−47.4	6.3	−8.0		
Senate, 1982	1.72	−1.17*	.25*	−.56*	1,758	60
		(.009)	(.001)	(.003)		52
Effect		−28.4	6.2	−13.4		
President, 1984	1.56	−1.76*	.11*	−.26*	1,004	67
		(.18)	(.05)	(.12)		58
Effect		−33.0	2.5	−6.1		
Senate, 1984	1.99	−1.68*	−.01	−.36*	1,355	67
		(.25)	(.05)	(.13)		67
Effect		−32.0	−0.2	−8.4		
President, 1988	2.30	−1.51*	.21*	−.48*	1,184	65
		(.16)	(.05)	(.13)		52
Effect		−36.0	5.2	−11.4		
Senate, 1988	1.92	−1.23*	.06	−.39*	1,139	59
		(.17)	(.05)	(.13)		56
Effect		−29.4	1.5	−9.7		
Governor, 1989	.43	−.78*	.09*	−.30*	1,375	68
		(.005)	(.001)	(.004)		62
Effect		−18.2	1.8	−7.0		
President, 1992	.36	−.97*	.15*	−.14	1,196	60
		(.16)	(.05)	(.14)		58
Effect		−21.7	3.4	−3.3		

Source: ICPSR, CBS News/New York Times, Election Day Surveys, 1982, 1984, 1986. ABC News/Washington Post, 50 State Poll, September–November, 1988. CBS/New York Times, New Jersey Gubernatorial Election Exit Poll, November 1989. Voter Research and Surveys, General Election Exit Polls, 1992.

Note: Dependent variable: 0 = Democrat, 1 = Republican; MLE coefficients; standard errors in parentheses; *p < .05; Effect = change in odds of voting Republican from moving x one unit at the means of the other variables.

nationally. The minority vote in the state rarely favors the Republican party. Nevertheless, in the county figures, race was much less of a factor in the 1981 and 1989 gubernatorial races than in the presidential contests. Kean may not have won the 1981 election had he ran in 1961 or 1982. He appears to have won on low Democratic participation and with the support of the Reagan Democrats—blue-collar voters who were fed up with the economic malaise and leaderless politics of the 1970s. As it turns out, though, the blue-collar support for Republican candidates would not last through the next year. Had this election been scheduled a year later, during the 1982 recession, James Florio would have won. Florio did win in 1989 on the strength of his name recognition and the unusually gaping contrast between his views and those of his opponent.

New York and New Jersey Compared

What do these patterns of persistence and change have to do with the organizational structure of the parties in New York and New Jersey? As it turns out, electoral change brought about a partial dissolution of the New Deal party coalitions and the influence of party organizations in New York. In New Jersey, Democratic organizations have lost influence as the inner-city populations that were once their source of strength have undergone significant change.

While New Jersey has seen no development of minor parties, gubernatorial primaries in the state are highly divisive. The crowded primaries are the result of the dissolution of old coalitions and the emergence of single-issue Republicanism at the state level. However, institutional changes cannot be discounted here. New Jersey has extended public financing to gubernatorial primary contestants since 1981.

The possible realignment of blue-collar voters threatened New Jersey's Democrats in the early 1980s. This threat was exaggerated. While blue-collar voters are perhaps more discriminating now than they have ever been, they have displayed a willingness to return en masse to Democratic candidates when they put up an attentive candidate. In New York, the greatest threat to party unity is from reformist insurgents in the state's Republican party. A conservative group calling itself "Change New York" has emerged to challenge the current moderate party leadership, and is apparently trying to situate New York Republicanism in a dominant stream of thought in the politics of the national party. This confusion about what to do with the conservatives has seriously affected party cohesion.

Candidates have now sensed that electoral rewards may go to those who organize their own autonomous and independent campaigns. Party organizations began to lose control of nominations and voters as the presidential base of partisanship moved away from the state and local base. Presidential politics became more conservative while state and local politics maintained their moderate trajectory. This development led to an increase in the frequency of contested primaries because there appeared to be more than one electoral pathway to the nomination.[39] Before the 1980s, appeals were occasionally heard that attempted to distance local politics from national politics, but close relations between the national and the state leadership ensured that these appeals made little difference to the outcome of state elections. Until national party choices more closely reflect state and local party alignments, one can expect that the electoral volatility that has undermined party unity will continue.

Deindustrialization and the Erosion of Party Unity: Ohio and Pennsylvania

Ohio: Electoral Background

SINCE THE 1930s, the consistent valence issue of Ohio politics has centered on labor interests and the maintenance of jobs. The Rust Belt issues of the 1980s were intensified as mass-production jobs were permanently lost. But Louis Stokes, an African-American politician from Cleveland, indicates that the state's interest in job creation and economic development has been a central plank of every politician's program for some time: "Over the last twenty years, I would rank the issues in Ohio as follows: the overall condition of the economy, jobs, health care, housing, education, and crime. Some of these issues may have changed priority from time to time, but the same issues have been there at the top."[1]

Mike Oxley, a Republican politician from north-central Ohio, concurs, "Jobs and job creation are by far the issues that are on the minds of most Ohioans. Economic issues are dominant and probably have been for the last twenty years."[2]

Senator Howard Metzenbaum, a Democrat who first entered Ohio politics as a state legislator in the 1940s, also agreed with the view that Ohio's number one issue has been jobs. He indicated, however, that the Ohio electorate has become more sensitive to issues more generally:

> When I first entered politics, I was an outsider. I would typically go into a political rally and say four things:
> 1. Good evening.
> 2. Vote Democratic.

3. Remember Howard Metzenbaum.

4. Goodnight.

There was no substance to politics then, even in the races for higher office. . . . Now my agenda is much more specific. What issues do Ohio voters care most about? Jobs, education, health care, and the environment.[3]

In discussing issues, politicians most often refer to those that are on everyone's mind. Valence issues such as the economy and crime prevention guide candidate campaigning in Ohio as elsewhere. Still, the state's politics do divide electoral groups on many matters and these divisions have a regional basis. The most Democratic area of the state is the north-northeast corner running along a diagonal from Toledo, through Canton, over to the Pennsylvania border (maps 4.1, 4.2). The twenty-two counties of this section include those that are most vulnerable to economic recession. In economic hard times like those of the early 1980s, the normally Democratic counties of Lucas (Toledo), Lake (Mentor), Cuyahoga (Cleveland), Mahoning (Youngstown), Summit (Akron), and Lorain (Lorain) tilt heavily Democratic (table 4.1). These six counties still contained about 30 percent of the state's population by 1990, so they remain a force in statewide politics.

The most lopsided recent gubernatorial contest was the 1982 race between Democrat Richard Celeste and Republican Clarence Brown. The northern tier of industrial counties lowered Brown's percentage of the vote by an average of 8.5 points when compared to the rest of the state (table 4.1). The large constants in the 1960, 1962, and 1980 contests show that had these industrial areas not been a part of the state, Republican candidates would have won by huge margins. Even in 1962, when James Rhodes won in a landslide over the unpopular incumbent Democrat Michael DiSalle, Republican percentages in the northern counties ran 3.7 points behind counties elsewhere. The best gubernatorial performance by a Republican in this area was that of George Voinovich in the 1990 race. As the former mayor of Cleveland and an ethnic Catholic, Voinovich was able to neutralize the Democratic voting tendencies of north-northeast Ohio. "Celebreeze wasn't Cleveland enough," wrote *Plain-Dealer* reporters of Voinovich's opponent, Anthony Celebreeze, following the 1990 election.

The regional foundations of Ohio politics are easily explained. According to John Fenton, the economic difficulties in the rubber and steel business caused the New Deal switch of northern Ohioans to the Democratic party. The prolabor features of the New Deal, including strike mediation measures

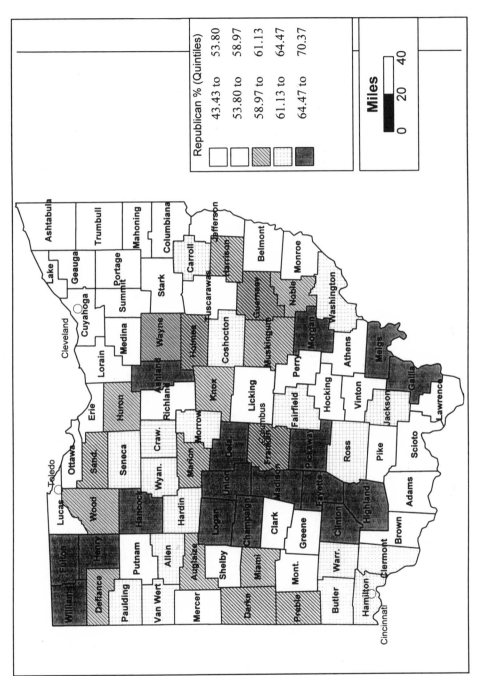

Republican % (Quintiles)

	43.43 to 53.80
	53.80 to 58.97
	58.97 to 61.13
	61.13 to 64.47
	64.47 to 70.37

Miles

0   20   40

Map 4.1   Average Republican Gubernatorial Vote in Ohio, 1962–1970

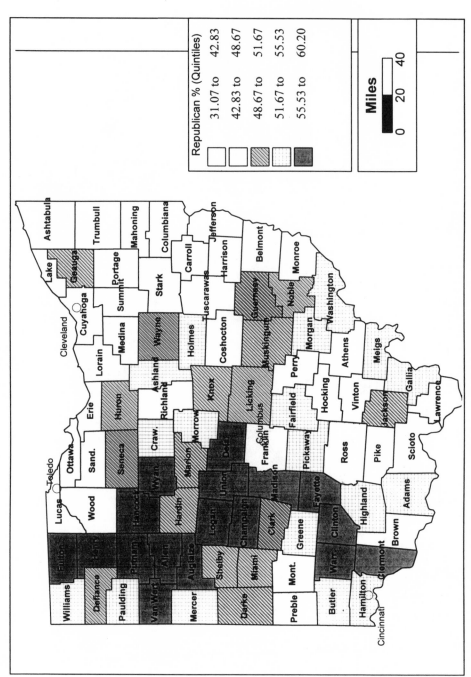

Republican % (Quintiles)

31.07 to	42.83
42.83 to	48.67
48.67 to	51.67
51.67 to	55.53
55.53 to	60.20

Miles

0   20   40

Map 4.2   Average Republican Gubernatorial Vote in Ohio 1982–1990

Table 4.1 The Influence of Northern Industrial Counties on Republican Presidential and Gubernatorial Voting in Ohio, 1960–1992

	Constant	Industrial Counties	Adj. R^2
President, 1960	61.9	−5.43* (1.76)	.09
Governor, 1962	64.8	−3.65* (1.59)	.05
President, 1968	51.8	−5.09* (1.70)	.08
Governor, 1970	51.8	−9.95* (1.63)	.29
President, 1972	66.6	−7.47* (1.44)	.23
Governor, 1974	56.2	−8.69* (1.80)	.20
President, 1980	57.4	−5.10* (1.62)	.09
Governor, 1982	46.2	−8.54* (1.83)	.19
President, 1988	62.4	−10.26* (2.14)	.20
Governor, 1990	58.2	−2.30 (1.91)	.01
President, 1992	42.4	−6.86* (1.69)	.15

*p < .05   N=88

Source: For election returns, Richard M. Scammon and Alice McGillivray, eds., *America Votes* (Washington, D.C.: Elections Research Center, various years).

Note: Linear regression, OLS estimation; unstandardized regression coefficients; standard errors in parentheses.

promoted by the national Democratic party, were the source of encouragement for rank-and-file laborers in their struggles against management.[4]

The Democratic party's base in Ohio is much like the foundation for the national Democratic party: urban liberals, Catholics, and blacks, blue-collar workers and whites in lower-income groups. Ohio is not wholly an industrial

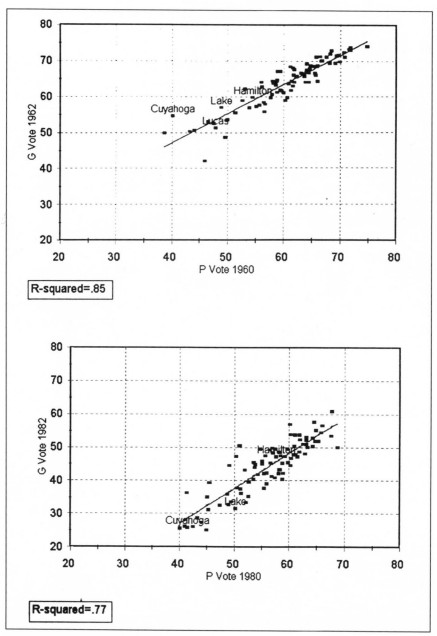

Figure 4.1 Relation Between Republican Percentage of the Vote for President and Governor in Ohio, by County, 1960–1962 and 1980–1982

Source: Richard M. Scammon and Alice McGillivray, eds., *America Votes* (Washington, D.C.: Elections Research Center).

and Democratic state, however. Balancing the northern industrial counties are the western rural counties and the Republican area around Cincinnati. Dayton (pop. 179,000), Springfield (pop. 70,000), Hamilton (pop. 65,000), and Columbus (pop. 566,000) also have Republican traditions. These cities sit among rural counties with deep Republican roots. Accordingly, the Republican tradition in these cities has been maintained because they attracted a well-educated labor force from the neighboring farms and communities.[5]

The rural base, running the entire length of the western third of the state, and in the southeastern corner, has been predictably Republican, as revealed by the dark shading in maps 4.1 and 4.2. Ohio farmers, like many midwestern farmers of the Corn Belt, are successful independent businesspeople that have little interest in government help. In the words of John Fenton, "Government was the bane of their existence, for it taxed away a large part of their earnings and, as they saw it, provided little in return save restriction and controls. The Ohio farmers found the Democratic party in alliance with the forces of restriction and control."[6]

The urban-rural political division is present in both presidential and state politics. Overall, as the scatterplots in figure 4.1 show, the relation between presidential and gubernatorial patterns in Ohio's counties has stood up well.

Party Organizations in Ohio Politics

According to David Mayhew's survey and other evidence, only five counties appear to have any semblance of organizational strength in recent times: Cuyahoga (Cleveland), Jefferson (Steubenville), Lucas (Toledo), Mahoning (Youngstown), and Franklin (Columbus). In spite of Cincinnati's reform government, the Hamilton County Republican organization remained strong well into the 1960s with jobs and money at the local, state, and national levels.[7] Due to Cleveland's size, the Cuyahoga County organizations maintain substantial autonomy from the rest of the state's politics. Campaigns and endorsements are handled locally, independent of any state party influence.

According to Louis Stokes, the rise of black power has eroded the influence big-city machines once exercised over the electorate. Candidate-centeredness in Ohio emerged upon an appeal to a particular electoral coalition—in this case, blacks—that had previously been excluded from traditional party politics:

> My brother Carl and I put together our own organizations in the 1960s. In the early seventies, we took blacks out of the local party as a protest. They wouldn't even give us an office, a vice-chairmanship. For four years we remained out of the party. Meanwhile, behind the scenes, I continued negotiations that Carl had begun—searching for

some common ground. For four years we didn't reach a meaningful agreement. Finally, they agreed that I would be a party co-chair in a troika that would run the party. They additionally agreed that one-third of the jobs would go to blacks, that the next vacancy on the elections board would go to a black, and they agreed to try to get a county official to retire early so a black could be appointed. None of these promises were kept. Shortly thereafter, I relinquished my spot in the party and gave up on them in exasperation.

According to Stokes, little has changed since then. The Cuyahoga Democratic organization remains strong. In recent years it has supported Stokes, but blacks have made few inroads into the party organization and continue to work independently.

Republicans never had to deal with the challenge of black power. In the 1960s, Fenton wrote that the Republican state organization was well organized because those identifying with it were culturally similar: "The residents of upper-middle-class neighborhoods were isolated from working-class people and arguments, possessed a common frame of reference, strong in-group attitudes, and emotions of loyalty to the business community and hostility to the 'out-groups.' "[8] During the 1960s, Republicans contributed substantial sums to their state headquarters because they wanted to remain on top.

"Today, the Republican state party has lost momentum because there are so few young people drawn to old-style partisan politics," Oxley points out. The old partisan issues aren't as important to the younger voters. Furthermore, "people don't rely on the party structure like they used to. . . . The party used to supply jobs, but all of this has been reformed out."[9] Metzenbaum agreed that the parties had few jobs compared to times past. He expressed more satisfaction, however, with the Democratic party's capacity to mobilize voters and schedule fund-raising events for candidates.

The statewide Democratic party has consistently drawn its strength from urban, ethnic, and blue-collar areas, but has been plagued with factionalism. Much of the factionalism was due to the diverse groups composing the party. Party leaders have worked through the local machines, labor unions, the state education association, and minority groups. In this connection, Democratic disorganization has been primarily the result of the large number of medium-sized cities with Democratic mayors. Metzenbaum said that the Democratic mayors don't even know one another: "The cities operate independently without reference to what is happening in the rest of the state."[10] At the state level, these competing power bases have translated into disunity as a number of equally powerful elites compete for the spoils.

Ohio Politics in the Post–New Deal Period

The hard-fought 1962 gubernatorial contest between incumbent Michael V. DiSalle, a Democrat and former mayor of Toledo, and James A. Rhodes, a Republican and incumbent state auditor from Columbus, illustrates the extent to which national cleavages divided the state. DiSalle was elected in 1958 on the strength of Democratic party organization and the Democratic registration edge. He won a solid plurality of 454,386 votes that year, facing an opponent he ran against in 1956.[11]

The first DiSalle administration between 1958 and 1960 proved highly unpopular because its cornerstone was a $150-million-a-year tax increase enacted in 1959. In reaction to the tax increase, the electorate turned many members of the Democratic General Assembly out of office in the 1960 election and Republicans gained a majority.[12] By election time in 1962, even DiSalle's hometown newspaper, the *Toledo Blade*, which had supported him up to that point, editorialized against him.

Voters have punished tax increases for decades.[13] DiSalle lost to James Rhodes in the 1962 gubernatorial contest on this classic valence issue. A tax increase, coupled with the perception of excessive spending, led to an abandonment of the DiSalle candidacy by thousands of middle-class Democrats. Note in table 4.2 that there is a noticeable absence of class cleavage in the 1962 contest. In addition, though, there is a clear sense that political party organizations affected the outcome. DiSalle lost the support of the Ohio Democratic organization. In the 1960s, most Ohioans were not issue voters. A substantial plurality streamed to the polls prompted by local organizations to vote a straight ballot based mostly on class and party identification. The nonissue orientation of these voters put a premium on party mobilization efforts. Since DiSalle had alienated many prominent members of his party with an unpopular tax policy, the withdrawal of party support in many quarters (including his home county and Cleveland) ensured a decisive defeat at the hands of a reinvigorated Republican party. Local party mobilization does not matter everywhere, but in the Ohio politics of the 1960s it surely did.

Emerging Candidate-Centeredness in Ohio Politics

Twenty years later, Ohioans are consumed by many of the same issues, but political parties have far less influence. As in other states, 1982 was a Democratic year. The outcome of the election placed the Ohio Democratic party in control of the state government for the first time since 1970; the Democrats not only won the governorship but also captured control of the Ohio House, won the attorney generalship, the offices of state auditor, trea-

Table 4.2   Influences on Republican Presidential and Gubernatorial Voting in Ohio, by County, 1960–1992

	Constant	Income	% Urban	Minority	% Mfg.	Adj. R²
President, 1960	72.2	.03 (.34)	−.07 (.07)	−.96* (.26)	−.23* (.06)	.56
Governor, 1962	70.0	.15 (.30)	−.16* (.06)	−.06 (.22)	−.11* (.05)	.35
President, 1968	67.0	.04 (.25)	−.03 (.06)	−.72* (.19)	−.42* (.11)	.42
Governor, 1970	90.4	−.65* (.31)	−.008 (.07)	−.56* (.24)	−.47* (.14)	.39
President, 1972	82.2	−.15 (.27)	−.07 (.06)	−.46* (.21)	−.22 (.12)	.35
President, 1980	58.7	.25 (.27)	−.06 (.06)	−.44* (.17)	−.19 (.13)	.33
Governor, 1982	61.5	.08 (.30)	−.06 (.07)	−.55* (.22)	−.48* (.16)	.28
President, 1988	25.2	1.25* (.23)	.15* (.06)	−.41* (.17)	.02 (.12)	.43
Governor, 1990	23.2	1.07 (.13)	−.11* (.04)	−.20 (.11)	.15* (.07)	.53
President, 1992	12.6	.98* (.20)	−.13* (.05)	−.11 (.14)	.005 (.10)	.28

*p < .05   N=88

Source: Bureau of the Census, *County and City Databook* (Washington, D.C.: GPO, various years); Richard M. Scammon and Alice McGillivray, eds., *America Votes* (Washington, D.C.: Elections Research Center, various years); *County and City Extra* (Lanham, Md.: Bernan Press, 1992).

Note: Linear regression, OLS estimation; unstandardized regression coefficients weighted for population; standard errors in parentheses; income is expressed in thousands of constant 1992 dollars.

surer, and secretary of state. All this occurred in a year when turnout was the largest for any nonpresidential election in Ohio history.

The 1982 Ohio gubernatorial race was a low-key mismatch for at least two reasons: (1) the economic recession of 1982 hit Ohio especially hard at the end of a period of Republican gubernatorial dominance, and (2) the Republican candidate, Congressman Clarence Brown, was a poor challenger to the better-known Lieutenant Governor Richard Celeste. Ohio's economic times were so hard that even the upper-income counties voted for Celeste. Given this massive economic protest, none of the conventional national cleavages predicted the 1982 gubernatorial vote with any degree of significance. Nonlabor areas voted against the obscure Republican as did the labor areas. Upper-income regions were about as hostile as lower-income regions. Furthermore, votes for Celeste were really votes against Reagan, not against the Republican gubernatorial candidate, whom nobody knew.[14] The week before the election, 656,000 Ohioans were out of work. At that point, Ohio had a higher unemployment rate than any other state in the country. In every county, Brown trailed Reagan's 1980 performance. Ohio's statewide patterns suggest that when the conditions of the Great Depression are duplicated by recession and a Republican president is in office, even Ohio's wealthy and most Republican areas will turn against their party's candidate. This tendency to punish governors for the shape of the national economy is weaker in states that are less tied to national economic trends. Recessionary forces hit some employment sectors with devastating losses, while others go almost untouched. The economic and occupational profile of some states makes them less vulnerable to downward economic spirals. With a large population and a significant industrial base, Ohio's economic fortunes have been central to the economic fortunes of the nation. This means that in Ohio negative trends in the national economy work against the party of the incumbent president more so than in other states.

The gubernatorial election of 1990 was marked by New Deal rhetoric of class cleavage, but was as devoid of party organization influence as the 1982 election. The Democratic attorney general, Anthony Celebreeze, tried to paint Cleveland's mayor George Voinovich as the voice of the privileged and the wealthy.[15] In response, Voinovich claimed that he was responsible for the revival of Cleveland, bringing thousands of blue-collar jobs into the city through tax abatement programs. Hoping that attitudes toward presidential politics would inform state-level balloting, Celebreeze tried to link Voinovich to the Bush administration, knowing that working-class Ohioans remained steadfast presidential Democrats. He made repeated reference to George Bush's promise not to tax the wealthy. The ploy worked insofar as most union voters remained loyal to Celebreeze (see table 4.3). Indeed, the UAW independently ran highly negative campaign ads against Voinovich throughout northeastern Ohio. Nevertheless, the attempt to exploit class divisions was not sufficient to the task of winning. Cuyahoga County Democrats, a group that Democratic candidates had to attract in order to win, voted solidly for Voinovich.

National Divisions in the Ohio Electorate

In the 1960s, there was a strong similarity between Ohio's gubernatorial and presidential voting (see table 4.2). The direction of influence for the urbanization, blue-collar, and race variables is quite consistent. Today, however, these cleavages are submerged in cases of sweeping landslide elections such as the gubernatorial race of 1982 where even a vast majority of white voters cast Democratic ballots. In closer contests, such as the 1990 gubernatorial race, class and labor divisions have persisted. From the beginning, my argument has emphasized that the common characteristic of old-party states is that they have had stable and predictable cleavages separating their electoral parties regardless of the office. There is little inconsistency in voting from one level of government to the next. There is no question that Ohio remains a highly divided state along some traditional lines of political cleavage. At the individual level, polarization between labor and nonlabor households is much greater in Ohio (table 4.3) than in New York and New Jersey (fig. 4.4). Ohio's least polarized contest divides union and nonunion households more than New Jersey's most polarized race. In the 1982 reelection of liberal senator Howard Metzenbaum, only one out of three union householders cast a Republican ballot, as labor householders were 23 percent less likely to vote Republican than their counterparts in nonunion employment. The class division between high- and low-income voters was also most pronounced in this race. Even though partisan divisions are durable, there are new signs that electoral divisions are forming around specific candidacies and therefore varying more from contest to contest (table 4.3). Finally, the elections held between 1984 and 1992 did not polarize Ohio by income and union affiliation as much as earlier contests.

If traditional coalitions are not present in local races, I would suggest that Ohio has developed a more autonomous political system. The 1982 race was certainly a departure from Ohio's competitive tradition. From today's vantage point, the landslide election of Celeste over Brown was a significant deviation brought about by voters' focus on economic conditions. Celeste did not win on the basis of a neat partisan split. The economic circumstances focused attention on who Celeste was (or was not), and even Republicans followed. In this sense, valence issues such as the economy promote candidate-centeredness when times are especially bad.

The national party system of the 1930s clearly projected itself into Ohio state politics. Because the divisions in the electorate have grown increasingly unstable, though, party organizations cannot rely on the same demographic groups today that they did thirty years ago. One change is worth noting, in particular. The aggregate data in table 4.2 suggest that the manufacturing

Table 4.3 Logit Analysis of the Influence of Race, Income, and Union Membership in Ohio Elections, 1980–1992

	Constant	Race	Income	Labor	No. of Cases	Predicted Null (%)
President, 1980	3.93	−2.14*	.33*	−.85	754	69
		(.01)	(.002)	(.005)		63
Effect		−46.2	6.6	−15.0		
Governor, 1982	1.44	−1.05*	.33*	−.74*	839	64
		(.01)	(.002)	(.005)		57
Effect		−26.0	8.2	−18.0		
Senate, 1982	1.71	−1.03*	.49*	−.99*	837	66
		(.01)	(.002)	(.01)		59
Effect		−24.8	12.2	−22.8		
President, 1984	4.91	−2.99*	.35*	−.83*	1,175	65
		(.29)	(.06)	(.14)		56
Effect		−46.7	6.6	−21.8		
President, 1988	3.31	−2.61*	.35*	−.57*	1,364	68
		(.28)	(.05)	(.12)		58
Effect		−56.3	8.7	−13.1		
Senate, 1988	2.42	−2.21*	.31*	−.53*	1,130	63
		(.30)	(.05)	(.13)		57
Effect		−46.1	7.6	−13.2		
Governor, 1990	2.02	−1.56*	.30*	−.73*	1,780	64
		(.006)	(.002)	(.004)		56
Effect		−36.2	7.5	−18.0		
Sec. of State, 1990	2.77	−2.09*	.13*	−.67*	1,370	63
		(.007)	(.002)	(.005)		50
Effect		−46.2	3.2	−16.4		
President, 1992	1.60	−2.25*	.29*	−.81*	1,142	66
		(.007)	(.06)	(.16)		60
Effect		−39.6	6.1	−12.3		
Senate, 1992	0.98	−1.57*	.22*	−.90*	1,388	64
		(.20)	(.05)	(.14)		60
Effect		−30.2	4.7	−12.5		

Source: ICPSR, CBS News/New York Times, *Election Day Surveys*, 1982, 1984. ABC News/Washington Post, *50 State Poll*, September–November, 1988. Voter Research and Surveys, *General Election Exit Poll*, 1990, 1992.

Note: Dependent variable: 0 = Democrat, 1 = Republican; MLE coefficients; standard errors in parentheses; *p < .05; Effect = change in odds of voting Republican from moving x one unit at the means of the other variables.

areas of the state are voting Republican in recent races. One must not be
misled into thinking that this data is evidence of a realignment of blue-collar
workers. Instead, it reflects the influence of deindustrialization in formerly
industrial areas. The more prosperous and originally Republican areas of the
state have maintained (or acquired) an industrial base. Democratic regions
have lost manufacturing jobs. Hence, the manufacturing areas that once
voted solidly Democratic are no longer swayed by the labor vote. Blue-collar
voters are still voting solidly Democratic (see table 4.2). This basic stability
has saved the party from the degree of multifactionalism and special interest-
centeredness that weak-party states consistently face. What has hurt party-
building efforts is the absence of a younger generation drawn to traditional
party building. Coupled with developments such as the loss of patronage jobs,
party organizations have increasing difficulty attracting a cadre of activists
motivated by the need for employment rather than by ideology. The upshot is
that Ohioans, while firm party identifiers, are more politically independent of
organizational politics. Ohio is a state where the foundation for unified organizations has weakened. The traditional partisans have aged and probably will
never be replaced.

Pennsylvania: Electoral Background

Pennsylvania's electoral divisions in the post–New Deal period have
been much like those of Ohio. Poorer, more urban and industrial areas vote
Democratic; wealthier and rural areas vote Republican. These states contain concentrated core constituencies of the New Deal realignment—blue-
collar workers in the cities and many conservative small-town and farm
voters. Reliance on manufacturing employment has made both states especially sensitive to souring economic conditions. Lopsided elections are
rare, but can emerge when unemployment rises and voters align themselves
against the party in power. Economic sensitivity is perhaps greater in Ohio,
but the competition for new industry has also been a persistent theme in
Pennsylvania politics. At least one-third of the labor force works in manufacturing in 44 percent of Pennsylvania's counties (54 percent of Ohio's
counties).

Maps 4.3 and 4.4 illustrate the geographic distribution of party voting in
gubernatorial races from 1962 to 1970 and from 1982 to 1990. In the 1960s
the areas of strong Republicanism included the northern tier of rural counties
and the suburban areas around Philadelphia. Philadelphia, Scranton, Erie, and
Pittsburgh were Democratic strongholds, along with the rural mining counties of the southwest. In the 1980s (map 4.4), the same regional patterns are

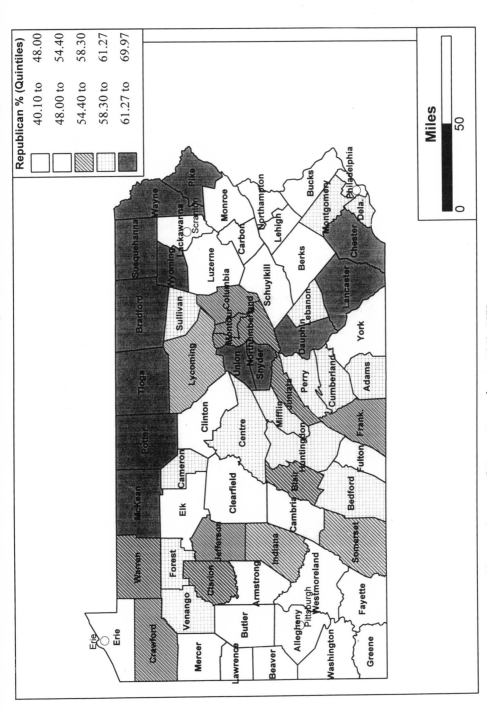

Republican % (Quintiles)

☐	40.10 to	48.00
☐	48.00 to	54.40
▨	54.40 to	58.30
▦	58.30 to	61.27
■	61.27 to	69.97

Miles

0   50

Map 4.3   Average Republican Gubernatorial Vote in Pennsylvania, 1962–1970

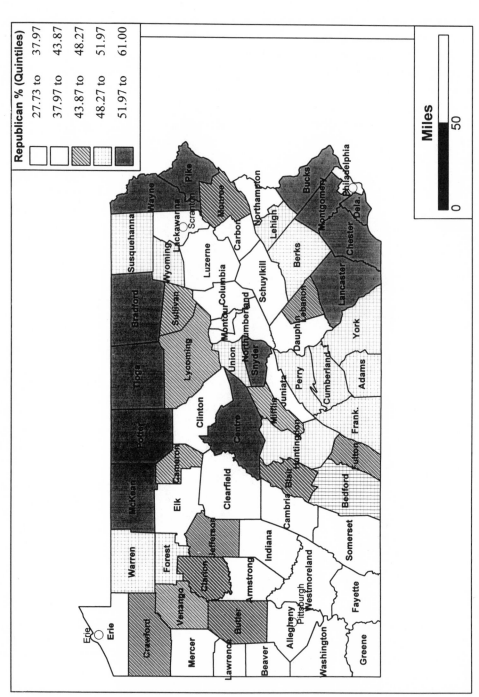

Map 4.4 Average Republican Gubernatorial Vote in Pennsylvania, 1982–1990

evident, although the drop in Republican prospects is reflected in the much
lower range of the quintiles defined in the map legend.

Both Ohio and Pennsylvania are bi-metropolitan states. The cultural and
political rivalry between East and West extends far back into the state's political history. For years, Philadelphia had a large and controlling bloc of votes in
the state legislature. And, like upstate New Yorkers in their attitude toward
New York City, "Western Pennsylvanians are convinced that all the money
goes to Philadelphia and is being poured down a rat hole," says Rep. Bob
Borski. "Western Pennsylvania looks at the candidates and chooses the one
from out West. Philadelphians don't have this bias. They look at the candidates and basically decide on the merits."[16] There are signs of change, and
Philadelphia's numbers in the state legislature have waned. But there are still
resentments. Bob Walker, a conservative politician from Lancaster County,
explained:

> The economics of the regions are very different. Western Pennsylva-
> nia has been adversely affected by deindustrialization. The East has
> been far more prosperous and much more successful in making the
> transition to the new service economy. . . . But there is also a cultural
> difference in much the same way that California is divided between
> north and south. Philadelphia and Scranton anchor the East. Pitts-
> burgh and Erie anchor the West. There is no overlap in the media
> markets. The two regions have very independent visions. . . . My
> district is wealthier and growing. We're different from the rest of
> Pennsylvania in that respect. Still, Pennsylvania's Republicans gen-
> erally care most about economic issues: government spending, reg-
> ulation, taxes and the preservation of jobs.[17]

The preoccupation with the size of government and the state of the economy is a perennial matter of partisan importance in the state legislature. Bob
Borski, a Democratic politician from northeast Philadelphia, now in Congress, recalled his days as a state representative in the mid-1970s. He remem-
bered that the most partisan issues in his years there were taxation, corruption, and welfare reform:

> The budget is due on July first, but in my first year we didn't get one
> passed until August twentieth. What struck me about the legislature
> was its intense and bitter partisanship. The Democrats had an over-
> whelming majority—an extra thirty votes or so, yet none of the
> Republicans would vote with us under any circumstances. It was
> extremely bitter.[18]

Apparently, Pennsylvania did not resist the New Deal realignment. The state's electoral movements have closely followed the national movements characterized by "long term stability extending over decades, followed by intense bursts of electoral reorganization."[19] Not only do aggregate electoral margins follow national trends, but voting in state politics has usually reflected voting in national politics.

Party Organizations in Pennsylvania Politics

Party organizations have been strong in eleven Pennsylvania counties: Bucks, Delaware, Montgomery, Philadelphia, Chester, Allegheny, Berks, Lackawanna, Dauphin, Luzern, and Schuylkill.[20] In these counties, party machines have been able to turn out a regular, reliable percentage of the electorate in election after election without worrying about issues that might crosscut national party alignments. In the 1962 gubernatorial race, Republican William Scranton repeatedly emphasized the role of the state and local party organization. In a final swing through the state the week before election day, Scranton reminded his rural audiences of the Democratic machines in Philadelphia and Pittsburgh, but then added, "This year we've got the people and that's what counts," as he urged rural Republican precinct workers to "work all day and all night to get out the vote."[21] Newspaper reporters guessed that weather would decide the vote in some places because bad weather would keep independent voters at home, while organization voters would turn out. On the Democratic side, Philadelphia machine boss William Green boasted that any Democrat, except Scranton's opponent, Richardson Dilworth, could beat any given Republican by 200,000 votes in the city. However, in recent years there have been signs of organizational decline in the old areas of strength. In Borski's words:

> The [Philadelphia] Democratic organization used to be an enormous force. It is much less of one today. The reason is that it is difficult to influence the electorate on election day standing at the polls. It does mobilize voters, and this counts in the 50–50 races, but it doesn't change many minds. The Republican organization, on the other hand, pours all of its resources into one area of the city—Northeast. I should know; this is my district and this is where all the Republicans live. They have been very successful in recruiting candidates and they have a following among younger and middle-aged people.[22]

Writing on the subject in the mid-1960s, Frank Sorauf indicated that the conventional description of American political parties as nonideological, decentralized, and pragmatic applied in the Pennsylvania case with "more than the usual accuracy."[23] This, too, may be changing, says Robert Walker. "The big change in Pennsylvania politics in the last twenty years has been the rise in citizen-action, or special interest, groups. The party organizations, big business, and big labor have all lost influence."[24] As voters become preoccupied with issues other than those of an economic nature, they become less predictable and more difficult to organize. The traditional economic themes that made organizational politics appear so consensual and unified are being replaced by divisive themes: abortion, womens' rights, racial issues, all of which invite intraparty strife and factionalism.

Pennsylvania Politics in the Post–New Deal Period

The 1962 gubernatorial race between Republican William Scranton and Democrat Richardson Dilworth is one of the best examples of how economic worries can steer a contest away from traditional partisan politics. Urban and rural areas of the state were squared off in a race that Scranton ultimately won by 486,651 votes (11 percent). Scranton was victorious primarily because Pennsylvanians were voting against the party that had been in power for two terms.

Industrial decline in the Northeast extends back at least to midcentury. By the early 1960s, Pennsylvania had stagnated economically and already jobs and industry had begun to trickle away. Voters looked to someone able to restore Pennsylvania's industrial economy, and throughout the campaign Scranton stressed the issues of industrial development and employment above all others. Campaigning in Pittsburgh, Scranton promised to restore Allegheny County's economic climate. He promised to work with coal miners on strip mine controls and pledged to get steel mills working again. Scranton also pledged to do away with state patronage jobs and move toward a merit-based civil service system. Scranton successfully painted the sitting governor as a tax-and-spend Democrat, saying that taxes and expenditures had doubled in Harrisburg over the last eight years while unemployment had remained unchanged. In the end, Dilworth's loss in the face of the Democratic registration edge marked the beginning of a trend toward candidate-centeredness. While the activist Democrats turned out for Dilworth in Philadelphia, Pittsburgh, the city of Scranton, and other cities, many weaker partisans voted against him—in effect holding him responsible for the policies of the Democratic Lawrence administration that had held office for eight years. Every one of the nine counties with double-digit unemployment gave Scranton a higher percentage of the vote than Nixon had won two years before. In four of these counties, the difference between Nixon and Scranton was five points or more. Republican Scranton won normally Democratic Allegheny County (Pitts-

Table 4.4 Influences on Republican Presidential and Gubernatorial Voting in
Pennsylvania, by County, 1960–1992

	Constant	Income	% Urban	Minority	% Mfg.	Adj. R²
President, 1960	43.2	1.40*	−.31*	−.50*	−.18	.72
		(.26)	(.04)	(.12)	(.13)	
Governor, 1962	44.9	1.30*	−.16*	−.46*	−.29*	.72
		(.17)	(.03)	(.08)	(.09)	
President, 1968	37.1	.99*	−.28*	−.29*	−.14	.61
		(.21)	(.05)	(.11)	(.13)	
Governor, 1970	42.4	.64*	−.19*	−.09	−.25*	.32
		(.20)	(.05)	(.10)	(.13)	
President, 1972	59.3	.55*	−.16*	−.45*	−.12	.72
		(.14)	(.04)	(.08)	(.09)	
President, 1980	42.2	.63*	−.13*	−.24*	.05	.62
		(.19)	(.04)	(.09)	(.12)	
Governor, 1982	17.7	1.52*	−.10*	−.10	−.09	.77
		(.20)	(.04)	(.10)	(.13)	
President, 1988	25.6	.89*	−.26*	−.07	.63*	.77
		(.10)	(.04)	(.07)	(.13)	
Governor, 1990	2.9	.95*	−.12*	.18*	−.02	.67
		(.08)	(.03)	(.06)	(.11)	
President, 1992	24.1	.43*	−.15*	−.16*	.42*	.63
		(.10)	(.04)	(.07)	(.13)	

*p < .05   N=67

Source: Bureau of the Census, *County and City Databook* (Washington, D.C.: GPO, various years); Richard M.
  Scammon and Alice McGillivray, eds., *America Votes* (Washington, D.C.: Elections Research Center, various
  years); *County and City Extra* (Lanham, Md.: Bernan Press, 1992).
Note: Multiple linear regression, WLS estimation; unstandardized regression coefficients weighted for population;
  standard errors in parentheses; income is expressed in thousands of constant 1992 dollars.

burgh), and carried a record seven wards in the city proper, although he lost
the city itself. He won his home county, Lackawanna, by 675 votes, even
though Democrats held a 50,000-vote registration edge. As expected, the
more rural areas voted overwhelmingly for the Republicans.

Overall, though, the interests defining state party conflict during this
period closely followed those defining national partisan conflict. About 72

percent of the variation in the Republican percentage of the 1962 Pennsylvania gubernatorial vote can be explained by the demographic characteristics identified in the county-level model (table 4.4). Racial divisions in the county data are stronger in the 1960s than they are in the 1980s and 1990s. This corresponds to the movement of minority voters out of inner-city areas. Because Pennsylvania's minority population is not as concentrated as it was thirty years ago, the influence of the minority vote on a given county's overall voting is not as strong. Like other states that followed the New Deal coalitional pattern, Pennsylvania is divided between rich and poor areas. In fact, income inequality distinguishes high-income from low-income areas more sharply than in New York and Ohio. The theory predicted that congruent cleavages reflecting the national parties' coalitional profiles are at the foundation of the political system in states with unified parties. Throughout most of Pennsylvania's history, reliable electoral coalitions have provided a stable underpinning for party cohesion.

Emerging Candidate-Centeredness in Pennsylvania

By the 1980s, though, candidate-centered electioneering had emerged in this strong party state. When the 1982 gubernatorial race began, Republican Governor Richard Thornburgh was as much as thirty-two points ahead of the Democratic challenger, U.S. Rep. Allen Ertel. Due to the economic recession of 1982, Ertel was able to close this enormous margin to three points, losing by a modest 100,431 votes. Like the race of twenty years before, this election focused considerable attention on candidates because of the state of the economy. Reaganomics lost, although Dick Thornburgh won; he and James Thompson of Illinois were the only two Republicans of the large industrial states to survive that year, and they did so largely through the powers of incumbency, name recognition, and the ease of fund-raising conveyed thereby. Unlike the race of twenty years before, there was little talk of party organization, and patronage had ceased to be an issue. The races were conducted according to current fashion—big money and television advertising making the difference. Thornburgh outspent his opponent by more than two to one.

Issues of the campaign were national ones: economic recession, high unemployment, and free and fair trade. However, simply because a state election echoes national themes does not mean that its politics are nationalized. The economy pulls voters' attention away from their own party loyalties to focus on candidates, candidate promises, and candidate party affiliations. In this case, the economy strengthened an otherwise weak candidate, making this race more competitive than it would have been otherwise. Ertel worked hard to connect Thornburgh to the economic policies of the Reagan administration, claiming that the latter was Ronald Reagan's "number one cheerleader." Boldly enough, Thornburgh made no effort to apologize for Reaganomics and remained a staunch supporter of the president's economic program. Ertel offered an economic redevelopment strategy as part of his program, but it was so complex that he failed to get the message out in stump speeches and TV spots. His other tactics included portraying his opponent as insensitive to the state's jobless and poor and emphasizing the flight of capital to the South and West.[25] Apparently some of this worked. Thornburgh lost the black vote in Philadelphia—he had won it in 1978. He lost the city by 147,000 votes, whereas four years earlier he had lost by a mere 35,000.

The 1990 gubernatorial race provides an even better example of the rise of candidate-focused electioneering in Pennsylvania politics. "[Barbara] Hafer loses 66 of the 67 counties," predicted David Buffington, editor of a Harrisburg political newsletter, only two days before the 1990 gubernatorial election.[26] The election, the most lopsided gubernatorial contest since 1926, was an overwhelming victory for incumbent Democrat Robert Casey. Oddly, Hafer desperately appealed for votes in Philadelphia in the closing days of the race, apparently conceding much of the rest of the state.[27] Observers claimed that in her drive to pick up liberal Democratic votes through such positions as her pro-choice stand on abortion (Casey was pro-life), she alienated significant segments of her Republican base. Democrats, though, remained unconvinced on election day and Buffington's prediction came true, as Hafer's only victory came in Montgomery County by a razor-thin 490 votes.

How could such a lopsided and candidate-centered election occur in such a traditional two-party competitive state? The answer lies in what the conservative presidential drift of the 1980s did to Republican organizations in northeastern states. The conservative and liberal wings of the Pennsylvania Republican party split in the wake of the rising conservative tide. Hafer barely won the May nomination against an inexperienced and unknown opponent. Emboldened by their presidential successes, conservatives failed to close ranks with their party leadership behind Hafer's candidacy. One conservative Lancaster County activist wrote, "I am unable to 'hold my nose' and support Hafer for governor." In several areas, Republican officials removed her name from sample ballots and palm cards so that the official party handouts listed no name at the top of the ticket.[28] In the end, even Robert Walker's very conservative Sixteenth Congressional District went to Casey by a three-to-one margin. After the election, conservative Republicans promised to mount primary challenges to those endorsed by the liberal party leadership. Thus, factionalism and candidate-centeredness arose as the result of an emerging discontinuity between national and state party movements.

National Divisions in the Pennsylvania Electorate

As in Ohio, traditional political divisions have clearly polarized Pennsylvania voters in recent elections (table 4.5). However, the extent of the polarization has tended to vary widely by contest and the candidates who ran. The probability that minorities would vote Republican remained low throughout the decade, but was lowest in the 1984 presidential race, in which whites were almost 40 percent more likely to vote Republican than nonwhites (table 4.5). Pennsylvania's racial polarization dropped with the landslide reelection victory of Robert Casey in the 1990 gubernatorial contest.

There is convincing evidence to indicate the candidate-centered nature of the earlier 1982 gubernatorial contest as well. There was a small nine-point gap between labor and nonlabor voting for Richard Thornburgh; apparently, the withdrawal of support for Thornburgh came across all occupational and demographic groups. Elections driven by valence issues often reduce the distance between rival coalitions.

Even with the aid of the recession, Allen Ertel, a four-term congressman with little recognition outside his central Pennsylvania district, could not overcome Thornburgh's high-profile media campaign, strong financing, and statewide name recognition. But Ertel's campaign made progress, considering his disadvantage when the race began. The economy helped him to pick up twenty-eight points on Thornburgh in a little over six months. Ertel was not a great fund-raiser and was vastly outspent by the incumbent. Due to Pennsylvania's sensitivity to economic decline, he made a competitive race out of what would have otherwise been a Republican blowout.[29]

The 1982 contest is historically noteworthy because it shows that in a state where the electorate is roughly evenly divided between the parties, a competitive election is not necessarily a party-centered contest. Sometimes the state of the economy appears to reinforce traditional party divisions by making a competitive contest out of what would otherwise be a low-key mismatch. At other times, however, the economy can make an otherwise competitive race a lopsided contest. That the economy matters in some elections is not a sign that the state's politics have been nationalized. To determine whether Pennsylvania's politics are nationalized, one must look to the coalitions comprising the parties and see if they resemble national coalitions. Often, the prevalence of the economy as a campaign issue will steer this and other states away from traditional coalition politics.

Table 4.5 Logit Analysis of the Influence of Race, Income, and Union Membership in Pennsylvania Elections, 1980–1992

	Constant	Race	Income	Labor	No. of Cases	Predicted Null (%)
President, 1980		−.99*	.19*	−.35*		65
	1.04	(.001)	(.0002)	(.0004)	966	51
Effect		−23.7	4.0	−8.7		
Senate, 1982		−.87*	.22*	−.45*		66
	.88	(.001)	(.001)	(.0004)	1,102	53
Effect		−20.8	5.0	−11.2		
Governor, 1982		−.69*	.23*	−.39*		66
	.85	(.001)	(.0002)	(.0004)	1,109	55
Effect		−17.1	5.5	−9.4		
President, 1984		−1.96*	.12*	−.33*		67
	1.38	(.25)	(.05)	(.06)	1,122	56
Effect		−39.5	3.4	−17.1		
Governor, 1986		−1.49*	.18*	−.68*		62
	1.98	(.01)	(.002)	(.004)	1,208	52
Effect		−32.6	4.6	−16.7		
Senate, 1986		−1.67*	.17*	−.44*		64
	2.31	(.01)	(.002)	(.004)	1,223	57
Effect		−38.6	4.2	−10.8		
President, 1988		−1.01*	.21*	−.41*		63
	.47	(.18)	(.04)	(.06)	1,377	51
Effect		−36.6	4.8	−20.3		
Senate, 1988		−1.67*	.15*	−.22*		72
	1.65	(.20)	(.05)	(.06)	1,307	68
Effect		−35.7	3.7	−5.5		
Governor, 1990		−.52*	.35*	−.77*		67
	.27	(.007)	(.002)	(.006)	1,526	68
Effect		−10.2	6.3	−14.6		
President, 1992		−2.23*	.19*	−.84*		64
	1.77	(.29)	(.06)	(.15)	1,139	59
Effect		−37.7	4.2	−12.4		
Senate, 1992		−.77*	.08	−.26*		55
	.57	(.17)	(.05)	(.12)	1,394	53
Effect		−18.2	2.0	−6.1		

Source: CBS News/New York Times, Election Day Surveys, various years. ABC News/Washington Post, 50 State Poll, September–November 1988. Voter Research and Surveys, General Election Exit Polls, 1990, 1992.
Note: Dependent variable: 0 = Democrat, 1 = Republican; MLE coefficients; standard errors in parentheses; *p < .05; Effect = change in odds of voting Republican from moving x one unit at the means of the other variables.

Summary: Congruent Cleavages as a Basis for Party Organization

The New Deal coalitional profile of New York, New Jersey, Ohio, and Pennsylvania is still present, although it is weaker in cases where the economy is everyone's preoccupation and where exceptionally strong incumbents (Cuomo, Casey, Kean) are running for reelection. In the 1962 races, sharp income differences divided three of the four states. By 1980, income cleavages divided New Jersey and Pennsylvania counties, but not counties in the other two states. In New York, the separation of black and Hispanic groups in New York City from white areas upstate overshadowed the income disparity that appeared elsewhere. Similarly, in the individual-level analysis, class cleavages in New York are less pronounced than in the other three states (see figs. 4.2 and 4.3).

Differences between manufacturing and nonmanufacturing areas were pronounced in Ohio and New Jersey elections in 1960. By the early 1980s,

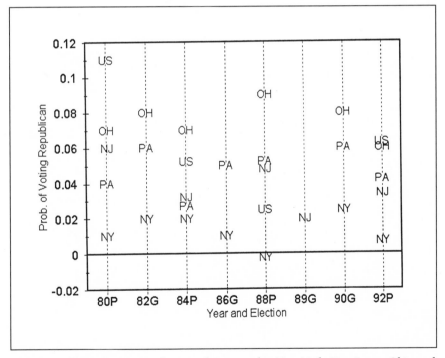

Figure 4.2 Class Cleavages in the United States and in New York, New Jersey, Ohio, and Pennsylvania Elections

Source: Probabilities computed from logit regression coefficients given in tables 3.2, 3.4, 4.3, 4.5, and A.5.

Note: Some data for New Jersey and Ohio are missing.

however, this cleavage weakened, with Lew Lehrman winning some blue-collar support in New York. This support turned out to be fleeting and temporary. In the late 1980s, the manufacturing areas in Pennsylvania and Ohio also leaned in a Republican direction. However, this is not evidence of a realignment of the labor vote; rather, it suggests that counties that have maintained a manufacturing base are now found in areas with a Republican tradition. As for the voters themselves, partisan differences between labor and nonlabor households are greatest in Pennsylvania and Ohio, and are of less significance in New York (see figs. 4.4 and 4.5).

Racial divisions remained as significant in the 1980s as they were in the 1960s. At the individual level, racial divisions in Ohio and Pennsylvania were generally stronger in presidential than in gubernatorial races because of the higher turnout of minority voters in presidential election years.

In the 1960s, presidential and gubernatorial voting were closely related, though this ceased to be true with the rise of conservative presidential candi-

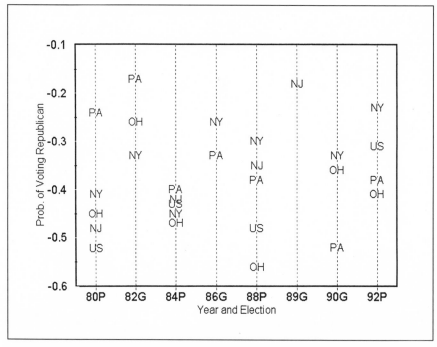

Figure 4.3   Racial Cleavages in the United States and in New York, New Jersey, Ohio, and Pennsylvania Elections

Source: Probabilities computed from logit regression coefficients given in tables 3.2, 3.4, 4.3, 4.5, and A.5.

Note: Some data for New Jersey and Ohio are missing.

dates in the Republican party. In the early 1960s, party organizations were influential, but they are far less so in the 1990s. Does the decline of party organizational strength follow from the emerging discontinuity between gubernatorial and presidential politics? Over time, as the parties were overtaken by factionalism brought about by the defections of party loyalists, the number of contested gubernatorial primaries has risen. In 1982, twenty-seven candidates were running in the primaries of these four states compared to only twenty-one in 1970 and sixteen in 1962 (counting the two nominated by convention in New York). By 1982, party organizations were not able to adapt to changing electoral settings and lost control over conservative politicians like Lew Lehrman, who stole the nomination away from party regulars. Candidate-centered and economy-centered campaigns are now the norm. Candidate-centered campaigning greatly favors incumbency, which has had an ironic impact on primary competition. In the late 1980s and early 1990s, primaries settled back down to fewer challengers than in 1982, but for an

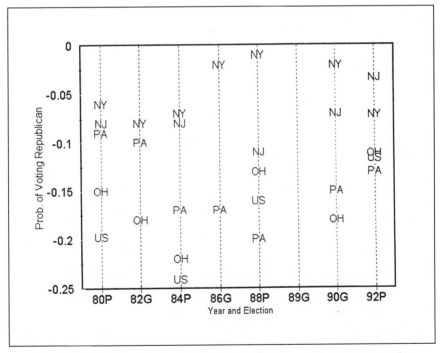

Figure 4.4   Labor Cleavages in the United States and in New York, New Jersey, Ohio, and Pennsylvania Elections

Source: Probabilities computed from logit regression coefficients given in tables 3.2, 3.4, 4.3, 4.5, and A.5

Note: Some data for New Jersey and Ohio are missing.

entirely different reason. Strong incumbents like Mario Cuomo (N.Y.) and Robert Casey (Pa.) and prominent names such as Ohio's Anthony Celebrezze (1990) and Pennsylvania's William Scranton III (1986) scared off serious opposition. A breakdown in party voting led to voting centered on name recognition. Consequently, incumbency is now stronger in these states than it has ever been.

Because of the changing electoral patterns of the early 1980s, party organizations splintered, then saw their influence over candidates wither. The resurgence of conservative Republicans at the presidential level continued to isolate presidential voting from voting further down the ticket in these ideologically moderate states. This presented new conflicts for voters, candidates, and organizations: do they follow presidential cues assuming that statewide voting will follow presidential voting? Or do they follow an independent route, insulating state from national politics? By the early 1980s, party orga-

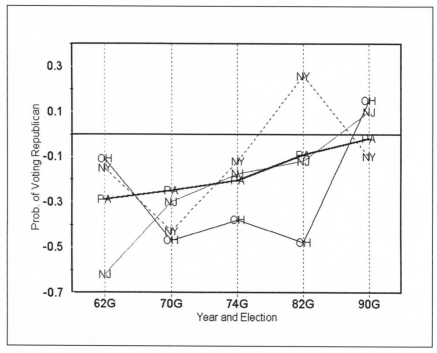

Figure 4.5   The Declining Democratic Vote in Manufacturing Areas of New York, New Jersey, Ohio, and Pennsylvania

Source: Figures based on regression coefficients for manufacturing employment given in tables 3.1, 3.3, 4.2, and 4.4.

Note: New Jersey data are for the 1961, 1969, 1981, and 1989 gubernatorial elections.

nizations no longer factored in the nomination process, as candidates like Lehrman won nominations without party support.

These states are in transition between an older politics of party-focused campaigning and the new politics of candidate self-sponsorship. Party positioning is being replaced by a politics whereby one of the two candidates attempts to latch onto a valence issue of universal appeal, which is easy to do if the traditional position issues have faded and the extent of the political division between rival social groups has diminished. The minority population of an Ohio county had only one-third the impact on voting in 1990 that it had in 1962. These county-level figures reveal something important about the concentration of minority groups in these states. The minority population is more geographically dispersed now than it was in the early 1960s. Unfortunately, there was no available polling data for statewide elections during the 1960s. But if minority voters are as likely to vote Democratic as they were thirty years ago, minority voters may not be as easily mobilized in their emerging suburban settlement pattern. In the late 1960s, the minority population was very concentrated—so much so that it sharply divided minority from nonminority areas in most large industrial states. However, by 1990, the influence of this factor had fallen and was statistically insignificant in New Jersey, Ohio, and Pennsylvania (see tables 3.3, 4.2, and 4.4). A similar pattern can be observed when one examines the impact of manufacturing activity on county political patterns. In the early 1960s, a high proportion of workers employed in manufacturing almost certainly implied a strong Democratic current in local politics. Now, however, the implications of manufacturing employment for a region's political orientation are far from clear. Figure 4.5 illustrates the change in gubernatorial elections between 1962 and 1990. As these states have deindustrialized, only the prosperous, historically Republican areas have maintained their industrial base. Owing to the forces of deindustrialization in large cities and the dispersion of manufacturing jobs to the hinterlands, the probability that a manufacturing area will go Republican is higher than it has ever been.

In these states, national coalitional loyalties remain, albeit in weaker form. Nevertheless, candidate-centered politics has emerged. What is behind this? The answer is that partisan groups that were once mobilized through low-cost, grassroots efforts, are now mobilized only with high-cost, high-technology campaigning that candidates themselves are best equipped to manage. Labor union voters are still drawn to the Democratic party; however, they are less often the dominant force in the areas where they live.

As for the influence of presidential politics, this, too, has produced change.

Presidential politics was once identical to the politics of these states. Perhaps this is why Lew Lehrman, Clarence Brown, James Courter, Herbert London, and Richard Thornburgh associated themselves with the Reagan legacy. The results were mixed. The presidential partisanship of 1980 did not evenly translate into gubernatorial partisanship in subsequent years, suggesting that state politics is increasingly separate from national politics. Thornburgh won his governor's race primarily because he had the advantage of incumbency that Brown, Courter, and Lehrman lacked. Thomas Kean, without the advantage of an incumbent's name recognition, decided to distance himself from the national ideological drift of his party and ultimately won twice, although his first race took place a year earlier than that of the other three candidates I have studied. The decision by Lehrman and Brown to attach themselves to presidential partisanship during troubled economic times, and in a period where state and national politics were increasingly separate, ended their political careers.

The Democrats' New Deal coalition was founded on some overlapping minority coalitions: the poor, blacks, union members, Catholics, Jews, and city dwellers.[30] When James Florio, Mario Cuomo, and Robert Casey won their governors' races by overwhelming margins, it was a sign that political divisions in these states were increasingly determined not by firmly anchored party identification, but by recognition of names and the emergence of fierce political divisions in the opposition camp. Today, when coalitional patterns in these states reflect older national themes, it is as much by the accident of who is running as it is by voter interests. Labor Democrats returned to the Democratic fold in state elections in the mid- to late 1980s in Pennsylvania, Ohio, and New York, but does this mean are they there to stay? Doubtful. And even if the shadows of the old coalitional patterns remain, it does not mean that state party organizations can regain a measure of influence. These states are not as geographically segmented by race and class as they once were. The labor bloc is smaller and more diffuse. The dispersed spatial location of these voters gives them smaller chances of compatible political support.[31] The social-psychological result is the chronic instability of their preferences and their attunement to candidates rather than parties. For candidates, the geographic diffusion of once solid coalitions means that they must sift more jurisdictions for votes than ever before. That sort of campaigning is done best on television, not through the door-to-door canvass.

PART III

The Western
Tradition of
Party Disunity

Introduction

THE development of political life in the established old- party states examined in chapters 3 and 4 followed the broad coalitional patterns established by the New Deal realignment. The 1980 presidential election challenged tradition. Republican parties in the Northeast lost a measure of their cohesion as conservatives and liberals feuded about which direction state politics should take. This put Democrats like Robert Casey, Richard Celeste, and Mario Cuomo in a position to win some unusually lopsided victories. Voters have not completely departed from their inherited party allegiances, but elections in this region are now showing some of the signs of volatility that have long characterized the West. Despite the existence of a trend away from once firm party foundations, traditional organization politics, characterized by an emphasis on mobilization of partisans rather than candidate-centered appeals, issue appeals, and sophisticated campaign technology, has endured longer in these states because voters have been regular in their behavior. In the early 1960s, politicians concerned themselves simply with getting out the vote—not with mobilizing new voters or particular factions through appeals to issues.

The intraparty squabbles and independent voting blocs emerging in the northeastern states are a phenomenon of the 1980s and 1990s. By most measures, party unity dissolved shortly after the 1980 election. Rival elites were attempting to locate an electorate displaced by the new coalitional pattern produced by the conservative presidential tide. The attempt to build on Ronald Reagan's victory completely backfired, proving that Republican victory in 1980 signaled no widespread conversion of Democratic voters. Democrats successfully seized upon valence issues in the 1982 contests to focus on the high unemployment generated by the recession.[1] While the Republican gubernatorial incumbent, Richard Thornburgh, won in the 1982 Pennsylvania race, it was not by nearly as much as his earlier leads predicted. The power of valence issues to decide elections demonstrates that campaigns are now decided by more than the balance of party registrants. A campaign strongly influenced by the state of the economy may work for or against either party's candidate. The anti-Reagan vote of 1982 showed that Republicans were willing to desert their partisan loyalties even in states where party attachments were strongest.

For most of the twentieth century, the assumption that gubernatorial and presidential candidates can draw on similar electoral bases has been a safe and proven one in the industrial East and Midwest. This has not been the case in every two-party competitive state. The next four chapters assess the congruence of national and state electoral parties in six of the eleven far western states: New Mexico, Arizona, California, Washington, Oregon, and Idaho. I have chosen these states because of their diversity. If V. O. Key was able to admit that the exceptions of southern politics made generalization hazardous, this must be even more true of the West, without the unifying themes of race and one-partyism.[2] These six states provide a sober challenge to the task of advancing some generalizations about candidate-centered political systems.

At minimum, what this analysis must show is that in competitive, weak-party states, state and national electoral bases are different and have been different for a long time. Counties that vote Republican in presidential elections have often voted Democratic in gubernatorial elections; at the individual level, the gulf between labor and nonlabor voters, white and nonwhite voters, and rich and poor voters, has not been as wide as in old party states.

Moreover, the coalitional profile of the electoral parties was probably different in the West even before the New Deal. These expectations draw directly from the theory set forth in chapter 1, that a well-defined, predictable partisanship in the electorate is a necessary condition for maintaining party unity and that the West has long lacked such an electorate. By evaluating significant indices of social and economic characteristics of substate regions and voters over time, my goal is to determine the extent to which the electorate divides along stable lines of cleavage.

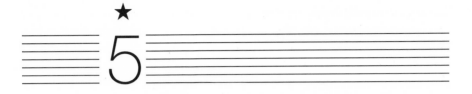

Candidate-Centered Politics in the Desert Southwest: New Mexico and Arizona

New Mexico: Electoral Background

FAMILIAR political science generalizations about the relationship of party competition to party cohesion would at first make New Mexico appear to be a political paradox. Several themes dominate the recent development of New Mexico's political setting. First, population growth has generated a competitive division between the "new" New Mexico and the "old" New Mexico. Second, a history of candidate-centered political organization has played a role in mobilizing strong turnout from time to time.

Because New Mexicans are informed about politics and elections are usually competitive, it might appear that strong organizations lurk behind a traditional party system.[1] However, while the state does have a tradition of fierce party competition, the parties are frequently splintered into rival factions. Crowded primaries emerge because the party hierarchies are inept at controlling the nomination process. Typical of a state where new populations have generated electoral volatility, the voters' partisan ties are shallow. A locally commissioned 1991 poll suggested that only half of the registered voters solidly identified with either of the two major parties, compared to over 60 percent in most states.[2]

One might think that New Deal labor legislation would have had some influence in defining the partisanship of the state's mining areas, where the labor movement periodically staged strikes against the potash, zinc, and copper industries in the 1940s, 1950s and 1960s. However, the labor disputes often did not translate into clear-cut Democratic majorities except in presidential elections. This suggests a state where national party positions and

99

ideologies may not influence local politics.[3] For example, class cleavages have not been particularly evident when controlling for other factors. The minority population of the state is so large and dispersed, that county-level figures on the size of racial groups bear an uncertain relationship to individual voting patterns. The rural Spanish-American areas in the north-central part of the state vote Democratic, a voting pattern that is a historical rather than an economic or sociological tradition. In other words, minorities are not voting Democratic due to their low socioeconomic status, as they might in large urban and industrial states. Urbanization here works exactly opposite to the pattern in older industrial states; voters in larger cities like Albuquerque tend to vote Republican.

According to local Republicans, the New Deal realignment had an impact on the state, but that impact was not lasting. The traditional appeals of Democratic candidates are not as popular as they once were. There is evidence at the presidential level that *national* Democratic themes have had less support, and the conservatism in the Mountain states is associated with antipathy to the expansion of Democratic social programs of the 1960s.[4] Republicans swept the region in the six presidential elections from 1968 to 1988, although Bill Clinton did win a narrow victory in New Mexico in 1992. Republicans have also steadily gained registrants in the state, rebounding from their pathetic nadir in the 1960s. However, New Mexicans show substantial independence from their own presidential voting behavior. Democrats won the governorship in seven of the last ten elections in a state where governors are limited to a single term. As an observer notes, this uncanny Democratic success suggests substantial differences between the constituencies of the national and local parties in the state:

> There appear to be two electorates: one group of voters is relatively undisturbed by the issues, policies, and mechanics of state and local government and makes its presence felt in the increased voting of presidential election years. The other group apparently attends to the issues and candidacies of statehood and local politics almost as diligently as it does to those involved in presidential politics.[5]

Steve Schiff, a Republican politician from Albuquerque, confirmed the differences between national and local parties in New Mexico. Schiff was a Democratic activist in Chicago's Forty-ninth Ward (Rogers Park) before moving to New Mexico to attend law school. He summed up his conversion to the Republican party as a combination of two factors: the "old boy" nature of the local Democratic party and what he considered to be the poor leadership in the national Democratic party: "Between the time I left Chicago and started working, my political views didn't change, but the party label sure did. The national Democratic party moved too far to the left and left me behind."[6]

The coalitions comprising New Mexico's electoral parties do not always reflect differences in income because many low-income farm workers are nonvoting migrants and undocumented aliens.[7] Because the poor in Mexico have been politically inactive, class cleavages are not as pronounced as they otherwise might be. New Mexico's two distinct political regions are best understood in sociocultural rather than economic terms. One region is the predominantly Republican area next to the Texas panhandle called "Little Texas." This area consists of the six southeastern counties and includes the towns of Roswell, Carlsbad, Hobbs, and Clovis (see maps 5.1 and 5.2). The second political region, predominantly Democratic, consists of the counties in the central part of the state north to the Colorado border. These are the Hispanic counties where a sizable proportion of the population is of Spanish-American ancestry. Both regions are part of what could be called the "old" New Mexico. The Hispanic counties, white areas in map 5.2, have had a solid tradition of Democratic voting since the late 1960s. In recent elections, these counties have been predictably Democratic. The 1982 gubernatorial race polarized the two regions most intensely, probably because a Hispanic, Democrat Toney Anaya, was running. Generally, conservative white Democrats such as Bruce King do better in "Little Texas."

Table 5.1 verifies that the Hispanic counties consistently vote more Democratic than the rest of the state. The patterns in table 5.1 bolster the point that there is increasing polarization between the two regions and strongly support the idea that ethnic patterns are present. In 1982, the Hispanic counties voted an average fourteen points less Republican than the rest of the state. Although not as cohesive as African Americans, Hispanics do share certain political opinions and grievances. In a November 1989 poll conducted by the University of New Mexico, 54 percent of Hispanic New Mexicans complained that it was "much harder for members of my ethnic group to get ahead than members of other ethnic groups." Only 15 percent of Anglos agreed with this statement.[8]

Electoral Turnout and Party Organization

Party affiliation is a poor predictor of voting in New Mexico politics, perhaps due to low turnout by Hispanics and Navajo Indian Democrats. One cannot predict elections by looking at party registration figures. Comparing 1962 party registration figures to the 1962 gubernatorial vote reveals no statistically significant relationship. Thirty years later, things have not changed much. A local poll in August 1992 showed that most New Mexicans

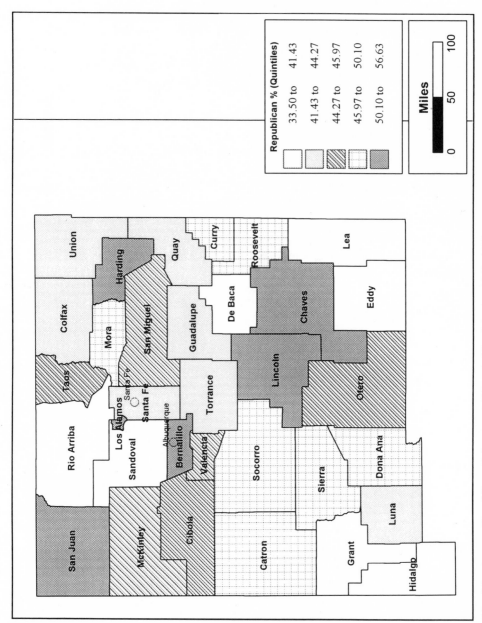

Map 5.1   Average Republican Gubernatorial Vote in New Mexico, 1962–1970

Republican % (Quintiles)

33.50 to   41.43
41.43 to   44.27
44.27 to   45.97
45.97 to   50.10
50.10 to   56.63

Miles

0   50   100

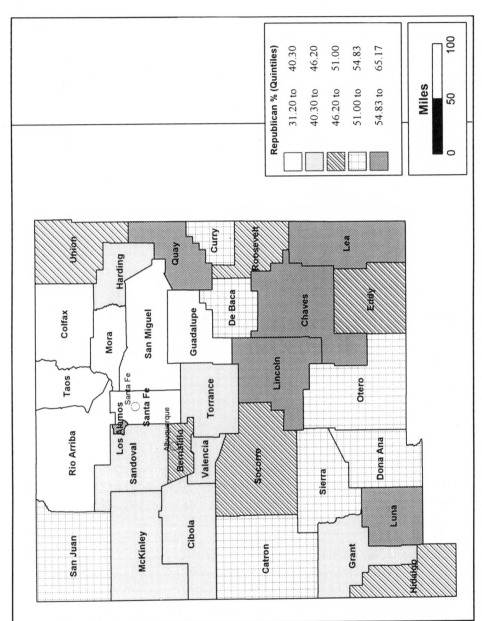

Republican % (Quintiles)

	31.20 to	40.30
	40.30 to	46.20
	46.20 to	51.00
	51.00 to	54.83
	54.83 to	65.17

Miles

0   50   100

Map 5.2 Average Republican Gubernatorial Vote in New Mexico, 1982–1990

Table 5.1   The Impact of the "Little Texas" and "Hispanic" Counties on the Republican
Gubernatorial Vote in New Mexico, 1962–1990

	Constant	"Little Texas"	"Hispanic"	Adj. R²
Governor, 1962	48.4	−.46 (3.01)	−3.25 (2.39)	.001
Governor, 1970	42.1	1.12 (3.58)	.90 (3.12)	.06
Governor, 1974	51.1	8.30 (4.81)	−13.02* (4.17)	.33
Governor, 1978	51.4	3.60 (4.75)	−8.41* (3.77)	.17
Governor, 1982	51.0	10.10 (5.22)	−13.82* (4.15)	.41
Governor, 1986	57.01	1.60 (4.53)	−9.27* (3.60)	.18
Governor, 1990	43.8	8.50 (4.58)	−5.20 (3.64)	.19

*p < .05   N=32

Source: Richard M. Scammon and Alice McGillivray, eds., *America Votes* (Washington, D.C.: Elections Research
   Center, various years).

Note: Multiple linear regression, OLS estimation; unstandardized regression coefficients; standard errors in
   parentheses.

were alienated from party positions. Sixty-one percent reported that the
parties did not do a good job of representing their views. According to former
Republican party boss Joseph Skeen, partisanship has failed to cue the votes
because the local parties have a different focus from the national parties.
Specifically, the ideological content of local elections is lacking. Gary Jacobson
has argued that in the West, Democrats were attracted to their party because
of the regulatory and distributive nature of New Deal politics, not for its class
or labor components.[9] When the Carter administration could no longer fund
projects and infrastructure for westerners, the Democrats suddenly lost their
buying power. Few had reason to vote Democratic unless it was for the sake of
race, ideology, or tradition. Ideologically, though, New Mexico is homogeneously conservative and individualistic. That left no compelling reason to
vote Democratic, except because of race and tradition. In this respect, New

Mexico is very much like Texas and other southern states where individually popular Republicans have been able to win votes independent of their party because the electorate is uniformly conservative.

Not only is the content of the partisan labels different at the local level, population change and the mobilization of new voters has placed an additional burden on party machinery. Joseph Skeen, who chaired New Mexico's Republican party organization from 1961 to 1965, commented on the importance of turnout and organization in a state where the electoral base changed daily:

> In a state where the population is changing so fast, it is crucial to have organizations with volunteers mobilizing new voters. We don't have an old ward boss system like the East and Midwest, but we do have precinct organization—especially in the cities. As for the Democratic registration edge, we could make that work for us in the areas where the most conservative Democrats were registered, as in "Little Texas."[10]

Given its sparse settlement, a history of steady party competition, and candidate-focused voting, it is somewhat surprising that New Mexico has had party organizations of any type at all. Skeen seems to indicate that party organizations remained a force in New Mexico politics. The successful and self-sufficient organizations, however, are personal organizations—committed to candidates rather than to abstract party principles, distribution of patronage, or the centralization of power. An elected official keeps the political base solid by doing favors for key constituents. The importance of mobilizing new voters is especially important. This activity is sponsored as much by individual officeholders as it is by the state organization.

While Skeen's concern is that of an "old" New Mexican who wants to mobilize the "new" New Mexico for Republican advantage, Steve Schiff is a "new" New Mexican. As a party outsider who won while running against entrenched Democratic and Republican party candidates and organizations, Schiff's perspective differs. He agreed that while there are organizations in New Mexico politics, they are not at all like traditional machines in the East. Schiff defeated the Republican party organization candidate in the 1988 primary for Manuel Lujan's congressional seat and then managed reelection in both 1990 and 1992. He explained that the difference between the New Mexico organizations and those of traditional organization states is that there is no bureaucratic nature to the traditional machine in New Mexico politics. Organizations are built around individuals with local followings, which resembles the southern pattern. In Schiff's words:

Albuquerque's machine wasn't like Chicago's. Chicago's was imper-
sonal, centralized. In Albuquerque, individuals controlled certain
factions of the organization. There was no central figure in the organizations. The system wasn't well organized. Instead, it was decentralized—built wholly around guys who had neighborhood followings, of maybe 100 people or so. A local leader was expected to deliver
personal favors for his followers. In turn, they expected city officials
to do personal favors for them. In my case, this wasn't like getting
their kids summer jobs or fixing things or getting the streets plowed.
They wanted you to get people off criminal charges—pretty serious
stuff. When my boss, the D.A. before me, refused to play along, he
was defeated.[11]

Between his boss's defeat by Democratic forces and his own run for district
attorney, Schiff switched parties. The decentralization of the organizations
and the candidate-centered nature of New Mexico politics worked to Schiff's
advantage in the 1988 Republican primary for the first congressional district
seat.

There were three candidates in the race, myself, Edward Lujan [Man-
uel Lujan's brother], and [Clarence] Budiger. This was a tough primary. I won 41 percent, Lujan won 37 percent, and Budiger won 22
percent. We have no run-off in New Mexico. Lujan was the party
organization candidate. He had the support of the machine. Traditional families in New Mexico politics have an advantage because
they've been around for so long and their names are well recognized.

I was able to beat Lujan because I was a recent migrant. I benefited
from the new population that had immigrated to Albuquerque and
didn't know of or care about the old traditional families in the state's
politics. From the start, Lujan emphasized his family's ties to politics.
His brother campaigned for him. He had a marvelous record of community service that was ignored for these appeals to family dynasty.
Eventually, the dynastic reign of the Lujans became an issue. I didn't
make it an issue, they did. People in Albuquerque, especially the
newcomers, resented this emphasis. The primary became a battle of
old arrivals versus new arrivals. New New Mexicans barraged the
newspapers with editorials against the "Lujan dynasty."

The strength of personalities has been a stable feature in New Mexico politics. New Mexico's candidate-centered races may not contain much more reference to policy and program than those in the Midwest and Northeast, but

the presence of important names has been a factor. Indeed, this case suggests a more refined typology of elections than the traditional issue-centered versus organization-dominated dichotomy. Similar to Key's observations about the old South, the New Mexican pattern suggests that a personality-dominated politics is often a nonprogrammatic politics. Arizona, California, Oregon, Idaho, and Washington (to be discussed later) have more progressive, pro-grammatic traditions, but are no less personality-centered. New York and Ohio are programmatic, but voter mobilization efforts have remained an important focus of party activity. New Jersey and Pennsylvania, at least through the 1970s, were organization-dominated but issueless.

The election of candidates without local roots is a sign that New Mexico's pattern of personality politics may begin to change. Once Steven Schiff won the primary, he went on to defeat another old New Mexico (and Arizona) political name by winning a narrow victory over Thomas Udall, the son of Stewart Udall and nephew of Morris Udall. The very population changes that made it so important for old New Mexicans to have registration drives and mobilization efforts also made it difficult to develop machine politics. Specifically, insurgent candidates were likely to be increasingly victorious due to the electoral shifts away from the old New Mexico. "My impression of the state's politics is that population changes have made it very difficult to really organize New Mexico politics," Schiff pointed out. "I am proof that old-style coalition politics doesn't work."[12]

The population instability and far-flung support won by candidates like Schiff promotes this kind of candidate independence and stands in the way of party unity: "The parties really are weak in New Mexico. Their main preoccupation has been just getting the rent paid." When asked whether the parties were weak because of the individual candidacies or if individual candidacies arose because the parties were weak to begin with, Schiff responded, "This is a chicken and egg question. My hunch is that individual candidacies split off because the parties were never very strong. But, in turn, the individual organizations have hampered the party from becoming centralized." Individual candidacies and weak party organizations perpetuate each other. There is something exogenous in this system generating the individual candidacies—population fluctuation prevents entrenchment of a party tradition in the electorate. Electoral shifts lead to the emergence of individual organizations that continue to sap the strength of a centralized party organization.

Other sources confirm that New Mexico is the only western state with any semblance of political organization. David R. Mayhew describes the essential features of a hierarchical party organization as bureaucracy, longevity, control over nominations, patronage, and autonomy. In New Mexico, how-

ever, contemporary parties have almost no control over nominations. Mayhew, for instance, calls attention to the Albuquerque race for mayor in 1974
where thirty candidates entered and the winners of the run-off tied with 12.8
percent of the vote.[13] With no control over nominations, there is no advantage for a candidate in uniting with the party organization. After all, the
organization cannot ensure victory.

At the state level, Republican and Democratic gubernatorial primaries
have often been crowded with four or five candidates. The parties sometimes
appear capable of self-management and occasionally stage strong mobilization efforts. Apparently, the strongest party organizations persist in the Hispanic counties in the north-central part of the state where, not coincidentally,
voting patterns are most durable. Still, campaigns throughout the state are
described as issueless, and the state's Republican party organization is given
credit for engineering surprising victories on mobilization alone. Newspaper
accounts from the 1960s suggest that Republican and Democratic party leaders were coaching party activists up to the last minute on strategies for
getting out the vote. Perhaps New Mexico is the kind of state, like the industrial Midwest and Northeast, where turnout is all that matters. More likely,
individual candidates work to mobilize voters, which sometimes gives the
illusion of party activity. A competitive election is not necessarily a partisan
one. The parties have been unable to control the nomination process, the most
important indicator of party influence.

New Mexico is distinct insofar as its historical pattern has been typified
by a personality-based, but issueless, politics. Voter mobilization, even by
candidate-oriented organizations, is important because issues will not bring
voters out. The population of the state has changed so rapidly in the population centers, that it is not always clear which issues might mobilize voters
anyway. One voting pattern, however, has remained stable since the 1970s—
the cultural tendency of Hispanics to vote Democratic. The rest of the state is
wide open.

New Mexico Politics in the Post–New Deal Period

What is so surprising about New Mexico politics is that contests are
barren of issues and strong party organizations in spite of their hard-fought
character. For instance, in the 1962 gubernatorial contest the race was very
close and yet devoid of highlights that would capture the voters' attention.
Unlike New York's contenders, candidates in New Mexico did not promote a
program. Unlike what occurs in other candidate-oriented states, New Mexico's candidates rarely used issues against one another, engaged in personal
attacks, or deployed any of the usual rhetorical tools of modern campaign-

ing.[14] The absence of a program advanced on either side reflects the fiscal conservatism of the state. The incumbent Republican governor Edwin Mechem
was described as running an administration that was fiscally sound and pay-
as-you-go. His opponent, Jack Campbell, the Speaker of the New Mexico
House of Representatives, had no program for meeting the deficits caused
by the failure of the Democratic legislature to appropriate money for the
everyday operations of state government. Against Mechem's record, which
included a sales tax increase, Campbell's empty campaign was better than
Mechem's "fiscal courage." Rather than a tax increase, Campbell promised
that he would "defer" or "postpone" payment of some of the state's bills.
Campbell claimed that he could put the state's finances back in order with
only a $1.5 million increase in revenue.[15] Mechem argued that an additional
$10 million was necessary. None of this discussion aroused the electorate.

New Mexico's statewide campaigns illustrate that competitive electioneering is not always associated with the involvement of party organizations.
But the nonparty character of the contest does not necessarily point to an
issue-oriented race, either. The symbolic talk about issues did not matter
much for a state that has historically entrenched candidate allegiances rooted
in familiar names. Mobilization mattered in the 1960s, as it does today, but
that does not mean that party organizations were behind it.

Perhaps New Mexico's politics is so hard to characterize because few of the
traditional electoral divisions appear to separate Republicans from Democrats. The regression coefficients for the contests of the early 1960s show that
none of the divisions typical of the national party system appeared in county-
level voting.[16] The indicator for industrialization (percentage employed in
manufacturing) was not only insignificant, it shows no consistent direction of
influence in recent history. Counties with large percentages of minority residents, mostly Hispanics, do lean toward the Democratic party, but not even
this tendency is universally true, once other variables are held constant.
Other major aspects of national party conflict seem to have very limited
relevance.

So how can even candidate-sponsored organizations persist in a climate
where the coalitions of national importance do not regularly appear? The
Democratic voting tendency of the Hispanic counties is reinforced by relatively stable patterns of voting between Catholics and Protestants. This religious division, while often less important than urban-rural and occupational
status differences, is present most clearly in a state with a large rural Catholic
population and a large urban Protestant population. Political divisions are
rooted in cultural and ethnic traditions that, in the case of the Hispanic
counties, make them predictable Democratic turf from the mid-1960s on-

ward in state-level races. Beyond this geographic pocket of interest, there are smaller pockets that candidates can draw upon for volunteers. These pockets are much more fluid than in earlier times, since population change has made their behavior more unpredictable. Large, centralized organization is impossible in a transitory setting. While most of the votes are in the cities such as Santa Fe and Albuquerque, there are enough votes in the outlying areas that even those counties must also be sifted. Some key areas, such as Las Cruces (Dona Ana County), are changing rapidly. An individual candidate may be able to put together a winning coalition of supporters in a home district, but, except for the Hispanic core of Democratic support, may not be able to carry those coalitions in the next statewide election.

Sustained Candidate-Centeredness: 1982 and 1990

The 1982 gubernatorial race was also an intensely candidate-centered election (see table 5.2). As in 1962, the traits one would usually associate with national party coalitions do not divide the state electorate. Presidential and gubernatorial cleavages similarly divide the counties, but not in the way in which coalitions appear elsewhere. Urbanization and the percentage of voters employed in manufacturing increase the margin of votes for Republican presidential and gubernatorial candidates. Albuquerque's traditional Republicanism accounts for much of this finding.

Press accounts suggest that Democrat Toney Anaya won the race on the strength of a personal campaign organization he had built in his unsuccessful Senate bid against Pete Domenici in 1978. He turned this organization into what was labeled "a vote gathering machine" that turned out more than 76 percent of the electorate.[17] In at least one rural county, Anaya supporters ran radio spots to tell voters where they could call for rides to the polls. Anaya's workers used four-wheel-drive vans to carry in elderly voters from the countryside. This type of organization apparently helped Anaya defeat Irick in Irick's home county—the first time a Democrat had carried the Albuquerque area in sixteen years.

Media attention focused primarily on the candidates, not issues or parties. When asked what mattered most in voting for governor, New Mexicans listed partisanship third behind the candidate's qualities and agreement on issues. As in races in the Midwest and Northeast, though, the economy was practically the only issue, generating considerable anti-Republican sentiment. County Democratic boss Emilio Naranjo, of predominantly Hispanic Rio Arriba County, advised voters to vote a straight ticket to change the economic picture of the nation.[18]

While local party figures framed the race as a response to economic condi-

Table 5.2   Influences on the Republican Presidential and Gubernatorial Voting in New Mexico, by County, 1960–1992

	Constant	Income	% Urban	Minority	% Mfg.	Adj. R²
President, 1960	45.1	−.02 (.37)	.10 (.09)	−.04 (.11)	−.17 (.49)	.01
Governor, 1962	44.7	−.05 (.27)	.04 (.06)	−.11 (.08)	.31 (.35)	.003
President, 1968	46.4	−.05 (.24)	.09 (.06)	−.26 (.73)	.12 (.43)	.03
Governor, 1968	47.6	.02 (.20)	.03 (.05)	.56 (.62)	−.19 (.36)	.00
Governor, 1970	23.3	.32 (.23)	.12* (.05)	−.77 (.71)	1.00* (.41)	.44
President, 1972	51.8	.29 (.28)	−.04 (.07)	3.66* (.86)	−.44 (.49)	.41
President, 1980	52.0	.12 (.34)	−.02 (.13)	−.01 (.15)	.30 (.51)	.02
Governor, 1982	30.0	−.10 (.47)	.21 (.18)	.08 (.20)	.55 (.72)	.10
President, 1988	52.1	−.21 (.37)	.12 (.12)	−.19 (.13)	.55 (.82)	.10
Governor, 1990	41.4	−.15 (.30)	.11 (.11)	−.19 (.10)	1.01 (.66)	.29
President, 1992	39.6	−.33 (.30)	.11 (.11)	−.07 (.10)	.31 (.67)	.01

*p < .05   N=32

Source: Bureau of the Census, *County and City Databook* (Washington, D.C.: GPO, various years); Richard M. Scammon and Alice McGillivray, eds., *America Votes* (Washington, D.C.: Elections Research Center, various years); *County and City Extra* (Lanham, Md.: Bernan Press, 1992).

Note: Multiple linear regression, WLS estimation; unstandardized regression coefficients weighted for population; standard errors in parentheses; income is expressed in thousands of constant 1992 dollars.

tions, it is not clear whether this Sun Belt state was suffering unusual economic hardship. New Mexicans remained optimistic about the Republican economic program. A voting majority of 57 percent claimed that Reaganomics would eventually help the state's economy.[19] Voters undoubtedly responded in sociotropic fashion to the general conditions of the economy. As in Ohio and Pennsylvania, national economic conditions took voters' attention off their own party identification and focused it on candidates' affiliations. It mattered little that conditions in the state were not as bad as in the Midwest and Northeast. Both Santa Fe and Bernalillo Counties (with unemployment at 6.6 and 8.3 percent, respectively) managed to avoid the double-digit unemployment rates afflicting urban areas elsewhere in the country. In the end, however, voters' fears about the national economy heightened existing candidate-oriented tendencies, and the 1982 race was decided in Toney Anaya's favor.

The presence of the recession as an issue in 1982 does not mean that New Mexico politics was nationalized. Citizen response to national economic conditions still varies with the local choices presented in an off-year state election. In this particular instance, Anaya's Hispanic surname and widespread anti-Reagan sentiment conspired to elect a Democratic governor.

By 1990, gubernatorial politics in New Mexico was still being described as issueless, with turnout of loyal voters playing the key role in Democrat Bruce King's victory. Polls showed that Republican Frank Bond was favored by new migrants to the state, whereas native New Mexicans and Hispanics favored King's election.[20] Name recognition was partially at work in this case (King had served two previous nonconsecutive terms as governor). For longtime residents, King was a familiar name. Bond pitched his campaign mostly toward new New Mexicans, stating that he represented a new generation of leadership. In the closing days of the contest, Bond turned to negative campaigning, charging in one ad that King played favorites and hired corrupt cronies in his two previous administrations. The ad went on to single out several of King's administrators involved in minor scandals. All were Hispanics. "It was the dumbest damn ad I've ever heard in my life," said former governor David Cargo, "All four [administrators] were from prominent Hispanic families."[21] With Hispanics alienated, the votes of Anglos and new migrants were insufficient to propel Bond to victory. King won with 54 percent of the vote.

In spite of Bond's ad campaign, the 1990 gubernatorial election saw much less divisiveness between Hispanics and white voters than the 1982 race (table 5.3). The magnitude of racial cleavage dividing the two candidates was less than half of what it was in 1982. Both Bond and King were Anglo cattle ranchers. By contrast, the U.S. Senate contest that year was almost twice as divisive. A Hispanic candidate, Tom Benavides, ran a losing campaign against Republican incumbent Pete Domenici. Given the remoteness of some New Mexican communities from the mass media, it is not surprising that racial polarization in New Mexico was still more dependent upon names than on the actual campaign tactics of candidates.

Table 5.3 Logit Analysis of the Influence of Race, Income, and Union Membership in New Mexico Elections, 1980–1992

	Constant	Race	Income	Labor	No. of Cases	Predicted Null (%)
President, 1980	2.25	−.82*	.28*	−.62*		65
		(.005)	(.002)	(.006)	858	63
Effect		−16.0	6.0	−12.0		
Governor, 1982	3.09	−2.03*	.20*	−.51*		72
		(.005)	(.002)	(.006)	863	55
Effect		−47.0	5.0	−13.0		
Senate, 1982	2.28	−1.30*	.22*	−.60*		66
		(.005)	(.002)	(.006)	998	53
Effect		−31.0	6.0	−15.0		
President, 1984	2.23	−.45*	.10	−.38*		65
		(.07)	(.06)	(.18)	951	62
Effect		−7.0	2.0	−7.0		
President, 1988	1.73	−.52*	.10*	−.35*		64
		(.06)	(.05)	(.16)	1,143	51
Effect		−11.0	2.0	−8.0		
Senate, 1988	1.36	−.49*	.04	−.43*		68
		(.07)	(.05)	(.18)	1,111	67
Effect		−12.0	1.0	−11.0		
Governor, 1990	.87	−1.15*	.20*			63
		(.005)	(.002)	—	902	54
Effect		−15.0	6.0			
Senate, 1990	1.76	−.85*	.29*			78
		(.005)	(.003)	—	892	77
Effect		−27.0	5.0			
President, 1992	−.13	−.82*	.30*	−.46		65
		(.16)	(.06)	(.26)	783	62
Effect		−18.6	6.3	−8.4		

Source: ICPSR, CBS News/New York Times, Election Day Surveys, 1982, 1984. ABC News/Washington Post, 50 State Poll, September–November 1988. Voter Research and Surveys, General Election Exit Polls, 1990, 1992.
Note: Dependent variable: 0 = Democrat, 1 = Republican; MLE coefficients; standard errors in parentheses; *p < .05; Effect = change in odds of voting Republican from moving x one unit at the means of the other variables. The 1990 Voter Research and Surveys poll did not include a question about the respondent's labor union membership.

National Divisions in the New Mexico Electorate

County-level figures suggest that one basis for party disunity in New Mexico has been the absence of national cleavages in state politics. Polling data drawn from representative samples of New Mexico voters are scarce. Fortunately, network-sponsored exit polls are available for several recent races. Table 5.3 presents a logit analysis of the influence of class, race, and unionization in recent elections.[22] National party divisions are present in the state, but are usually not as divisive (compare table 5.3 to appendix table A.5). When a Hispanic surname appears on the ballot (1982 gubernatorial, Anaya; 1990 Senate, Benvenides), the gulf separating minority from Caucasian voters is about as wide as it is in the older industrial states of the Midwest and Northeast. Otherwise, many minorities do not follow the national profile. Reagan had won almost half of the state's minority votes in 1980—far more than he had in any eastern or midwestern state. Two years later, however, Jack Irick won only 16 percent of the minority vote against Anaya. In spite of the higher turnout for presidential contests, racial divisions were less pronounced in 1980, 1984, and 1988 (table 5.3). This, too, is a pattern opposite to that found in traditional party states where presidential voting sharply divides racial groups. Clearly, the minority vote in New Mexico has not been as consistently Democratic as elsewhere. The composition of the minority population accounts for this. Less than 5 percent of the state's voting population is African-American, while 29 percent is Hispanic.

While national coalitions are present in the New Mexico electorate, racial and economic cleavages generally explain much less of the total voting than in New York, New Jersey, and other competitive old-party states. In the 1980 and 1984 presidential contests, the race, class, and labor variables in table 5.3 combine to just barely explain more than ordinary guesswork. While minority voters in New Mexico vote solidly Democratic in gubernatorial contests, they are not nearly so Democratic in presidential races (fig. 5.1). The attraction of rural Hispanic voters to Ronald Reagan's presidential candidacy explains the ups and downs in the divisiveness of racial cleavages.

The polling data temper any extreme conclusions about the complete absence of national cleavages that might be drawn from the weighted county-level data. We learn that traditional aspects of national partisanship are not absent in New Mexico, but other influences divide Republicans from Democrats. Part of the weakness of the national coalitional model is that local party constituencies do not reflect national party constituencies. There are far fewer union and African-American households in New Mexico, for instance, than in the more populous industrial states. Moreover, the aggregate data suggest that black, union, and low-income households are not concentrated in any particular county. Instead, these populations are dispersed throughout urban and rural areas and are less likely to turn out consistently or be as consistent in their voting. In response to an inconsistent partisanship that is acutely sensitive to local conditions, New Mexico politics has followed a familiar path of development. Personal organizations form and are dominated and perpetuated by individuals.

In conclusion, New Mexico's pattern of party competition falsifies the competition/cohesion thesis. The state's elections are often competitive, despite the solid Democratic registration edge, but this has not always led to a corresponding cooperation among candidates. In the 1990 Democratic gubernatorial primary, Bruce King had to battle fierce intraparty opposition from a former attorney general. Factionalism results when candidates can sense that there is more than one electoral pathway to office. With the influx of new

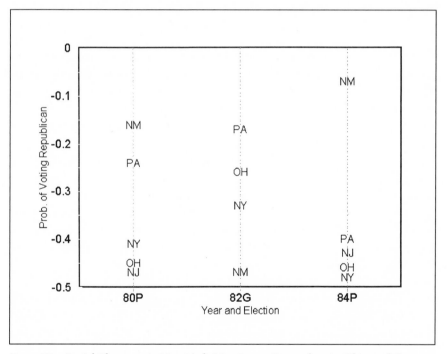

Figure 5.1   Racial Cleavages in New York, New Jersey, Pennsylvania, Ohio, and New Mexico Elections

Source: Probabilities computed from logit regression coefficients given in tables 3.2, 3.4, 4.3, 4.5, and 5.4.

Note: Data from the 1981 New Jersey gubernatorial election were unavailable.

migrants, the winning coalitions are not obvious. There is one exception. Democrats have found a reliable bastion of support in the Hispanic counties. The rest of New Mexico is much less predictable due partly to the shallow partisan loyalties of new voters and the tendency for old voters to abandon party ties when they recognize well-established names. The end result is that New Mexico can be described as a place where personalities stand out but issues do not. The hold of prominent family names on the state was broken, for a time, by the elimination of gubernatorial succession (a governor can run again only after being out of office for four years), but that has been repealed, and a governor can now serve two consecutive terms. Names are growing less important, though, because they mean little to new residents entering the state. New Mexico's politics is likely to become more issue-centered, but will continue to lack organization until it can stem the flow and socialize new arrivals. Without a doubt, the current setting favors the personal appeals of candidates to voters.

The Arizona Electoral Context

Arizona is one of the most urban states in the nation. In 1960, 53 percent of the state's population lived in one urban county, Maricopa, site of Phoenix. As of 1990, about 27 percent of the state's population resided in Phoenix itself. Geographically, the state is divided among the seven Democratic counties of the southeastern corner and the more Republican counties around Phoenix and in the northwest. In the 1960s, the axis dividing Republican from Democratic areas could be drawn diagonally across the southern part of Apache County, through Gila County and Pinal County to the Mexican border well to the west of Tucson (maps 5.3 and 5.4).

As in New Mexico, registration figures are not a precise predictor of aggregate-level voting behavior. Party loyalty has been weak for years. For example, in 1960, overwhelmingly Republican Maricopa County reported that only 36.3 percent of all registered voters were Republicans. In solidly Democratic Greenlee County, Republicans consistently poll about a third of the votes, but voter registration figures from 1960 indicate that only 4.7 percent of all voters were Republican at that time. By 1980, that number had risen to only 12.2 percent. In spite of the Democrats' registration edge, Republicans have always run well statewide and in congressional districts. Bob Stump, a conservative politician from Arizona's western Third Congressional District, found it easy to switch from the Democratic to the Republican party in 1981. He explained that he had always had support from Republicans in his district:

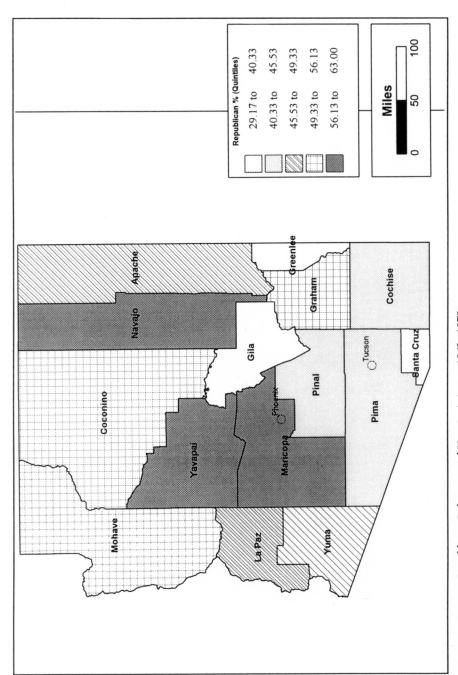

Republican % (Quintiles)

29.17 to	40.33
40.33 to	45.53
45.53 to	49.33
49.33 to	56.13
56.13 to	63.00

Miles

0   50   100

Map 5.3   Average Republican Gubernatorial Vote in Arizona, 1962–1970

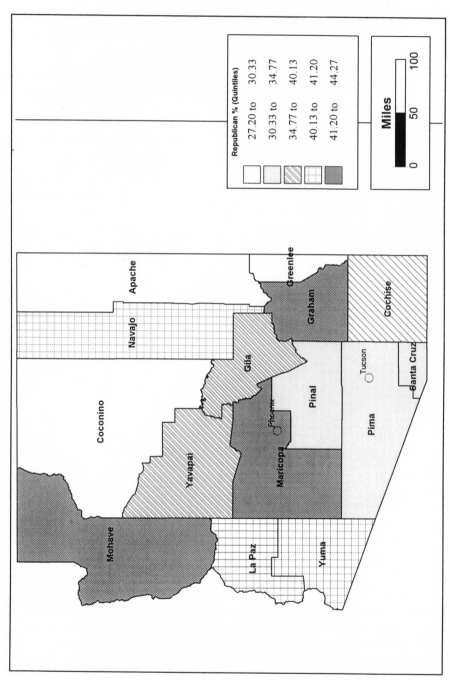

Legend:

Republican % (Quintiles)

□	27.20 to 30.33
▨	30.33 to 34.77
▨	34.77 to 40.13
▨	40.13 to 41.20
▨	41.20 to 44.27

Miles

0   50   100

Map 5.4 Average Republican Gubernatorial Vote in Arizona, 1982–1990

Even when I first ran back in 1976, I never got any support from labor or traditionally Democratic constituencies. You see, for three terms I was a boll weevil ["pinto"] Democrat. When Reagan was elected, we switched during the first year of his administration. We were always under pressure from the Democratic leadership. The Democrats had always tried to beat me in the 3rd District.[23]

He said that even if he was active in local politics, in the state legislature where he labored from 1959 to 1976, he might still have switched parties: "The state legislature is more liberal now than it was back in the 1950s and 1960s. Understand that in Arizona, party loyalty is weak. Arizonans are independent and the Democrats used to be pretty conservative." Stump's easy switch stands in strong contrast to the account of the party switch in the late 1970s of Peter Peyser, a Republican House member from New York. Peyser's switch was described as a "metamorphosis" that forced him to seize upon completely new issues.[24]

From Stump's testimony, however, one obtains the impression that the issues and cleavages dividing the parties in Arizona may not be as clear as those dividing the parties in places like Peyser's New York. Arizona would fit V. O. Key's description as having been rendered homogeneous by the issues of national politics.[25] Democrats and Republicans here share a generally conservative outlook. This uniform world view distances the state's politics from national political orientations. As former governor Bruce Babbitt explained to political scientist David Berman, "Whenever the chairman of the Democratic National Committee came to town, I made it a point to be in the bottom of the Grand Canyon and to leave behind a telegram welcoming him to Arizona." In a similar vein, Stump's state director, Lisa Jackson, emphasized Stump's conservatism, but described it as a *nonpartisan* conservatism in the context of Arizona politics: "Many issues that are divisive elsewhere, are not issues here because there is a conservative consensus among voters."[26]

In the 1960s, divisions in Arizona state politics appeared to emerge along class or occupational lines. The regional division between the parties reflected the separation of the mining from the nonmining areas of the state. The three counties with the most dependence on mining, Greenlee, Gila, and Pinal, were also among the most Democratic (see map 5.3, above). The importance of mining to the state's economy has declined sharply, but these counties have maintained their Democratic traditions. While this occupational pattern may be similar to the New Deal cleavages dividing labor from nonlabor voters, Arizona's urban voting patterns are the reverse of those in states like Ohio, New Jersey, New York, and Pennsylvania. Maricopa County has been solidly

Republican for many years although migration may slowly alter that in the 1990s. Throughout the 1950s and early 1960s, Maricopa County was more Republican than the state as a whole.[27] Rural areas, conversely, have tended to vote more Democratic. Even with these reversals of conventional national party alignments, there has been an ideological compatibility between city and countryside that does not exist in all states. For example, Bob Stump's political turf encompasses part of Maricopa County and the entire western third of the state. It contains myriad economic interests, from the Phoenix suburbs to the timber in Mohave County to agriculture to basic infrastructure and economic development along the Colorado River. The nonpartisanship of Arizona politics, says Bob Stump, may have surrounded the mutual interest of city and countryside in economic and infrastructural development:

> Party labels have never been that important. The key issues have not been the national party issues. Together, Arizonans have fought for years to obtain infrastructure and water development. Discovery and pioneering are the keys to Arizona politics.
>
> Partisanship, however, is growing. Now the decisions are becoming more lifestyle oriented. Now that local issues about infrastructure and water are close to resolution, lifestyle conflict will emerge. We will see partisanship grow as it has in California.
>
> We are nearing the top of the development curve. This is when states can have the luxury of party politics. For years, we were fighting just for the basics. We needed postal offices, shopping centers . . . we were resolving land use questions and involved in water transfers.
>
> I would guess that many of the western states are about where we are. Colorado is at the top of the development curve, and partisanship is taking over Colorado politics. Wyoming is about where we are. So are Utah, Nevada, and New Mexico. Now that our freeway is complete, we are probably at the top of our development curve.[28]

A more class-based partisanship has emerged, and consensus is dissolving with the advance of development. For most of Arizona's history, though, voters with rural and urban interests agreed that development was necessary. In this context, Stump added, "When I was in the state legislature, there were only seventeen members in the Senate. Water was a big issue then. We had consensus on most things." Others confirm the existence of this consensus. In the state Senate, where Stump served from 1967 to 1976, Ross Rice observed that there really was no minority bloc. The general approach was to "keep new legislation to a minimum, hold down appropriations, and adjourn."[29] The

common organizational pattern in the 1960s and 1970s was a coalition between conservative Democrats and Republicans.

Because development has been a dominant concern in state politics, the
more divisive issues of national partisan politics have not meant very much.
This interpretation of Arizona politics is bolstered by a multivariate regression analysis of the gubernatorial and presidential votes (see table 5.4). Not
one of the demographic variables typical of the national party system is
statistically significant. Upon dropping variables out of the equation to avoid
multicollinearity, the demographic variables remained statistically powerless.
In more recent elections, Arizona's wealthier counties had a slight tendency
to vote *against* Republican candidates due to the candidate-centered nature of
Arizona elections.

Candidates, Not Organizations, in Arizona Politics

Unified party organizations are not present in accounts of Arizona's political history. There is no ward or city organization in the system upon which
to build a party machine. The only city with a long history of partisan elections is Tucson. Without a seniority system in the state legislative committee
structure, party power is not concentrated in any particular place for any
duration. Political organizations belong to individuals and lack the autonomy
and cohesion of the traditional machines of the Midwest and East. As in
New Mexico, patronage is dispensed by individuals rather than by political
machines.[30]

Several accounts have suggested that the development of unified parties
has been inhibited by the persistence of strong personality politics. Both
Republicans and Democrats have feuded within their parties over issues and
leadership. In the 1960s, the Republicans split between the right wing, represented by controversial conservative Evan Mechem, and the more moderate
faction led by former representative John Rhodes and former senators Barry
Goldwater and Paul Fannin (also former governor). Following the 1980 election, Republicans split again into left- and right-wing camps. The right wing
maintains socially conservative positions, such as opposition to abortion; in
contrast, the moderate faction reflects the increasingly libertarian views of
Goldwater.[31] Moderate U.S. Senator John McCain hastened some of this intraparty split when he tried to seize control of the state party. The right wing
of the party suffered most in recent years with the impeachment of ultracon-
servative Governor Evan Mechem in 1987. Similarly, Democrats had both
liberal and right-wing factions within their party. The liberal wing was led by
Governor Bruce Babbitt and Morris and Stewart Udall. The more conserva-

Table 5.4 Influences on the Republican Presidential and Gubernatorial Vote in Arizona, by County, 1960–1992

	Constant	Income	% Urban	Minority	% Mfg.	Adj. R²
President, 1960	13.5	1.35	−.08	.13	.99	.44
		(1.32)	(.15)	(.17)	(.51)	
Governor, 1960	9.2	1.77	−.09	.18	.74	.28
		(1.56)	(.18)	(.20)	(.60)	
Governor, 1962	−25.8	3.56	−.35	.27	.89	.15
		(2.17)	(.25)	(.28)	(.84)	
President, 1968	41.2	−.03	.09	−.45	.59	.38
		(.96)	(.15)	(2.03)	(.30)	
Governor, 1968	26.9	.27	.01	−.54	1.48*	.68
		(1.22)	(.20)	(2.59)	(.39)	
Governor, 1970	27.5	.44	−.21	.80	1.54*	.63
		(1.14)	(.19)	(2.42)	(.37)	
President, 1972	28.2	1.06	−.17	1.08	.75*	.58
		(.83)	(.14)	(1.76)	(.27)	
President, 1980	85.9	−1.33	−.05	−.09	1.65*	.23
		(1.49)	(.26)	(.20)	(.67)	
Governor, 1982	53.3	−1.26	.02	−.07	1.41*	.35
		(1.11)	(.20)	(.15)	(.50)	
President, 1988	43.1	.42	.07	−.08	−.59	.01
		(.64)	(.19)	(.17)	(.93)	
Governor, 1990	23.9	−.75	.04	−.04	−.39	.19
		(.74)	(.21)	(.19)	(1.08)	
President, 1992	23.5	.71	−.05	−.11	−.30	.52
		(.39)	(.11)	(.10)	(.56)	

*p < .05   N=14

Source: Bureau of the Census, *County and City Databook* (Washington, D.C.: GPO, various years); Richard M. Scammon and Alice McGillivray, eds., *America Votes* (Washington, D.C.: Elections Research Center, various years); *County and City Extra* (Lanham, Md.: Bernan Press, 1992).

Note: Multiple linear regression, WLS estimation; unstandardized regression coefficients weighted for population; standard errors in parentheses; income expressed in thousands of constant 1992 dollars.

tive or "pinto" wing of the party was comprised of mostly rural legislators and conservative Democrats like Stump. This factionalism has made for lively intraparty competition but little party cohesion.

Arizona Politics in the Post–New Deal Period

Many of Arizona's recent gubernatorial elections have been low-key events, which is why the weighted regression coefficients presented in table 5.4 show that Arizona's counties rarely divide along the traditional lines of national politics. Even when gubernatorial races occur in presidential election years, as in 1960 and 1968, the political cleavages are dissimilar in important respects. So just what are the local issues that have uniquely divided Arizona politics?

In 1962, the gubernatorial race was between Tucson's Sam Goddard, a Democrat, and incumbent Paul Fannin from Maricopa County. This case provides a good illustration of the regional and ideological split between Tucson and Phoenix. Besides the mining areas, the bastion of Democratic party strength has been Tucson (Pima County)—home of liberals Morris and Stewart Udall. Stewart Udall represented Arizona's second district before his appointment as secretary of interior under John F. Kennedy. His younger brother, Morris Udall, took his place in the House in 1962 and stayed there until ill health forced him to retire in 1991.

It is not immediately obvious why Tucson and vicinity would be the Democratic stronghold in the state. Two, possibly three, explanations come to mind. First, the southeast is the mining region of the state. Much of Tucson's economy was originally related to mining, although only about 3 percent of the Pima County population worked in the mines by 1960. Second, Tucson is dominated by a university; in Arizona politics, as in much of the nation, university towns such as Flagstaff, Tempe, and Tucson tend to vote Democratic. Finally, while the presence of large numbers of Indians in the northern counties is not associated with a clearly partisan pattern, the presence of Spanish Americans in the southeast may consistently pull down Republican margins, as in the New Mexico case. Republican dominance throughout the 1960s and 1970s could be attributed to the lack of a large labor vote in the state and the steady in-migration of elderly citizens who tended to import Republican party identification.[32]

At a glance, Arizona's divisive state issues appear to be similar to those elsewhere—how state government should be financed and how the money would be spent. In addition, school aid has been an issue at least since 1959 when Democrats split on the proper method of financing additional state aid to school districts.[33] But the youth of the state and its underdeveloped infrastructure suggest a more complicated political setting. Not only has Arizona's transportation and water infrastructure lagged far behind that of older and more settled states, but the state has also struggled to keep up with the demand for basic government services brought on by rapid growth.[34]

Generally, infrastructure could be considered a valence issue in Arizona, where widespread consensus prevails. Still, development issues occasionally lead to serious side-taking. In 1962, for instance, a major election issue concerned the location of a medical school, and there was considerable pressure in the legislature to expand the system of higher education. Fannin contended that the state could not afford a medical school and that the expansion of the junior college system was more important. Fannin did suggest that if there was to be a medical school, it should be located in Tempe at Arizona State University. Goddard, who was from Tucson, insisted that it be located at the University of Arizona in Tucson. This was sufficient to mobilize Tucsonans against Fannin and in favor of Goddard, while Maricopa's superior numbers remained in the Republican column.

The absence of party unity also contributed to Goddard's defeat. In the end, he lacked the complete support of his party, and the other candidates on the Democratic ticket campaigned with their own personal organizations. Congressional candidate Morris Udall and incumbent Senator Carl Hayden joined forces, endorsing each other on billboards and in newspaper advertising, while leaving Goddard's name out of the publicity. Late in the campaign, Goddard put Hayden and Udall's name on his advertisements, but they did not reciprocate.[35] The Udall and Hayden campaigns realized quickly that promoting Goddard's election over the popular Fannin was a lost cause. They could expect to win their races, but knew that in such a candidate-centered state as this, Goddard could not beat Fannin. Rather than risk losing with Goddard, they campaigned without him. Goddard's personal campaign organization was no match for Fannin's widespread name recognition and the state's economic prosperity. Goddard lost, but Udall and Hayden won.

The failure to campaign as a cohesive slate in this instance illustrates the history of intraparty strife and candidate independence in both Arizona parties. The Democrats have, since statehood, engaged in wide open primary contests—especially if no strong personality was present. In the 1960s, Democratic party leaders came together to try to form a system of preprimary endorsements by the amateur organization, the Arizona Democratic Council.[36] The attempt was ultimately unsuccessful because it came from the liberal wing of the party where only about half of the party's voters were located.

Sustained Candidate-Centeredness: 1982 and 1990

Twenty years later, the low-key 1982 gubernatorial race was a mismatch, much like that of 1962, but for different reasons from those which made the 1982 Ohio contest so lopsided. In Ohio, a Democratic challenger won on a valence issue—the weakness of the economy—which unified much of the electorate against the party in power.[37] In Arizona, a Democratic incumbent won, independent of trends in the national economy. The economy was a valence issue at some level, and it may have helped scare off serious Republican opposition. As in New Mexico, however, the state of the national economy did not nationalize this race. If anything, it focused more attention on the Democratic incumbent's successes. Unlike the situation in Ohio and other Rust Belt states, complaints about the condition of the economy did not ring as true locally. Arizona's boom in migration and employment suggested that it was moving opposite of national trends.[38]

The early 1980s were hard in some areas of Arizona but not where most of the people lived. Maricopa County's unemployment rate was at 7.9 percent—two points lower than the state and national average. Pima County's (Tucson) unemployment rate was slightly lower than the state average at 9.6 percent. Those counties where unemployment had risen most were traditionally Democratic areas holding to the position that the Democrats are always better at handling income security issues. Governor Babbitt would have done well in these areas despite the trends.

The upshot is that incumbent officeholders, regardless of party, may not be hurt by national recession if the recession is not truly local. Bruce Babbitt won reelection victory based primarily upon his no-nonsense approach to grappling with growth issues that were subject to substantial local consensus. While candidates in eastern and midwestern states were bemoaning their economic woes, Babbitt could point out that Arizona had moved from the twenty-eighth to the eighth most desirable state for business relocation. A coalition of business leaders even put together a "Republicans for Babbitt" organization to help finance his reelection with Republican money.[39] In a state where there was already a strong tradition of candidate-centered politics, the economy made this election even more centered on names.

Intraparty strife and interpersonal rivalry have been a consistent theme in more recent elections, too. Arizonans desperately wanted a low-profile contest in 1990: "The passion this year clearly is to stop having Arizona be the subject for one-liners on the Carson show," said Phoenix mayor Terry Goddard, the Democratic gubernatorial candidate (and son of Sam Goddard who ran for governor in 1962).[40] It was not to be. On the Republican side, the impeached governor, Evan Mechem, launched a comeback bid. He managed to finish second behind Phoenix developer and political novice Fife Symington in a five-way race that also featured the feisty libertarian Sam Steiger.

Early polls showed Goddard with a commanding seventeen-point lead over Symington. By late fall, however, his lead had evaporated. Goddard had some natural disadvantages. His name was most recognizable in the Phoenix area, which tended to lean Republican. Observers claimed that the challenge was to get his name out to the strong Democratic areas of the state, in Tucson and the north. Polls late in the race showed that Goddard and Symington had swapped some blocs of support.[41] Goddard did surprisingly well among high-income voters, and he also managed to attract 25 percent of the Republican votes, while Symington was able to pull over only 15 percent of the Democratic vote. Still, Republicans outnumber Democrats in the state, and Symington narrowly beat Goddard by 4,200 votes.

The story did not end there. A Mechem ally, Max Hawkins, had entered the race and won just enough write-in votes to deny Symington a majority. Ironically, a simple majority rule was passed as an anti-Mechem measure in the 1988 legislative session.[42] Mechem had won the 1986 election with a plurality. The law required a runoff election of the top two candidates if neither candidate won a simple majority. The legislature failed to attach any enabling legislation to the law, and for several weeks following the 1990 race the election remained up in the air as the legislature went into special session to figure out how to conduct a runoff election.[43] Once the runoff was held, Symington came out the winner, with a slightly larger margin, 52 to 48 percent. Lower turnout for the runoff contributed to Goddard's defeat. Seventy-two thousand fewer Democratic voters showed up for the runoff, compared to only thirty-one thousand fewer Republicans. Momentum or "bandwagoning" may also have contributed to the Symington victory. Wanting to side with the front-runner, many independent voters may have switched their vote when the runoff came around.

National Divisions in the Arizona Electorate

The county-level data are not especially revealing, given that the county jurisdictions in Arizona contain vast land areas and, in the case of Maricopa and Pima Counties, large populations. They may suggest, however, that the traditional New Deal cleavages of race, urbanization, income, and occupation have little relevance as *sectional* cleavages. The national coalitions do not surface to divide counties and regions of the state. Unfortunately, Arizona is one of the states where polling data are scarce. Network exit poll data are

Table 5.5 Logit Analysis of the Influence of Race, Income, and Union Membership in Arizona Elections, 1986–1992

	Constant	Race	Income	Labor	No. of Cases	Predicted Null (%)
Governor, 1986	2.64	−1.52*			269	76
		(.32)	—	—		70
Effect		−35.0				
Senate, 1986	1.28	−.65*			507	66
		(.16)	—	—		62
Effect		−16.0				
Governor, 1990[a]	.74	−1.06*	.15*		1,314	57
		(.005)	(.002)	—		50
Effect		−25.0	4.0			
President, 1992	1.20	−1.46*	.14	−.49	552	60
		(.27)	(.08)	(.29)		54
Effect		−31.9	3.4	−10.3		
Senate, 1992	1.26	−.70*	.08	−.20	814	66
		(.20)	(.07)	(.25)		66
Effect		−16.6	1.9	−4.8		

Source: ICPSR, CBS News/New York Times, *Election Day Surveys,* 1986. Voter Research and Surveys, *General Election Exit Polls,* 1990, 1992.

Note: Dependent variable: 0 = Democrat, 1 = Republican; MLE coefficients; standard errors are in parentheses; *p < .05; Effect = change in odds of voting Republican from moving x one unit at the means of the other variables. The 1986 CBS/New York Times poll did not include questions on the respondent's labor union membership and income. The 1990 Voter Research and Surveys poll did not include a question on labor union membership.

a. The Republican vote includes the vote for independent conservative candidate Evan Mechem, a former Republican governor.

available only for a few recent elections (table 5.5). The 1986 poll did not ask questions about family income or labor union membership, and the 1990 poll failed to ask about union membership.

Racial divisions are unmistakably present in Arizona voting at the sub-presidential level (table 5.5); however, the distinction between minority (black and Hispanic) and white voting was more pronounced in the 1986 gubernatorial race than in the U.S. Senate race of that year. Compared to white, middle-income voters, minorities were 35 percent less likely to vote Republican in the gubernatorial contest, but only 16 percent less likely to vote for the Republican senate candidate. This suggests a volatility to race-based voting that has been typical of the southwest. Only around 2 percent of

Arizona's voting population is black, and the Mexican-American and Indian populations more evenly divide their vote between the two parties. The number of union households is below 13 percent. Economically, the electorate is homogeneously middle class. Like elsewhere, higher-income voters tend to cast Republican ballots; the low-income voters, however, do not constitute a strong counterweight. Similarly, Native Americans and Hispanics comprise some 17 percent of the population but cast only 9 percent of the ballots.[44] Neither the labor nor the class cleavages are statistically significant in the 1992 presidential and U.S. Senate races.

As in the 1960s, there is no sign of party cohesion in the more recent races. In fact, third-party candidacies have had strong appeal in Arizona. Late October polls in 1986 suggested that independent candidate Bill Schulz led both major party candidates for governor. The major party candidates had won by beating candidates backed by party organizations in divisive primary contests. Many Republican regulars turned and backed Schulz, who inevitably lost to conservative ideologue Mechem. Amazingly, third-party challengers in Arizona races consistently draw between 5 and 25 percent of the vote. Typical of weakly institutionalized party systems is the success of ex-Republicans like Steiger and Schulz, and write-in candidates like Hawkins, at winning votes in general elections. If American political institutions encouraged it, Arizona might have the strongest multiparty system of any state.

Arizona's primary system of nomination is not the cause of its absence of party unity. In Arizona politics, third-party candidates like Steiger and Schulz would emerge in any case. V. O. Key understood that the mere presence of a primary did not guarantee competition for the party nomination. Contests develop in primaries, according to Key, when incumbents retire, when issues divide the community, or when there is a disturbance such as a realignment.[45] In Arizona, the first two causes of primary activity are important, especially the second. Incumbents find themselves challenged in the primary due to divisions in the community produced not by national conditions, but by local ones.

Summary: Party Weakness in the Desert Southwest

Arizona and New Mexico are unified by their apparent independence from national trends and forces. Thanks to network television and radio, the electorate in the desert Southwest follows the rest of the nation on many valence issues. These societies, however, are relatively homogeneous. Unique local coalitions wield substantial influence in separating national from local politics: Hispanic population groups, conservatives, environmentalists, the elderly, developers, mining interests, Native Americans, cattle ranchers. Without a large black population and without a concentrated and politically active low-income population, social welfare programming is a low priority. Much of Arizona's post–World War II politics has concerned distributive and regulatory issues such as adapting to population growth and ensuring water availability and quality.[46] Finally, what unites Arizona and New Mexico is that the foundations for two-party competition are not the urban-rural foundations of the Northeast and Midwest. Cities are prosperous trade centers with successful service and high-tech industries—not the aging, declining Rust Belt cities of the Northeast and Midwest. Rural areas, on the other hand, are neither the productive nor the heavily subsidized farming areas of the Midwest and Northeast. National farm policy has little relevance in a desert populated with cattle and mines.

New Mexico, nevertheless, has been able to maintain some semblance of candidate-based organization strength. Voters are not mobilized by issues in New Mexico, but they are mobilized by candidate-centered organizations. Toney Anaya drove elderly rural voters to the polls in Jeeps in his 1982 gubernatorial election. In Arizona, there is no evidence of coordinated candidate efforts. Regions of the state show short-term durability and predictability in their voting behavior, but in the long term, the volatility is dramatic—electing Republicans by wide margins in one election, then turning to Democrats by similarly wide margins in another. This points up the weak-party state's candidate-centered orientation.

For these states to have developed strong parties, the coalitional social group profiles of the local parties would have had to match those of the national parties. As it stands, partisanship is a very partial guide for citizen voting behavior. Substantial congruence of national and state partisanship would have forestalled the generation of a consciousness in the electorate that is sensitive to the appeals of individual candidates. At the very least, for party organizations of any strength to have emerged, the voting behavior of the electorate would have to have been more predictable.

Migration of new population groups to both states has contributed to electoral unpredictability. Thad Brown's insightful analysis of the effects of migration on a citizen's political thinking is especially applicable to these states. Migrants often drop their partisan ties as they move. Their voting becomes more individualistic, more independent: "Migration is a source of progressive dissolution of the party system."[47] Party labels in Arizona have declined in significance with the influx of citizens from other states: "Without the mediating function of partisanship, voters are more likely to look directly at the candidates."[48] This is how massive migration to Arizona has driven candidate-centered, consensus-oriented elections such as that of Bruce Babbitt in 1982.

Clearly, some national themes are present in local politics, such as jobs and economic growth. Without the degree of geographic social and economic stratification of the East and Midwest, however, elites must represent large dispersed constituencies where class has not been a prominent force and race takes on a different meaning. This electorally misshapen political environment does not necessarily make for issue voting, if issue voting is understood as distinct from candidate voting. The effect is that candidates definitely stand out. With a state-level distribution of ideology that differs from that of the national party system, politicians are left to construct personal coalitions that are only as permanent as the candidates themselves.

Both New Mexico and Arizona are heading in the direction of a more programmatic and perhaps more partisan politics, but one just as devoid of party organizations. In Arizona, distributive and regulatory issues may turn into redistributive issues as the frontier is filled and technology can no longer satisfy the demand for scarce resources. In addition, as some infrastructural problems have been resolved, formerly ignored issues have arisen to take their place. These issues divide rather than unify the community and may serve to extend national political divisions into local politics. In New Mexico, the conflict that has emerged to obstruct party cohesion is also related to migration. The division between the "new" New Mexico and the "old" New Mexico fragments both parties. Whether one party will become the party of the old, while the other the party of the new, is doubtful. The new voters have too many resources (votes) to be ignored by either party. The Hispanic counties of New Mexico's north-central region will probably continue to lose power and population, shifting the action of New Mexico politics even more toward the population centers of Albuquerque, Santa Fe, and Las Cruces.

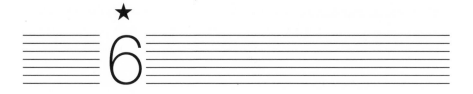

★

6

Panning for Partisans in a Turbulent Environment: California

California: Electoral Background

ASK THE governors from Warren to Wilson, and they'll tell you that California is a difficult state to manage. In a 1948 article, Governor Earl Warren was quoted as saying that every time he made a trip to the Midwest, East, or South, astonishing numbers of people would tell him, "As soon as I can cut loose, I'm coming West to live."[1] For Warren, the West Coast's biggest political problem was trying to keep up with the pressures of in-migration.

Politically, California has become the most important state in the nation and is now the most populous. For forty years now, states in the Northeast and upper Midwest have lost U.S. House representation to California. Between 1960 and 1990, California grew by 89 percent, as compared to 6 percent for New York and 11 percent for Ohio.

As for political sections, the state looks much different now than it did at the turn of the century. The state is home to more high-income Democrats than any other. Most of these voters live on the coast. Maps 6.1 and 6.2 illustrate the changes in the geographic distribution of party support between the 1960s and the 1980s. Note that the coastal counties are decisively Democratic.

Vic Fazio, a Democratic politician from the Davis area and co-founder of the *California Journal*, a periodical on California politics and issues, explained the mentality of this significant bloc of voters:

> The wealthy Democrats live on the coast. They are Democrats because they are socially liberal. They want to protect their quality of

life against the spoilers of the environment—developers, oil drillers. They are for free speech and privacy. They live around centers of intellect. Many of these people are willing to live with the negative consequences of their ideology. They will even live with higher taxes to a point. Many are interested in helping the "downtrodden." Some cynically say this is guilt. I tend to think these people have a "global" perspective. They think globally and act locally. They also vote globally. They are politically interested, active, and they do wield clout.[2]

Like the coast, much of California north of the San Francisco Bay area is Democratic. In Humbolt County, Democratic registration exceeded Republican registration by 21.6 points in 1980. Like the Oregon and Washington coastal counties, many residents of this region work in lumbering, fishing, and dairy farming. The Bay area itself is environmentally sensitive and Democratic. In 1980, 58 percent of the four-county region (Marin, Contra Costa, San Francisco, and Alameda) were registered Democrats, but for no apparent economic reason. The economy of the Bay area is as strong as it is diverse. No one industry dominates, although the high-technology corridor south of San Francisco continues to prosper and bring Republican voters to the region. Still, the people are heterogeneous, and the Bay area has large African-American, Asian, Hispanic, and Italian populations.

Central California was politically transformed by the migration of southwesterners ("Okies, Arkies") in the 1930s and 1940s. Today, this region, including San Joaquin County, southward to Fresno and Bakersfield, is largely two-party competitive, and the northern valley is dominated by agricultural interests. Modesto, Stockton, and Merced are centers for agricultural trade, food processing, and wine. In the south, oil fields operate near Bakersfield and refineries in several coastal towns.

Southern California has been described as sprawling, ethnically diverse, and municipally fragmented.[3] Los Angeles County leans Democratic, but not for the same reasons that, for example, Cuyahoga County, Ohio, is Democratic. Only around one-fifth of the population is employed in industry; the aircraft industry has been the largest employer for most of the post–New Deal period. Orange County is a Republican stronghold and has been dependent, until recently, on government markets for military-related products. This area has the lowest rate of worker unionization of any county in California.[4] The rest of southern California, including San Diego and Riverside Counties, is heavily Republican and has been subject to rapid growth.

California's size and heterogeneity make it unique among the western states. It has a larger African-American population than any of the others and

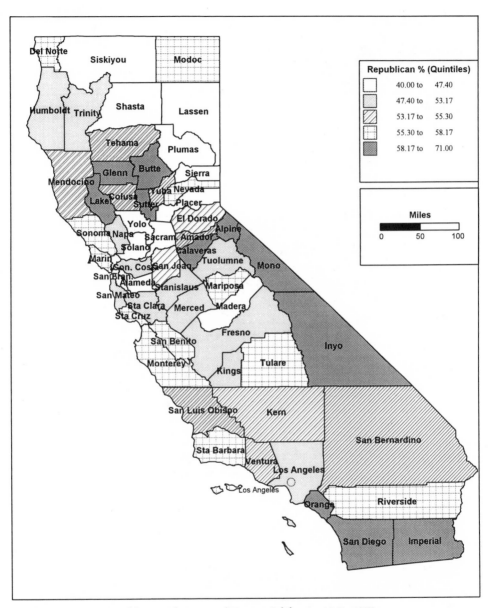

Map 6.1   Average Republican Gubernatorial Vote in California, 1962–1970

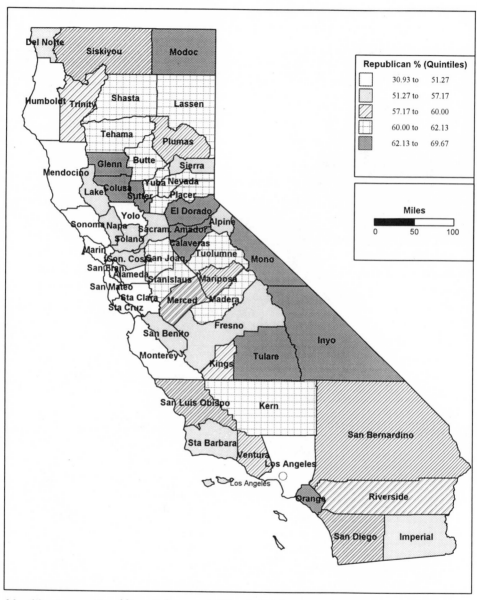

Republican % (Quintiles)

30.93 to	51.27
51.27 to	57.17
57.17 to	60.00
60.00 to	62.13
62.13 to	69.67

Miles

0   50   100

Map 6.2   Average Republican Gubernatorial Vote in California, 1982–1990

has a larger Asian population than any state except Hawaii. Although it is the most industrial state in the West (15 percent employed in manufacturing in 1990), it has never been as industrialized as states in the Northeast and Midwest, where employment in manufacturing amounted to 28 percent of the total employment in 1990. California's unique constellation of characteristics formed a distinct politics. In the words of Rep. Vic Fazio, "California is very ethnic now. It is not a melting pot, but a conglomeration of distinct groups."[5]

California's History of Weak Party Politics

Almost no one would argue about the famed weakness of California political parties. At various times in the state's history, powerful interests—the Southern Pacific Railroad, Pacific Gas & Electric, proponents of old-age pensions, and lobbyist Arthur Samish—have been said to absorb the state's parties. No one person or group, though, has held control for very long. As a result, the state has been "almost entirely devoid of any well-defined, responsible leadership." Policy is determined by "many influential individuals who gravitate from one amorphous alliance of interests to another."[6]

Candidates do their own fund-raising, hire their own campaign managers, and only occasionally does one candidate coalesce with others on the ticket. Vic Fazio explained that slate making has never been an important aspect of party activity in the state. Instead, slates became the province of amateurs and then professional consultants:

> The original reason for the creation of the amateur political clubs was to form slates. Today, consultants peddle slates to candidates. There are three or four Republican slates and three or four Democratic slates. They are up for grabs by the local candidates. This kind of activity works sensibly only in California's crowded and wide-open primaries.[7]

There is an increasing tendency, nearly unique to California, for candidates and interest groups to market statewide endorsements through the mail.[8] Since parties are prohibited from making primary endorsements, consultants have stepped in to fill the void. There are several competing explanations for the weakness of parties and the strength of groups. The institutional argument suggests that the weakness of parties was due to progressive reforms enacted during the early twentieth century. These reforms took power away from the political parties, giving it directly to the people. One of these reforms, crossfiling, was passed in 1913 to introduce a strong measure of nonpartisanship into the state's primary system. In elections, this put the emphasis on a candidate's name recognition and heavily favored incumbency. Republicans Earl Warren and Hiram Johnson effectively used crossfiling to win both party nominations in the primary, and because they were the only candidates appearing on the ballot, they won near unanimous victories in general elections. This reform, so it is argued, destroyed party control and party responsibility by allowing a candidate to run in the opposition party's primary as only a name—without having to list party affiliation. Why work to build a party if party does not cue the votes on election day? In turn, without official party machinery to limit the influence of special interests on politicians, special interests abounded—successfully obtaining direct influence over legislation. Campaign funds flowed directly to candidates rather than through party organizations.

Professional campaign managers first emerged in California in the vacuum left by the absence of party leadership. In a 1989 Supreme Court case, *Eu v. San Francisco County Democratic Central Committee*, certain Progressive Era regulations controlling the internal operation of party organizations were struck down as violations of the First Amendment. As a result, both parties may have renewed potential for influence.[9] Hence, to cut the argument short, the roots of candidate-centered politics lay in institutional reforms. Removing these institutional barriers will strengthen the parties.

The institutional argument stands tall because political scientists like to think that institutions and institutional reforms matter. The relevant question here is whether California would have developed strong parties without institutions like crossfiling. There is reason for doubt. While they are surely not irrelevant, institutional reforms are not sufficient to explain party weakness. In Oregon, Nevada, Arizona, Wyoming, Colorado, and New Mexico, crossfiling was never a part of the institutional framework of the system, but candidate-centeredness persisted. In several strong-organization states, such as Connecticut, Pennsylvania, and New York, progressive institutional forms were adopted with little corresponding impact on the strength of organizations. In Cincinnati, one of the most reform-oriented cities in the nation, machine politics persisted into the 1960s.[10]

The most compelling explanations for party weakness, given these counterexamples, seem to be demographic ones. It is difficult to build an effective precinct organization in California because the state grew so quickly, it has so many suburban areas, and people move around frequently. Vic Fazio suggested that Californians in his region are hard to organize principally because of their suburban lifestyle:

People work a long way from where they live. They don't participate actively in community groups or organizations that could provide a base for political organization. They are contributors to the community in some sense, but they are not joiners. There's not a lot of "there" there. California's rootlessness has been well chronicled. People don't develop a strong sense of community identity in the suburbs. Part of this has to do with the rise of households where both parents work.[11]

In a 1951 article, one commentator pointed out that, over a two-year period in a typical Los Angeles County precinct, 19 percent of the people had moved away, 3 percent had died, 3 percent had changed their party registration, and 17 percent had been purged from the rolls for failing to vote.[12] This 42 percent cumulative change in two years indicates what challenges a precinct captain would face in organizing. According to U.S. census figures for 1980, 30 percent of California residents had moved from one area of their county to another between 1975 and 1980. No other state equaled California in this tendency. Thirteen percent of the population had migrated from a different state in the previous five years, in striking contrast to the movement of Midwestern and Eastern populations.[13] Only around 7 percent of the population in the five upper Midwestern states had moved in from a different state during this period.

These rapid population shifts add confusion to the political party system. When electorates change, issues change. Population growth may become an issue itself, as it has been in the Bay area and in southern California. More important, when electorates change, party balances of counties and sections change.[14] In California's case, areas around San Francisco that were Republican strongholds in the 1950s quickly became Democratic bastions in the 1970s and 1980s. Some of those areas south of San Francisco are changing yet again. Rapid redistribution of party support leads to a weakening of the party organization's influence over candidates. Electoral change inhibits an organization's capacity to offer cohesive slates and to win elections. In these cases, there can be little planning for the task of electing candidates. The party system is directed by little more than a loose cadre of "free-marketeers," known also as consultants. Candidates have no choice but to go out on their own. No party organization could possibly keep up with the pace of change in so large a state. This has contributed to a "notable absence of broad coalitions capable of building political alliances across space, class and ethnicity."[15]

Evidence for the degree of change that can occur over a twenty-year period appears in figure 6.1. The scatterplot shows the relationship between the 1960 and 1980 Republican presidential voting by county. Both Republican candidates those years were from Southern California and both were from the conservative wings of their state party. Note that while the slope is upward, there is a wide scatter of counties around the line of regression. A similar regression comparing the 1962 to the 1982 gubernatorial vote indicates even greater disparity (not shown). The 1962 gubernatorial vote explains less than 3 percent of the variation in the 1982 gubernatorial vote.

The Rise and Fall of California's Club Movement

The story of political parties in California in the post–New Deal period is largely the story of the rise and fall of the amateur club movement. I will not fully summarize the role of the amateur here.[16] Generally, three things can be said about the amateur: the amateur is ideological and believes that parties

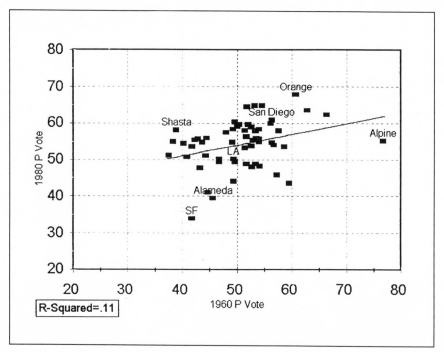

Figure 6.1   Relation Between the 1960 and 1980 Presidential Vote in California, by County

Source: Richard M. Scammon and Alice McGillivray, eds., *America Votes* (Washington, D.C.: Elections Research Center).

should be programmatic; the amateur is opposed to the "old politics" of patronage; and an amateur is generally an "out" rather than an "in." These three characteristics are comprehensible when we understand that the motivation of the amateur is to set purposeful individual goals, rather than material ones. The amateur is fighting for a cause. In the case of the California Democratic Council (CDC), the cause was to elect Democratic candidates in what had been a lopsidedly Republican state.

There are certain electoral conditions under which a club movement succeeds and fails. In the California instance, both movements arose from defeats at the polls. In the Democratic case, the club movement took hold in the 1950s in the form of the California Democratic Council (CDC). An earlier movement, called the California Republican Assembly (CRA), was organized in the 1930s, when Democrat Culbert Olson won the governorship, to maintain the Republican domination of state and federal offices that had persisted almost unbroken from statehood on. The CRA was successful as a means for endorsing certain candidates but not well enough organized to do precinct-level work. The CRA lacked the ideological fervor and devotion to cause that characterized the California Democratic Council. The CDC was working against the long tradition of Republican domination—a powerful motivator. The CRA had been organized largely to protect the status quo, so it never gained a mass membership. At its peak, membership reached 25,000. It helped candidates occasionally through the 1940s and 1950s by making pre-primary endorsements. By the 1960s, the CRA had been taken over by extreme elements; it has since disappeared.

The California Democratic Council, on the other hand, was a far more powerful and influential movement. The rise of the CDC in the early 1950s was primarily responsible for the coming of two-party politics to California. The CDC began when state senator George Miller in 1953 called a meeting of Democratic partisans in Asilomar. Alan Cranston claims that after moderate Republican Governor Earl Warren left California politics, the Democrats acquired a renewed sense of urgency that bolstered their drive to organize. The conservative wing of the California Republican party then took over, and the Democrats had something ideological to organize against.

> What pulled us together was defeat. We had the governorship only once in the twentieth century [Culbert Olson]. In the early 1950s, when we began, the state Assembly and Senate were very lopsided against us: 77–3 and 37–3, respectively. What happened was that George Miller called a meeting to discuss the wrongs and the rights of the Democratic party. Pat Brown was there briefly. We invited

anyone who wanted to come—not just party leadership. At this
point, the volunteer club movement began.

Once Earl Warren left California politics to serve on the Supreme
Court, the Nixon-Knowland-Knight faction of the Republican party
took over. This gave us an imperative we didn't have when the more
moderate Warren dominated the scene.[17]

Following the meeting at Asilomar, party officials launched a full-scale
organizational effort in northern California.[18] Cranston drew up a blueprint
for developing organizational machinery and introduced it at a Stockton
party convention. Cranston's blueprint called for the creation of county and
congressional-district Democratic Councils comprised of delegates from the
chartered clubs, including women's clubs, Young Democrats, and all other
recognized groups, as well as county central committees. The councils would
then seek to coordinate the policies and activities of the clubs, to encourage
and expand existing clubs, to organize new ones, and to cooperate with the
existing county-level, central committees.[19]

The design was tailored to a California electorate that was young, issue-
oriented, and rapidly growing. The clubs were comprised mainly of younger
voters who joined partly because they found the suburbs lonely and they
wanted social contacts. The movement was distinct from the national Democratic party because it was homogeneously middle-class; low-income groups
and unskilled workers were not attracted to the movement.[20] This illustrates
just how distinct California Democratic activists are from the dominant coalitions comprising the party elsewhere. The CDC thrived in areas that one
would expect to be heavily Republican—namely, the middle-class suburbs—
effectively crosscutting the economic cleavages that defined the national
party system. It was not surprising that supporters of Lyndon Johnson later
left the movement and factionalized the party. The club types were social
liberals who were part of the later antiwar movement. The more socially
conservative Democrats—blue-collar voters—supported the war and backed
the right wing of the California party led by Los Angeles Assemblyman
Jesse Unruh.

The club movement left little room for "coal scuttle" politics. California
was "short on oppressed minorities and breathed the confidence of a long
postwar boom."[21] One journalist, writing in 1962, summed it up this way:

> In booming Orange County, where the typical resident is 26.5 years
> old, only one family in ten makes less than $8,000 a year, and one in
> four makes $10,000 to $15,000. In San Francisco, one person in every

four owns capital stock, the nation's highest ratio. In [Jesse] Unruh's own Los Angeles, there are so many cars that everybody could have a front-seat ride at the same time. Every child is guaranteed a tuition free college education to fit his taste. Even the migrant farm laborers, though low men on the pole, make higher pay than farm workers in other states.

Here, men expect and get their place among the masses clustered around a high median income. Millions of success stories add up to the near achievement of a utopian dream: economic equality at a high income level.[22]

While the notion that have-nots had vanished into a society of near-equal haves, was probably exaggerated even in 1962, it is true that California was and still is a prosperous state. Democratic party leaders pinning their hopes on building a party movement on class oppression would not succeed. Even Jesse Unruh realized this and grudgingly worked with the CDC in general elections, though he tried to beat them in the primaries.

The CDC suddenly succeeded because there really had never been a forum for political participation other than directly at the polls. By creating a forum for the exchange of Democratic ideas, the CDC provided an avenue for furthering participation, and policy goals and advancing party endorsements. The CDC introduced a measure of organization that previously had been rare in the state. Before the early 1950s, Democrats, as a party, had no program or political objectives. Since the New Deal, they had held a majority of total registrants, but there was no New Deal cause to mobilize voters. While Earl Warren's moderation and nonpartisanship was partly responsible for this, California's prosperity didn't generate the class-consciousness Democrats possessed elsewhere.

Furthermore, there was no reason to build official party machinery. Under state law, the parties could not endorse candidates. Different interest groups and candidates had programs and policies, but the party did not. This diffusion of disparate groups and the legal constraints on the official party led to a complete lack of control over primary system nominations. Cranston, Miller, and others realized that getting control over their primary system would be the key to winning elections—especially under crossfiling.[23]

What the CDC provided was the extralegality to get past state laws and the all-important forum for the cooperation of rival Democratic interests. The CDC did not get bogged down in intricate policy debates. When debates did emerge, they were handled by a democratic convention process much like that of a national party convention. Ultimately, the goal was to meet to endorse excellent party candidates, not to dissect the fine points of policy.

At the Stockton meeting of amateurs, Cranston's plan was adopted and he was elected president of the CDC. From there, the organization met with considerable success through the 1950s and early 1960s. The organization gave Democratic partisans a voice they had never had before. There was now a Democratic organizational presence to take advantage of Republican party factionalism. Before this time, opportunities to exploit Republican weakness were always lost because the Democrats had no organization. Now things were different, at least for a while.

What caused the decay of the club movement? Two things led to the rise of the Democratic club movement in the 1950s: issues and the failure of Democratic party candidates to win elections. Issues and success, however, also led to decline. Ironically, much of what brought the club movement into being was also its undoing. Senator Cranston elaborates:

> It was unfortunate that once the Democrats won, we factionalized. Jesse Unruh and I were dire enemies. Unruh hated volunteers and hated the CDC. He wanted to build old-fashioned, patronage-based politics. The problem with volunteers, you see, was that you really had no control over them. Once Jess entered California politics, he sat about to destroy the CDC.[24]

Of course, the further irony was that Unruh could initiate this destructive work because the CDC had broken the Republicans' lock on state government. This is what Cranston meant by success destroying the CDC. Once Democrats had their foot in the door, there was much more room for bickering. They proved that they could win, so the goal of winning no longer unified them. Democratic unity, in this diverse state with population centers both north and south, was tenuous enough even when Democrats were losing. Once in power, though, issues arose that initiated the organizational decomposition. Why did the issues arise to split the party? Probably because each faction of the party thought it could now win without the other. The Republicans were on the run, and each side of the Democratic party claimed it was responsible for victory. Vietnam was the watershed issue, says Cranston.

> Vietnam really tore apart the CDC. Our attention to grassroots activities died because the Democrats split on Vietnam. Unruh, and more conservative Democrats, supported President Johnson. I was an opponent of the war.
>
> In 1964, the Democrats split in the primary between me and

Pierre Salinger. Unruh helped Salinger get into the primary precisely to beat me. Salinger did and then lost in the general election. In 1966, Reagan won big. I was the designated hatchet man. I went around the state beating up on him, hoping he would not win. However, it was obvious he would win two weeks before the election. I scrambled at the last minute, just to save my post as comptroller, but lost. Only one Democratic candidate, the attorney general Tom Lynch, won that year.

By 1968, the CDC was a shadow of its former self. I did manage to make peace with Jesse Unruh. With Unruh consistently opposing me, I had to make peace with him. Unruh wanted to run for the Senate seat but didn't. In a meeting I had with him, he said that he wouldn't support me in the primary, but if I won, he would support me in the general. He did, and I won.

The general election did bring some grassroots support back to life. I won on a "get out of Vietnam" platform. I was also for open housing, which was an important issue at the time. I had the support of widespread name recognition and the volunteers. A large number of liberal Republicans supported me.[25]

These party splits did not happen in states where the Democratic party was unafflicted by the kinds of socioeconomic and demographic diversity that divided the California party. The CDC never represented a cross-section of Democratic voters. As a middle-class movement, it did not represent lower-bracket interests. Vic Fazio summarizes the differences:

> Jesse (Unruh) was originally a Texan. He was from the South. . . . He had a blue-collar ethic. [Alan Cranston's] background, and that of Pat Brown too, was more upper-middle class—from the Los Altos area. Cranston's people were intellectuals, limousine liberals, Stevenson supporters. In fact, that's why Unruh was so comfortable with Lyndon Johnson and with the Kennedys—he supported Jack Kennedy, and later was a strong backer of Robert.
>
> So there was a class difference between the CDC, which had this war-peace and environmental dimension, and Unruh's blue-collar politics, which looked more like conventional national party politics of the 1960s.[26]

Traditional Democrats like Unruh saw themselves as representing those who were not participants in the club movement: labor, farm workers, and more conservative Democrats. Unruh sought to build a traditional organization from the top down. He fought the clubs in primaries from the beginning, usually beating them in Los Angeles County, joining forces with them only temporarily in general elections.

California Politics in the Post–New Deal Period

The bitterly fought gubernatorial race of 1962 serves to illustrate the complexity of issues and cleavages in California politics. The race that year was between Richard Nixon and Democratic incumbent Edmund G. "Pat" Brown. Nixon was a strong candidate. He had the name recognition associated with his run for president two years earlier. In the state, he defeated John F. Kennedy by 35,000 votes. He had been vice president under Eisenhower for eight years. Never had he been defeated in a California election. Major newspapers recognized his credentials, and he won the endorsements of both the San Francisco *Chronicle* and the *Los Angeles Times*.

The issues in the campaign were potentially quite divisive. Brown's emphasis was on education, vocational training, and expansion of welfare programs. Brown advocated a conservation program to counteract the tendency for unemployed youth to drift from idleness to delinquency to permanent unemployment.[27] He supported an expanded program of vocational training for welfare recipients—a form of "workfare" to get the poor "back on their feet." Brown proposed that the state extend more assistance to local mental health centers and increase funding for vocational rehabilitation programs for the disabled—a plank designed to win labor support. The program was clearly left-of-center but closely corresponded to President Kennedy's national proposals of Medicare, social programming, and welfare statism. Brown's major weakness was his policy on crime. He appeared to be "soft" on crime when he ordered a sixty-day stay of execution for convicted sex offender and death row inmate Caryl Chessman, hoping the legislature would abolish the death penalty.

Nixon's campaign, on the other hand, lacked a coherent theme. Apparently, the Nixon camp assumed they could win on the candidate's celebrity status and name recognition alone. Instead of offering a positive program, in the waning days of the campaign Nixon charged that Brown forces had falsely accused him of "being anti-Semitic, anti-Negro, and anti-Catholic." Nixon's campaign manager H. R. Haldeman filed suit against the Democrats for distributing two controversial anti-Nixon leaflets in black and Jewish sections of Los Angeles.[28] Nixon's own forces were not guiltless of this kind of activity. Democrats had gone to court and obtained restraining orders against the distribution of smears circulated by Nixon forces. But Nixon did almost nothing to attack Brown's four-year record as governor.

As a self-styled, middle-of-the-road Republican, Nixon also alienated the far right wing of his party just as the Republican right was reaching its peak in southern California. The Brown campaign ran a series of question-and-answer telethons. On one of these, Earl Warren, Jr., son of the chief justice, appeared to take questions on behalf of Brown. According to press reports, this underlined a Nixon problem. Liberal Republicans were also alienated from the campaign, and while they may not have endorsed Brown, they were not out actively working for Nixon.[29] Nixon was left with a campaign lacking any of the ideological causes that form the stuff and substance of California politics. There would be no way to combat an overwhelming registration edge by the Democrats without the Republican loyalists.

As the votes rolled in, it became clear that among Nixon's principal deficits was in the area of higher education, where the CDC had some of its strongest clubs. Club activity in Riverside, San Mateo, Santa Barbara, and Alameda Counties was especially detrimental to what might otherwise have been better Republican margins. Nixon won only two of the eight counties having the most highly educated populations.

Except for the rural northern counties where Brown won solid majorities, Nixon did well in agricultural areas. He also won a solid majority of 58.9 percent in Orange County and 55.8 percent in San Diego. Although Nixon was expected to do poorly in Los Angeles County, he did even worse than expected. In Los Angeles and Alameda Counties, both with large proportions of the voting electorate, Nixon's 1962 performance trailed his 1960 presidential margin by 2.5 and 4.8 points, respectively, losing majorities in both.

Dominant national cleavages clearly did not determine the Nixon vote (see table 6.1) in California. In the model of the 1960 presidential race, only the minority variable had the usual influence after weighting the cases for population. Higher-income counties voted Democratic, and more urban counties leaned Republican. California's political divisions were similar in both the presidential and gubernatorial races, even though they did not resemble the coalitional patterns of eastern and midwestern states. Since the same person was running on the Republican ticket in 1960 and 1962, some similarity was to be expected. The precise relationship between Nixon's 1960 presidential and 1962 gubernatorial votes can be depicted in a scatterplot diagram (fig. 6.2). While the relationship is strong, the constant (not reported) is large enough to show that Nixon's 1962 performance consistently trailed his 1960 performance by an average of four percentage points. More

Table 6.1   Influences on the Republican Presidential and Gubernatorial Vote in
California, by County, 1960–1992

	Constant	Income	% Urban	Minority	% Mfg.	Adj. R²
President, 1960	64.2	−.62* (.25)	.18* (.05)	−1.09* (.14)	−.05 (.08)	.52
Governor, 1962	61.4	−.83* (.30)	.23* (.06)	−1.17* (.17)	.06 (.10)	.48
President, 1968	52.8	−.60* (.20)	.19* (.07)	−1.23* (.17)	.39* (.10)	.55
Governor, 1970	54.7	−.22 (.18)	.13 (.06)	−1.20* (.15)	.17 (.10)	.54
President, 1972	61.1	−.58* (.20)	.19* (.06)	−1.13* (.16)	.36* (.10)	.48
President, 1980	72.9	−.71* (.23)	.20* (.08)	−.78* (.12)	.28* (.13)	.43
Governor, 1982	72.8	−.55* (.19)	.11 (.07)	−.69* (.10)	.13 (.11)	.49
President, 1988	66.7	−.67* (.21)	.40* (.12)	−.89* (.15)	.33* (.17)	.39
Governor, 1990	70.4	−.84* (.20)	.40* (.12)	−.84* (.15)	.37* (.16)	.38
President, 1992	50.4	−.53* (.15)	.22* (.09)	−.55* (.11)	.16 (.12)	.34

*p < .05   N=57

Source: Bureau of the Census, *County and City Databook* (Washington, D.C.: GPO, various years); Richard M. Scammon and Alice McGillivray, eds., *America Votes* (Washington, D.C.: Elections Research Center, various years); *County and City Extra* (Lanham, Md.: Bernan Press, 1992).

Note: Multiple linear regression, WLS estimation; unstandardized regression coefficients weighted for population; standard errors in parentheses; income expressed in thousands of constant 1992 dollars.

important, in some of the larger counties, Nixon's losses were decisive. Still, the former vice president did have areas of strength. He won votes in the smaller cities of the Central Valley where the population had strong roots in the social conservatism of the southwestern migration.[30] Nixon's support in these agricultural regions was not completely uniform, but he did consistently better there than in any other region in the state.

Sustained Candidate-Centeredness: 1982 and 1990

Some twenty years later, the hard-fought gubernatorial race between Attorney General George Deukmejian and Los Angeles Mayor Tom Bradley, was even closer than the Nixon-Brown contest. California's Democrats had maintained a solid statewide registration edge of 18.5 percent.[31] With the exception of San Diego and Orange Counties, Democrats completely dominated the state's urban areas, holding a twenty-six-point registration edge in Los Angeles County, a forty-point lead in San Francisco, a twenty-seven-point lead in Sacramento County, and a thirty-seven-point lead in Alameda County. These four heavily Democratic counties constituted 46 percent of the state's Democratic electorate and accounted for 41 percent of all registered voters.

Unlike the climate in Ohio and Pennsylvania in 1982, many doubted whether Reaganomics was an issue at all with voters in California. The *Fresno*

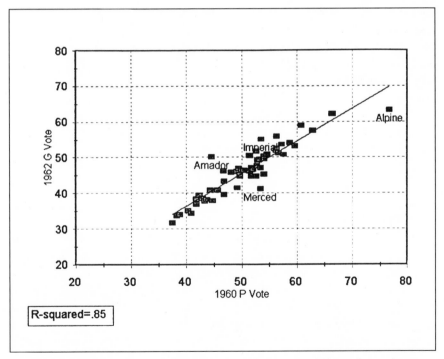

Figure 6.2 Relation Between the 1960 Vote for Richard Nixon for President and 1962 Vote for Governor in California, by County

Source: Richard M. Scammon and Alice McGillivray, eds., *America Votes* (Washington, D.C.: Elections Research Center).

Bee reported on the day before the election that the economy had been over-blown as an issue.[32] California was running neck-and-neck with national averages on leading economic indicators in 1982. The state's overall unemployment rate was 9.9 percent, compared to 9.7 for the nation, 12.5 in Ohio, and 10.4 in Pennsylvania. On election day, 60 percent of California voters expressed optimism that Reagan's economic reforms would eventually benefit the state.

Economic times were perceived to be bad enough, however, that Tom Bradley made the economy a central campaign issue. The problem for the Bradley campaign was that where the economic message would play best—namely the rural hinterlands, which were experiencing the highest unemployment rates, Republicans successfully blamed the recession on sitting Democratic governor and U.S. Senate candidate Jerry Brown. On election day, 56 percent of those polled blamed Brown for the economic recession, compared to just 44 percent who blamed the president.

The 1982 race, like the one twenty years earlier, presented a clear candidate choice. Deukmejian, as the incumbent attorney general, emphasized a platform dominated by law-and-order issues.[33] For many years, his theme had been the death penalty and stiffer sentences. When he first arrived in Sacramento as an assemblyman in 1962, he found that "there was nobody who was really sort of specializing" in crime.[34] A month later, one of his first crime bills called for the death penalty for armed robbery. Much later, he was almost singlehandedly responsible for putting the death penalty back on California's books. In the gubernatorial race, he criticized the Brown administration for appointing liberal judges who were soft on crime. Deukmejian supported a Victim's Bill of Rights initiative that Bradley opposed, and he opposed a handgun control initiative that he argued favored criminals rather than potential victims. Deukmejian's most controversial law-and-order program was to create prison industries so that convicts would be forced to pay for their room and board. Bradley argued that this would place prisoners in direct competition with private enterprise, sneering, "I suppose his [Deukmejian's] slogan now will be, 'Want a job? Go to prison.' "[35]

Deukmejian scored points with the California electorate by criticizing the antigrowth policies of Jerry Brown's administration. The tension between economic growth and environmental degradation had been an issue in gubernatorial races throughout the 1980s and 1990s.[36] During stable economic times, candidates tried to straddle the issue as best they could. During economic recession, a position favoring economic growth was usually more popular, and Deukmejian seized upon it with more credibility than Bradley could muster. He argued that Bradley would simply emulate Brown, harassing business rather than promoting it. Deukmejian promised to eliminate unnecessary state regulations and bureaucracy. The state's budget deficit was also a problem issue. In response, Deukmejian stopped short of promising not to raise taxes, but argued he would cut government spending as the first step. The attorney general also criticized Bradley for being a Los Angeles "aid junkie," claiming that Bradley sought perpetual bailouts from the state and federal governments for his own bad management practices.[37]

Press accounts pointed out that while Bradley had considerable support among blacks, he was reluctant to take controversial positions that would alienate the white Los Angeles citizenry, most of the city electorate. In the 1970s, for instance, he refused to take a stand in the Los Angeles school busing controversy, urging all sides to obey court orders, regardless. Pro-busing advocates criticized him for failing to provide leadership on the issue. Simeon Booker, the Washington bureau chief of *Ebony* magazine, editorialized that Bradley was one individual "who has least capitalized on the color of his skin." Bradley understood that a coalition of black voters would not be sufficient to elect him to anything in California. He was, as *Los Angeles Times* reporter Bella Stumbo wrote, a "colorblind candidate."[38] His campaign slogan, "He doesn't make a lot of noise. He just gets a lot done," summarized his approach as one of calm competence.

There was no talk of party organization in this race. Each candidate drew support from predictable areas of the state, but cooperative efforts among candidates probably had little to do with the vote. The day following the election, in an article on the editorial page of the *Fresno Bee*, Peter Schrag lamented the death of parties in California and the "atomization of the entire political process."

> In effect, every politician has become a lone ranger, a free-lance operative appearing every two years and then vanishing again, a man or woman with no base, and often no connections, other than a mailing list and growing amounts of cash from well-heeled political action committees based outside the home district.[39]

Of course, this observation was made about California politics in previous times. Except for the brief presence of the Democratic clubs in the 1950s and 1960s, it was probably true that a candidate never turned to a party organization rather than a special interest. In the early years of California politics, organizations were the captives of special interests.

When the votes were tallied, Deukmejian had won by a mere 93,345 votes (1.2 percent); surprising, because polls taken immediately before the election had predicted that Bradley held a solid seven-point lead. Deukmejian won this open-seat contest partly because the economy in California was not as bad as it was elsewhere. Turnout levels tended to help Deukmejian. Thanks to the lower off-year turnout, Republican percentages in counties with a high proportion of minorities and blue-collar workers were larger in 1982 than in 1980. Deukmejian's vote in Los Angeles and Imperial Counties, both with sizable minority populations, was higher than Reagan's from two years earlier. Deukmejian won consistently higher percentages of the vote in the high-income regions as well. Bradley won major victories in traditionally Democratic northern California, including Marin, Alameda, San Francisco, Santa Cruz, Sonoma, and Santa Clara Counties. In the Bay area, the sectional origins of Bradley's candidacy did not matter much, since Deukmejian was a native of Long Beach. Looking back on such a narrow loss, one could argue that Bradley could have improved his margins in many areas. He had almost no appeal in rural northern California, where Democrats had often done well in the past twenty years. Rural areas in central California also voted Republican.

California's 1990 gubernatorial contest was the most closely watched race in the nation that year. Issues and candidates were up front, but party organizations were not, as U.S. Senator Pete Wilson squared off against former San Francisco Mayor Dianne Feinstein. Wilson had the edge going into the fall, since Feinstein had to wage a costly primary battle against Attorney General John Van de Kamp. Taking a page from Deukmejian's book, Wilson made crime a dominant theme in his campaign. Fortunately for him, it turned out to be the number one issue on the minds of voters too. Feinstein's central theme was education, but polls at the end of the race showed that this was an issue of declining concern.[40] The race would ultimately come down to undecided voters: blue-collar workers, older women, and suburban voters. The race became tighter in the waning days, and polls showed a substantial gender gap, with Wilson winning as little as 36 percent of the female vote.

As votes were counted, Wilson won with a narrow margin of 186,000 votes. As in 1982, Republicans managed to out-organize Democrats with some one million absentee ballots. Turnout played an influential role. Exit polls showed that Wilson was doing more poorly than Deukmejian had in 1982 among certain Democratic constituencies, including minorities and union members. Central Californians were less enthusiastic about Wilson than they were about Deukmejian, as the former performed more poorly than might have been predicted from 1982 and 1986 results in places like Kern (Bakersfield), Yuba, and Calaveras Counties. The comparison of the 1982 and 1990 results shown in table 6.1 shows that Wilson did far better in urban areas of the state than Deukmejian had done. A ten-point increase in the percentage of people living in cities increased Wilson's vote about four points, compared to just one point for Deukmejian in 1982. Counties with higher levels of manufacturing employment also went more strongly for Wilson than they had for Deukmejian. In addition, low turnout of Democratic blocs ensured that Wilson's sizable deficits with women, union members, and minorities would not tip the election for Feinstein.

National Divisions in the California Electorate

The weighted county-level data presented in table 6.1 support the contention that California parties are weak because cleavages defining partisanship in the state are incongruent with the national party system. Because partisanship does not always crystallize around cleavages of national importance, voters have focused on candidate qualities and issues. Tests of the impact of unionization, race, and income on voting appear in table 6.2. Not surprisingly, the coefficients show that the 1986 gubernatorial race was the most racially polarized. In this celebrated rematch between Bradley and Deukmejian, Deukmejian won a mere 21 percent of the non-Caucasian vote that year. Reagan had won about one-third of the minority votes in 1984 and 1980. In spite of Tom Bradley's presence on the ballot, however, the racial cleavage was more divisive in old-party states such as New York, where white gubernatorial candidates ran in both parties in 1982 and 1986. Ohio, New York, and New Jersey also exhibited more decisive racial cleavages in the three presidential elections.

The magnitude of difference between labor and nonlabor voters fluctuated wildly through the 1980s. California's blue-collar population cast ballots along racial lines. When asked their reasons for candidate choice in the 1982 and 1986 contests, most of these voters said that "race of candidate" or their "dislike of opponent" were the most influential criteria. These shifts in labor's support for Republican candidates are reflected in the coefficients in table 6.2. In the 1982 Bradley-Deukmejian contest, labor households were only 5 percent less likely to vote Republican than nonlabor households. Labor's resistance to Tom Bradley's candidacy explains the narrow gap. Such drastic inconsistencies from office to office and election to election have been less common in eastern and midwestern states.

Finally, class differences are readily apparent as influences on California voters in every election. Like unionization, though, there is considerable variation in the division separating rich from poor voters. Furthermore, the California electorate was not polarized by class as much as in some traditional party states. In Ohio, a state where class patterns are very strong, the cleavage between rich and poor was more divisive in every recent contest.

Table 6.2 Logit Analysis of the Influence of Race, Income, and Union Membership in California Elections, 1980–1992

	Constant	Race	Income	Labor	No. of Cases	Predicted Null (%)
President, 1980	1.48	−1.34*	.23*	−.33*		63
		(.004)	(.001)	(.003)	2,213	65
Effect		−32.0	6.0	−8.0		
Governor, 1982	1.44	−1.40*	.14*	−.18*		60
		(.004)	(.001)	(.003)	2,610	51
Effect		−32.0	4.0	−5.0		
Senate, 1982	1.84	−1.35*	.29*	−.41*		70
		(.004)	(.001)	(.003)	2,225	55
Effect		−32.0	7.0	−10.0		
President, 1984	1.92	−1.43*	.20*	−.35*		68
		(.12)	(.03)	(.11)	1,965	54
Effect		−34.0	5.0	−9.0		
Senate, 1986	1.06	−1.08*	.27*	−.59*		63
		(.004)	(.001)	(.003)	2,137	52
Effect		−25.0	6.0	−15.0		
Governor, 1986	1.78	−1.37*	.22*	−.41*		66
		(.004)	(.001)	(.003)	2,150	58
Effect		−33.0	6.0	−10.0		
President, 1988	2.17	−1.28*	.22*	−.53*		62
		(.13)	(.03)	(.11)	2,083	58
Effect		−30.0	5.0	−12.0		
Senate, 1988	2.18	−1.32*	.16*	−.41		62
		(.13)	(.03)	(.11)	2,009	55
Effect		−31.0	4.0	−10.0		
Governor, 1990	1.07	−.79*	.20*	−.69		58
		(.003)	(.001)	(.004)	2,882	50
Effect		−19.0	5.0	−17.0		
President, 1992	−.12	−.96*	.21*	−.42*		69
		(.14)	(.04)	(.15)	1,580	54
Effect		−18.5	3.9	−6.8		
Senate, 1992	.58	−1.00*	.08*	−.15		62
		(.12)	(.04)	(.12)	1,856	62
Effect		−21.8	1.8	−3.3		

Source: CBS News/New York Times, *Election Day Surveys*, 1982, 1984, 1986. ABC News/Washington Post, *50 State Poll*, September–November, 1988. Voter Research and Surveys, *General Election Exit Poll*, 1990, 1992.
Note: Dependent variable: 0 = Democrat, 1 = Republican; MLE coefficients; standard errors in parentheses; *p < .05; Effect = change in odds of voting Republican from moving x one unit at the means of the other variables.

Ecological Versus Individual-Level Analysis

The voter-level data show that California voters resemble the national electorate in some respects (for comparison with the national electorate, see Appendix table A.5). The California case, therefore, provides an excellent example of how ecological analysis and individual analysis bring out different aspects of a state's politics. The comparison of national party coalitions to state party coalitions must take account of both coalition size and voting tendency, but also concentration. Specifically, county figures suggest something about how interests are concentrated by capturing settlement patterns—that is, the distribution of minority voters or manufacturing workers in counties. That the income cleavage is often a weak predictor of the divisions between California counties does not necessarily suggest that low-income voters voted for Deukmejian, while the wealthy turned to Bradley. What it does suggest is that, unlike Ohio, New York, and other eastern and midwestern states, the poor population was not concentrated in an area where voters' only interest was economic. If the poor were dispersed, they would be less likely to mobilize and vote their interest. Since manufacturing jobs were spread around the state, rather than concentrated such as in northeastern Ohio, it was far more costly to organize blue-collar voters into a cohesive and powerful bloc. Like large eastern and midwestern states, California is heterogeneous. The state differs from other states because it lacks the cohesive pockets of class interest that can be found elsewhere. There is a strong tendency for affluent Bay area and coastal residents to vote for Democrats. Exit polls show that 55 percent of those in the Bay area earning over $100,000 voted for Democrat Leo McCarthy against Pete Wilson in the hard-fought 1988 U.S. Senate race, a much lower percentage than in the rest of the state. This trait is a sectional one, and it hinders the cohesion of both parties. The split between Unruh and Cranston was a split over just what to do with these middle- and upper-income voters. For Cranston, they were the key to his volunteer movement. For Unruh, these voters were undisciplined, uncontrollable, and dangerous.

Summary: The Organizational Challenge of California

The challenge for a California party organizer has always been to stay on top of an unpredictable population. The result of this electoral flux is that coalitions of constituent interest are not easy to locate. Unlike New York, where an urban-rural cleavage persists because upstate New Yorkers resent the payment of a large proportion of their taxes to support programs that go to New York City, the situation in California is different. There are several

poles of influence of almost equal power: San Francisco, Los Angeles, Orange
County and San Diego. The urban-rural rivalry cannot take on New York
proportions because there are too many urban areas—some of them affluent
and some Republican. A 1990 poll revealed that one-fourth of Republican
party identifiers in California lived in cities of over 500,000 people, compared
to only 11 percent for the national electorate.[41] The confusion of the California political scene can be explained by its heterogeneous electoral interests,
rapid in-migration, and an even geographic distribution of party votes.

It is no wonder that California pioneered media-style, candidate-centered
Other states certainly had to contend with massive waves of in-migration.
Ordinarily, though, this migration was into urban centers. The migrants
settled in concentrated areas and were politically socialized by the prevailing
powers. Later they trickled out of the city and into rural regions, but the
dispersal into the hinterlands was gradual. By contrast, California's waves of
migration hit urban and rural areas about equally. Resettlement was dispersed from the very beginning.[42] Furthermore, most of the established Californians at midcentury were themselves transplants from other areas from
earlier waves of migration. As a population of non-natives became a solid
majority of the state's population in the 1930s, 1940s, and 1950s, the state's
partisan patterns became impossible to decipher. Migration is associated with
a detachment from party and an increase in individualistic voting patterns
that emphasize candidate rather than party loyalty.[43]

It is no wonder that California pioneered media-style, candidate-centered
campaigning. Old-style grassroots party efforts work best when votes are
concentrated in a small geographic area composed of stable neighborhoods.
Would-be party bosses in California such as Unruh could never command the
entire California party. His Los Angeles electoral base was not sufficient to
the task. Similarly, Alan Cranston's club movement served as a voice for a
portion of his party, but not all participated. Nixon could not hold the right
and left of his party together and suffered at the polls when neither faction
would work for him. Tom Bradley narrowly lost to Deukmejian largely because he had little appeal for California's rural Democrats, whose origins were
the Dust Bowl states of the South and Southwest. Wilson's 1990 victory,
however, was built on coalitions quite different from Deukmejian's, as Wilson
did far better in urban areas. These cases indicate that California parties and
candidates are confronted with an electoral conundrum that has proved in-
scrutable to would-be organization builders.

7

Where Federalism
Is a Solvent of Party:
The Pacific Northwest

Washington State: Electoral Background

WASHINGTON is one of only seventeen states that currently hold major statewide elections in presidential election years, making it an excellent test case for evaluating whether local party elites escape the impact of national partisan tides. Like other western states, Washington's political system violates the competition/cohesion thesis. In the post–New Deal period, the state's party organizations have been weak and decentralized in spite of steady two-party competition marked by serious contests at all levels of government.[1]

While the state's voters have a longstanding reputation for unpredictability, certain regions exhibit distinct behaviors. Eastern Washington's economy used to be entirely agricultural, and therefore solidly Republican. Spokane is now the largest trading center in the northern Rocky Mountain region and is also central to the economies of Montana and Idaho. In-migration has diluted its Republican leaning, although it remains the most Republican city in the state.

The most solidly Democratic area lies west of Seattle on the Olympic Peninsula and includes Jefferson, Grays Harbor, and Pacific Counties (maps 7.1 and 7.2). This is lumbering country, where the depletion of natural resources has been a persistent threat to the local economy since the 1920s.[2] Here, environmentalists and loggers continually battle each other over whether the forests should remain open for development.

The remaining central section of the state is a patchwork of sparsely

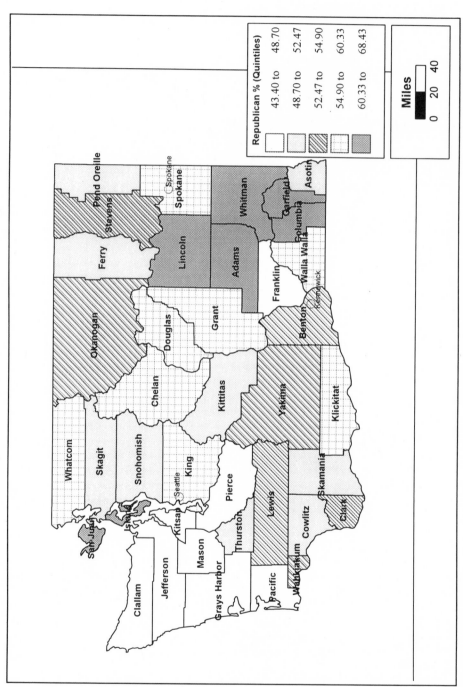

Republican % (Quintiles)

	43.40 to	48.70
	48.70 to	52.47
	52.47 to	54.90
	54.90 to	60.33
	60.33 to	68.43

Miles

0   20   40

Map 7.1   Average Republican Gubernatorial Vote in Washington State, 1960–1968

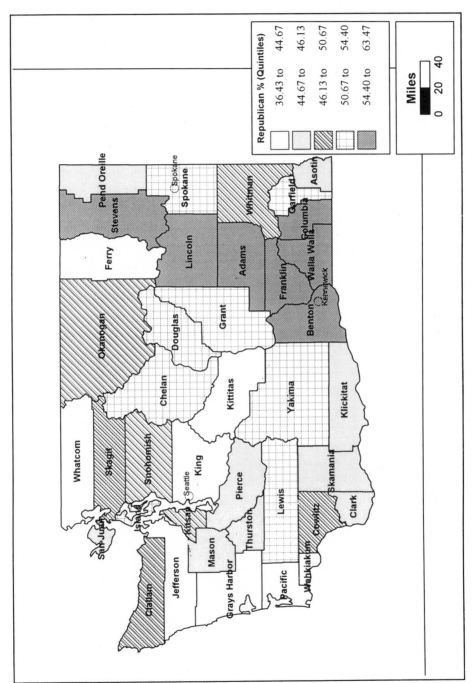

Map 7.2 Average Republican Gubernatorial Vote in Washington State, 1980–1988

Republican % (Quintiles)

36.43 to 44.67
44.67 to 46.13
46.13 to 50.67
50.67 to 54.40
54.40 to 63.47

Miles

0   20   40

settled counties that lack a dominant political tradition. They tend to swing back and forth with statewide political tides.

Several features of Washington's pattern of socioeconomic development distinguish its politics from that of eastern and midwestern states. First, the most industrial areas are not the most urban areas. The largest concentration of those employed in manufacturing in recent decades live in Cowlitz County, a rural timbering area in the southwest. Second, cities in the Pacific Northwest did not develop around heavy industry, but instead developed around trade and transportation. Because of the unique economy of the Pacific Northwest, several rural counties vote solidly Democratic—in contrast to most rural parts of the nation. Third, the state of Washington has never developed a persistent pattern of racial conflict comparable to that found in states like Ohio, Illinois, or New York. Seattle's African-American population was a comparatively low 20 percent in 1990 and just 9 percent ten years earlier. The largest concentration of minorities was in rural Adams County in the eastern part of the state, with a large Hispanic population. Finally, the state is not highly class stratified. While upper-income counties tend to support Republicans, many middle-income counties provide a base for both parties and some lower-income counties vote Republican. Neither settlement patterns nor redistributive politics have had the same impact on Washington politics as they have had further east.

The Weak Party Tradition in Washington State

Washington, by all accounts, is a candidate-centered state. Its uniqueness lies in the unusual relationship among the party in office, party organizations, and the voters. Republican and Democratic party leaders in office are usually moderate in their ideology, and voters are moderate as well, but both party organizations have frequently been dominated by extremists from the right and the left.[3] In other words, the party in office and the electorate are aligned, but party organizers are not. Many have suggested that institutional factors are responsible for the irrelevance of parties: voters make no declaration of party affiliation when they register; split-ticket voting is neither an exceptional nor recent development; the blanket primary allows voters the freedom to vote in the primary without revealing their political party preference; and there has never been any party control over who enters the primary. Machine politics has never developed in the cities for any length of time. Rarely do candidates band together to form slates. Races are bitterly competitive, often focusing inordinate attention on the personal characteristics and qualities of candidates.

Party weakness and the intensely personal campaign style may be rooted in the electoral foundations of the state's politics. There is sometimes a sharp separation between state and national politics, as local issues divide national coalition groups in unusual ways. This skewed juxtaposition of national and local views makes it more difficult to identify supportive coalitions. Voters, in turn, are free from the pressures of political socialization that exist in states where social characteristics coincide with party identification. In Washington, labor does not always goes Democratic, city residents do not vote monolithically for one party, and the affluent areas do not vote consistently Republican. Local political parties have rarely been able to count on the firm and undivided loyalty of any particular demographic or socioeconomic group.

If voters are on their own, so too are candidates. Sid Morrison, a Republican politician from Washington's tri-cities area (Pastco, Kennewick, Richland) and a 1992 gubernatorial candidate, pointed out that parties were not really factors in his elections: "We have an open primary, a weak party system, and one [the Republican party] that is controlled from the far right. There is something called the Legislative Council in Washington which is sort of a coalition of political elites that helped me get some early financing. But we had to figure that out on our own."[4]

John Miller, a liberal Republican politician from the north Seattle suburbs, was a member of the Seattle Council before being elected to Congress in 1984. He agrees that Washington's party system is weak and could not identify just who the Republicans are in his area. This may suggest, he said in an 1990 interview, that candidates are insulated from traditional coalition politics:

> My coalition groups are hard to pinpoint because they are not readily identifiable like Democratic coalition groups. We never did a survey to find out how my voters were different from or similar to Reagan's in 1984. But, in general, Democrats practice coalition politics and can identify distinctive blocks: environmentalists, labor, teachers, and so forth. But my support came from all over. . . . When you think of traditional Republican coalition groups, you think of business and the religious right. My views are too much at variance with the religious right, and I was a neighborhood activist that never received much business support. I would say that I received support from elements of all of these Democratic and Republican groups but probably not from the hard core activists or ideological purists.[5]

While this tendency to draw voters from many groups may be true of the Republican party more generally, it seems especially true of Washington State.

As in Arizona, the parties in Washington are frequently split among feuding right-wing, moderate, and left-wing factions. When Republicans pull together and Democrats split, Republicans are in a better position to win. When the opposite happens, Democrats can reap the benefits. Recent Washington politics is the history of this competitive seesaw battle over which party can maintain cohesion long enough to get to the next election. Long-term stability is an elusive goal. Sid Morrison acknowledged that party splits are a problem:

> Right now, the Republican party in the state is in complete disarray. In the legislature, the Republicans have dwindled to a precious handful. They only represent about 14 percent of the electorate. Part of the problem is that the state party is out of touch with the party leadership in federal office. Take the abortion issue. Our state has always been liberal on abortion. State funding of abortion will win in Washington—and will almost win in a district as conservative as ours. Voters in Washington approved a pro-abortion law in 1970.[6]

Morrison points out that the state's Republican party was taken over in the mid-1980s by extreme right-wing factions. John Miller indicated in 1990 that the party machinery has been controlled by the right for twenty-five years, going back to Goldwater's nomination for president, and that former governor Daniel Evans always had difficulty working with the party organization in the late 1960s and 1970s. During the mid-1980s, the right wing split between Pat Robertson and Ronald Reagan, or between right and further right. The ideological gap between candidates who win and the party activists is part of weak organization politics. The right-wing takeover was the result of a party system in which organization is not central to governing. If organizations really made any difference, there would be less tension between organization leaders and party officeholders.

Brett Bader, a former state party employee who is now a political consultant, claimed that the 1992 Republican party platform was "more far out there than any platform I've seen." He called it "off-base and reckless" and admitted that the candidates simply ignored it and that it really didn't matter. Rod Chandler, the unsuccessful Republican candidate for U.S. Senate, denounced the right-wing takeover of the party in the strongest terms: the platform was "rooted in the dark ages."[7]

Fortunately for Republican moderates, candidates have never had to rely on party machinery to propel them into office. Consequently, organizational support is not a major focus of candidate effort. Campaign appeals in the state are cast directly to unattached, independent voters. John Miller pointed out that the Democrats have the same problem with extremism in their party.

The hard core of party activists are much more left-wing than the average voter: "A candidate can win the vote of the environmentally concerned, regardless of whether the hard-core environmental activists are supporting that candidate, much like Republican candidates can win without the support of the Republican organization."[8] The majority of voters are in the middle. They are cued by issues but not necessarily by the single-issue appeals of interest group activists.

Morrison and his state director, Gretchen White, indicated that politics in Washington State was different from that in other states because of issue voting and voter independence caused by state-level matters that often failed to reflect dominant national themes. The urban-rural division in the state is a recent development, according to White, because Seattle has always been such a prosperous city. Morrison added that in the late 1980s, Republicans strongly supported social services because lingering high unemployment rates made them necessary.

John Miller amplified the point that state and national coalitions are different by denying that there is a sharp class cleavage in the state. He pointed out that Seattle is both affluent and liberal. When asked to compare it to an eastern city, he responded, "Seattle is like Manhattan, it is Democratic, affluent, and liberal. Seattle constitutes 20 percent of my district. In the Seattle precincts, I am lucky if I win 46 percent. To survive in Seattle, I would have to become like Lowell Weicker—a Republican who never voted with the President on anything."[9]

The congruence of state and national cleavages varies— sometimes following national trends and interests, sometimes not. Drawing on his experience in Seattle city politics, John Miller claimed that the issues dividing the Seattle City Council were different from city politics elsewhere and that conventional coalition politics was not always in place:

> When I was on the Seattle Council, several issues divided the council, including neighborhood issues, environment, energy regulation, and zoning. Race relations and the substance of city politics in the East was not as relevant because the city's minority population is about 20 percent of the total, and that includes all minorities: blacks, Asians, Hispanics. . . . I never had any labor support on the council because I was too environmental. Democrats can bring these two blocs [labor and environment] together at the national level, and sometimes they can at the state level, but often this is a source of friction.

These conflicting intraparty coalitions are present in state politics elsewhere, but in few other states are the labor and environmental blocs of equal size and influence. There may be foundations for the New Deal coalitional structures between labor and business, rich and poor, but the cleavages that divide state politics more consistently in the East are not as evident in Washington State.

The fact that Washington holds its gubernatorial elections in presidential election years makes it simple to examine the extent to which the state's politics differs from its national politics. In 1960, for instance, there is a close correspondence between state and national voting. In 1980, there is a substantial difference. We might expect state-level voting in Washington to follow the presidential vote quite closely. Examples of recent gubernatorial politics, however, suggest that the two offices are separable from one another.

Washington State Politics in the Post–New Deal Period

The inconsistent alignment of national and local cleavages is apparent in a review of the 1960 race between Democrat Albert Rosellini and Republican Lloyd Andrews. In spite of the highly visible presidential contest of that year, the news accounts of the gubernatorial race indicate a hard-fought politics full of issues and programs, charges and countercharges, with no mention of precinct organizations, endorsements, or the usual fodder of strong party politics.[10] Rosellini's vote in the urban areas was enough to give him the edge in a race he won by a mere 17,865 votes (1.4 percent). As in Arizona, much of the debate centered on the proper strategy for providing basic state services in the face of population pressures. Trying to outflank his opponent on the issue of infrastructure, Republican Andrews promised to provide more and better schools for the rapidly growing Washington population. Andrews suggested diverting $20 million from public assistance funds to school construction while resisting new taxes and any increase in existing taxes.[11]

Rosellini charged that Andrews's proposals to expand the school system did not make any sense, given his aversion to taxes. Rosellini also emphasized economic development. Several days before the election, he announced a plan to complete a geological map of the state's raw material resources—many of which remained untapped. Rosellini argued that such a map would provide incentives for businesses to come into the state and, since businesses would not have to go elsewhere to find coal, oil, and gas, would ensure a secure industrial base. Andrews's critics claimed he was the pawn of big western Washington business interests, such as the forest products industry, that favored right-to-work laws, though Andrews had repeatedly denied that he favored antiunion legislation.

In the 1960 gubernatorial race, the state failed to divide along lines that would be found in Ohio and New York (table 7.1). The size of the urban

Table 7.1   Influences on the Republican Percentage of the Presidential and Gubernatorial Vote in Washington State, by County, 1960–1992

	Constant	Income	% Urban	Minority	% Mfg.	Adj. R^2
President, 1960	36.8	.13 (.23)	.12* (.04)	−.52 (.26)	.59* (.10)	.49
Governor, 1960	38.6	.08 (.23)	.11* (.04)	−.59* (.26)	.50* (.10)	.41
President, 1968	39.7	.62* (.23)	−.03 (.04)	−1.40* (.50)	−.58* (.10)	.48
Governor, 1968	18.9	1.63* (.26)	.10 (.06)	−1.84* (.59)	−.69* (.12)	.56
President, 1972	58.3	.27 (.17)	−.05 (.04)	−.07 (.37)	−.38* (.07)	.40
Governor, 1972	19.3	1.31 (.92)	−.14 (.20)	−.71 (2.05)	−.28 (.41)	.05
President, 1980	73.4	−.36 (.24)	−.004 (.05)	−.09 (.20)	−.47* (.15)	.38
Governor, 1980	64.1	.002 (.18)	.007 (.04)	−.05 (.16)	−.40* (.12)	.21
President, 1988	62.2	−.27 (.16)	−.02 (.04)	.07 (.13)	−.13 (.14)	.20
Governor, 1988	73.7	−1.06* (.23)	.04 (.06)	−.08 (.18)	.34 (.20)	.45
President, 1992	55.3	−.61* (.14)	.02 (.04)	.09 (.12)	−.05 (.13)	.46
Governor, 1992	87.2	−.92* (.14)	.02 (.04)	−.35* (.12)	.002 (.13)	.73

*p < .05   N=39

Source: Bureau of the Census, *County and City Databook* (Washington, D.C.: GPO, various years); Richard M. Scammon and Alice McGillivray, eds., *America Votes* (Washington, D.C.: Elections Research Center, various years); *County and City Extra* (Lanham, Md.: Bernan Press, 1992).

Note: Multiple linear regression, WLS estimation; unstandardized regression coefficients weighted for population; standard errors in parentheses; income is expressed in thousands of constant 1992 dollars.

population and the percentage employed in manufacturing *increased* Republican percentages. As John Miller suggested in my interview, though, there did not appear to be a significant income division in the state.

Oddly, the sick state of the local economy in 1960 tended to work against Republican gubernatorial candidate Andrews more than it did against presidential candidate Richard Nixon. For instance, as unemployment rose across the state, the difference between Nixon and Andrews grew as Andrews's margins dropped. In areas of highest unemployment—in the western and more urbanized areas—presidential Republicanism exceeded gubernatorial Republicanism.

In instances where the state's presidential and gubernatorial voting are related, neither is especially reflective of dominant national party cleavages. National loyalties are simply not reinforced by the issues of state politics. As early as 1950, a state poll asked respondents whether they voted for candidates from one party or from more than one party in the primary and general election. Seventy-eight percent reported splitting their tickets in the primary and 73 percent did so in the general election.[12] Voters in Washington do make distinctions on the basis of personality and issues more than citizens in other states.

Sustained Candidate-Centeredness: 1980 and 1992

The intense focus on candidates in Washington politics is best illustrated in recent years by the 1980 gubernatorial campaign between Republican John Spellman, the King County executive, and liberal state senator James McDermott, a Seattle psychiatrist (later elected to the U.S. House in 1988). This was a bitter, open-seat contest where the opponents sought to expose by smearing each other's reputations and trying to take advantage of electoral cross-pressures. There was no evidence of the importance of national economic issues and trends. Reagan narrowly defeated Carter in the state while winning landslides elsewhere.

Spellman's initial strength was his name recognition. He had run for governor once before, in 1976, and lost to Democrat Dixy Lee Ray. Ray had since become unpopular in her party and suffered an unprecedented loss in a primary challenge by McDermott. In the 1980 general election, Spellman was better known and far more confident. In the end, Spellman won on the strength of the vote from independent-leaning Democrats, including Governor Ray, and influential Republicans like former Governor Dan Evans.

In the closing days of the race, McDermott fiercely accused Spellman of creating divisions in the state electorate.[13] Sensitive to his unpopularity in conservative eastern Washington, McDermott accused Spellman of playing off one half of the state against the other. He was responding to a campaign ad that Spellman had run labeling McDermott as a "liberal *Seattle* psychiatrist." Spellman had repeatedly mentioned McDermott's occupation to diminish his credibility as a representative of the state's electorate. In the midst of an October gubernatorial debate, Spellman turned to McDermott and asked him if he was "psychoanalyzing" him, a remark that, according to the media, was calculated to make McDermott appear suspect.[14]

Aside from the focus on the candidates' personal qualities, local issues and candidate positioning apparently had an impact independent of the presidential race. The influence of the presidential contest on local balloting was not strong, especially if measured by eastern and midwestern standards.[15] Although the gubernatorial and presidential margins are comparable on a statewide tally, when the data are disaggregated by county, the similarities end. Spellman did substantially better than Reagan in the traditional Republican areas. He consistently outperformed Reagan in urban counties, and McDermott did better than Carter in the most Democratic areas.

As a postscript to this description of Washington State's lack of party unity, in the 1982 midterm elections John Spellman turned against twenty-four state legislators in his own party, dubbing them "troglodytes" for opposing his initiatives.[16] Three retired, and he assisted in defeating eight others, making the legislature more liberal, Democratic, and amenable to his fiscal program.

In the 1992 gubernatorial race, one of the more ideologically polarized contest in recent memory, a liberal former House member, Democrat Mike Lowry, ran a successful campaign against conservative attorney general Ken Eikenberry. In September Eikenberry had won a narrow primary victory over moderate Congressman Sid Morrison, thanks to the turnout of ideologically conservative Republicans. Morrison and his supporters remained bitter about the loss and did not close ranks behind the nominee. For his part, Lowry had campaigned for statewide office two previous times, losing U.S. Senate bids in 1988 and 1983.

Bill Clinton's lopsided twelve-point win over George Bush in 1992 undoubtedly helped Lowry, although the gubernatorial race was much closer. Eikenberry led Bush in winning over Democratic constituencies. He won about 34 percent of the non-Caucasian vote, while Bush only polled 25 percent. As Bush was able to poll only 24 percent of the environmentalist vote, Eikenberry won about a third: he won 35 percent of the votes cast in King County, while the president came in at 28 percent. Due to the closeness of the contest, race and class emerged as stronger determinants in the gubernatorial than the presidential race. The constants in table 7.1 tell much of the story. Had none of these traditional elements of New Deal partisanship influenced the 1992 gubernatorial vote, Eikenberry would have averaged a whopping 87 percent of the vote across Washington's thirty-nine counties. Bush, however, would not have done nearly so well, averaging only about 55 percent of the vote. This is an odd result, but not altogether atypical of Washington State, given the clear distinctions state voters have often drawn between presidential and gubernatorial politics.

National Divisions in the Washington State Electorate

Polling data from recent elections provide a more precise means of evaluating the presence of national coalitions in Washington State politics. The most racially divisive contests were the 1988 gubernatorial race and the 1986 U.S. Senate election (table 7.2). In these races, only one out of three minorities cast votes for the Republican candidate. By contrast, Ronald Reagan and George Bush received about half the minority votes cast in 1984 and 1988. The magnitude of the labor cleavage varied considerably from 1984 to 1988. Voters from labor union households were much more likely to vote for Reagan than for Bush. As in the county-level results, an income cleavage does not consistently divide the electorate in these elections. Income differences are simply not a statistically significant determinant of the vote except in 1992, where there is a slight 3.8 percent increase in the probability of voting Republican as one moves from the lowest income cohort (under $15,000 per year) to the second lowest ($15,000–$29,000).

Compared to eastern industrial states, Washington's racial divisions do not polarize the electorate nearly as much (fig. 7.1). The state's most racially divisive election split the community only as much as the least racially divisive contests in New York and Ohio. Washington's minority electorate is diverse and consists of fewer African-American voters (3.1 percent) and relatively more American Indians (1.6 percent), Asians (4.3 percent), and Hispanics (4.4 percent). The extent to which union activists vote Democratic in Washington varies more from election to election than in older states. To summarize, electoral coalitions in Washington State are often a confusing jumble. Because candidates can find electoral support in many places, they possess little ideological cohesion. For this reason, candidates are not drawn to organization politics. One cannot assume that even in states where elections for governor and president occur in the same year, electoral foundations for these offices are similar. One reason for party weakness in Washington is that certain national constituencies are very small. The second reason is that these constituencies, where they do exist, are dispersed, not concentrated. The

Table 7.2 Logit Analysis of the Influence of Race, Income, and Union Membership in Washington State Elections, 1984–1992

	Constant	Race	Income	Labor	No. of Cases	Predicted Null (%)
President, 1984	2.00	−.55*	.10	−.35*		63
		(.28)	(.06)	(.15)	830	64
Effect		−11.0	2.0	−6.0		
Senate, 1986	1.84	−1.08*				58
		(.36)	—	—	905	51
Effect		−26.1				
President, 1988	2.85	−.56*	.09	−.77*		59
		(.25)	(.05)	(.14)	967	50
Effect		−10.0	1.5	−12.0		
Senate, 1988	3.39	−.77*	.04	−.77*		61
		(.25)	(.05)	(.25)	989	54
Effect		−12.7	.6	−11.0		
Governor, 1988	2.91	−1.03*	−.02	−.64*		60
		(.33)	(.06)	(.17)	735	60
Effect		−24.0	−.4	−14.0		
President, 1992	−.45	−.48	.16*	−.21		63
		(.25)	(.05)	(.15)	1,073	63
Effect		−10.4	3.8	−4.4		
Senate, 1992	−.20	−.47*	.18*	−.34*		57
		(.21)	(.05)	(.12)	1,399	57
Effect		−11.1	4.2	−7.5		
Governor, 1992	−.02	−.57*	.16*	−.17		55
		(.21)	(.05)	(.12)	1,410	55
Effect		−13.4	3.8	−4.1		

Source: CBS News/New York Times, *Election Day Surveys*, various years. ABC News/Washington Post, *50 State Poll*, September–November, 1988. Voter Research and Surveys, *General Election Exit Polls*, 1992.

Note: Dependent variable: 0 = Democrat, 1 = Republican; MLE coefficients; standard errors in parentheses; *p < .05; Effect = change in odds of voting Republican from moving x one unit at the means of the other variables. The 1986 CBS/New York Times poll did not include questions on the respondent's labor union membership and income.

result is that the nationally partisan divisions between urban and rural, labor and business, minority and white, rich and poor, are not dominant patterns in Washington State.

Such inconsistent electoral behavior has had an impact on party organizations. Confusion and factionalism result when a party cannot count on clear

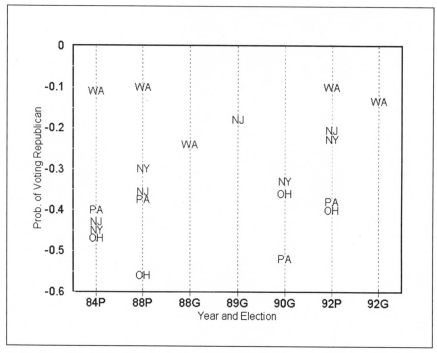

Figure 7.1   Racial Cleavages in New York, New Jersey, Ohio, Pennsylvania, and Washington Elections

Source: Probabilities computed from logit coefficients given in tables 3.2, 3.4, 4.3, 4.5, and 7.2.

Note: Washington gubernatorial race = 1988; New Jersey = 1989.

and consistent electoral divisions. Party elites splinter into competing intra-party groups, each in search of the proper course for electoral victory. The task is complicated, and successful candidates are those who moderate their message, avoid becoming linked to extreme elements in their party, and win over diverse and heterodox constituencies.

Oregon: Electoral Background

When asked to describe his state's economy, Senator Mark O. Hatfield claimed that it was tri-cultured, "built around timber, agriculture, and tourism."[17] In this respect, the two Pacific Northwest states look very much alike. In 1960, roughly 23 percent of the work force in both states was employed in manufacturing, compared to over one-third in Pennsylvania and 35 percent in Ohio. By 1990, the proportion of workers employed in manufacturing had dropped drastically in both Washington and Oregon, but were nearly identical: about 13 percent. In spite of the statistical similarity, Oregon's economy is neither as strong nor as diverse as Washington's. One-third of Oregon's manufacturing jobs are in the timber industry.[18]

Oregon's political geography is similar to that of its neighbor: there are three basic regions and the city of Portland (see maps 7.3 and 7.4). Eastern Oregon is rural, Republican, and conservative. Writing in the 1960s, Donald Bogue and Calvin Beale called much of this region "a vast wasteland which as yet has been put only to a very limited economic use."[19] Most of this region is federal land and is leased primarily for cattle and sheep grazing. Wheat farmers make up much of the population of the northern row of eastern counties running along the Columbia River. The major city of the region is Pendleton (Umatilla County), a trade center for the shipment of cattle and wheat. The western coastal area is the most liberal and most Democratic area of the state. These contrasts are clearly displayed in map 7.4. The coastal counties are grouped together in the first quintile, having the lowest average gubernatorial vote from 1982 to 1990. The eastern counties are shaded solidly in the Republican quintiles.

Just inland, in the Willamette Valley region stretching from Lane County (Eugene) in the south to Portland in the north, the parties are competitive in gubernatorial elections. This area has four medium-sized cities: Albany, Corvallis, Eugene, and Salem. Each of these cities is a trade center known for food processing, lumber, pulp, and paper. Salem (Marion County) is one of the more Republican cities in the valley, whereas Eugene (Lane County) votes Democratic. Finally, there is Multnomah County (Portland), the most urban county of the state. Like Seattle, Portland is liberal and Democratic, although not as affluent. In 1990, Multnomah County trailed King County, Washington, by $11,000 in median family income. As for the cities themselves, median family income in Portland is substantially less than that in Seattle. Generally, this is because Portland is more industrial and blue-collar, with a narrower manufacturing base in the forest products industry.

Oregonians cast their ballots with little regard for party affiliation. Many counties do not follow their presidential voting patterns in local races. As figure 7.2 reveals, the 1980 presidential vote explains less than 40 percent of the variation in the 1982 gubernatorial vote. In rural Gilliam County, which generally votes Republican, the 1982 Republican gubernatorial incumbent Vic Atiyeh exceeded Ronald Reagan's percentage by over twenty-five points. In heavily Democratic Lincoln and Tillamook Counties, on the coast, Atiyeh's percentage exceeded Reagan's percentage by 14.9 and 17.9 percent, respectively. Even in Multnomah County, Atiyeh ran 16.4 percent ahead of Reagan, and all this in a year (1982) that was supposed to be bad for Republicans.

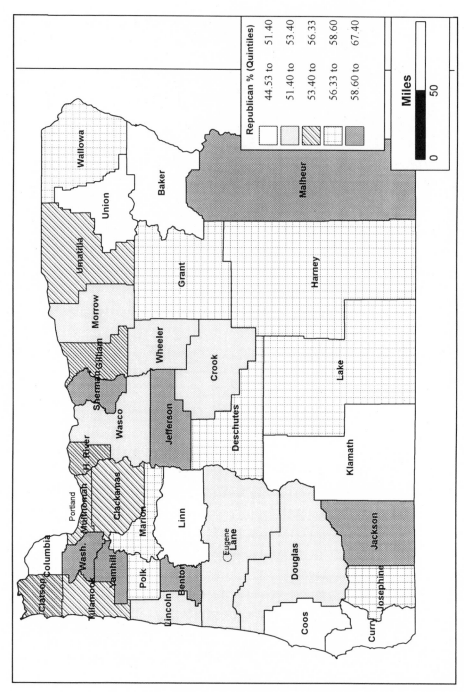

Republican % (Quintiles)

	44.53 to 51.40
	51.40 to 53.40
	53.40 to 56.33
	56.33 to 58.60
	58.60 to 67.40

Miles

0   50

Map 7.3 Average Republican Gubernatorial Vote in Oregon, 1962–1970

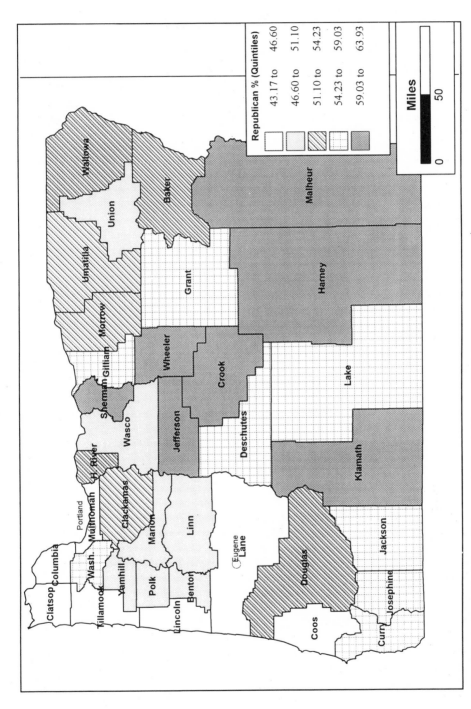

Republican % (Quintiles)

	43.17 to 46.60
	46.60 to 51.10
	51.10 to 54.23
	54.23 to 59.03
	59.03 to 63.93

Miles

0   50

Map 7.4 Average Republican Gubernatorial Vote in Oregon, 1982–1990

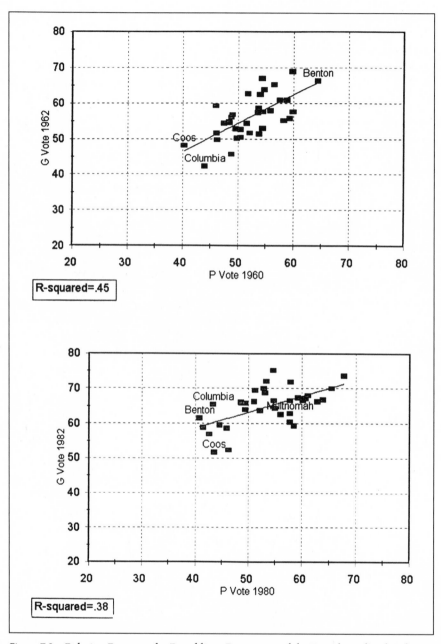

Figure 7.2 Relation Between the Republican Percentage of the Presidential and Gubernatorial Vote in 1960–1962 and 1980–1982 in Oregon, by County

Source: Richard M. Scammon and Alice McGillivray, eds., *America Votes* (Washington, D.C.: Elections Research Center).

Oregon's Weak Party Past

It hardly seems necessary to join the chorus of voices that have repeatedly emphasized the weakness of Oregon's political parties. The parties are not weak because of a lack of party competition. Candidates from both parties compete and win. Instead, the party organizations are structurally weak and do not have a reliable coalitional profile from election to election. David Henderson, a Republican political operative from Salem, summed up the state of Oregon's parties in the 1980s as an "every-man-for-himself" system.[20]

The influence of Oregon's electoral uniqueness on party elites is evident in Henderson's statements about how to run elections by drawing from diverse segments of the electorate. He explicitly mentioned the tendency for Republicans to exploit the conflict between timber interests and environmental preservation in state politics:

> It is possible in Oregon to be a conservative and be for the environment. But you have to remember that timber is the main industry and always will be. Environmental interests cannot upset or shut down the timber business. This has happened from time to time because the state legislature is dominated by liberal Democrats. As a result, there are aspects of the Oregon political landscape that are hostile to business; . . . workman's compensation rates are miserable. The tax system is against business.

Yet Republicans in Oregon are not exclusively the pro-business party. In 1986, Democrat Neil Goldschmidt won the governorship by relying on his home base, Portland, while running in the rest of the state on a pro-business, economic development platform. Other accounts of Goldschmidt's administration echo this account of his independence. Goldschmidt's politics was described as a contrast both to Reagan's conservatism and the labor liberalism of the national Democratic party.[21]

In state politics, the dominant issues are school finance, sales taxes, environmental preservation, and economic development. Race relations and welfare expenditures have emerged in some of the more recent contests; however, they are usually not foremost in the minds of voters. The influence of national issues has been consistently watered down by local concerns.

Not surprisingly, then, candidates typically run alone without the support of party organizations. In one study of the state's political elites, Oregon parties were found to be virtually impotent in the recruitment and selection of candidates.[22] Most state legislators are described as self-starters, having never been recruited by anyone. Others claimed that they were recruited by a faction or inner-circle "clique" of personal friends. A still smaller number were recruited by interest groups. Not one legislator claimed to have been recruited by the organizational machinery of the state party system.[23] In Oregon, *party* is only a label for partisanship. Party organization serves as no intermediate filter or screen to political candidacy.

In response to the void left by the weak, factionalized parties, many candidates form personal organizations of considerable strength and sophistication. When interviewed in 1989, Mark Hatfield claimed to have an organization that outnumbered the activists in the Republican and Democratic party organizations combined. At any one time, he has 10,000 volunteers available. At election time, that number triples to about 30,000. He pointed out that parties had no voice in Oregon because there was no patronage and no strength in the nomination process: "What that means is that we have to spend a lot of time back in the state, always having an extensive schedule of trips and spending money on personnel." In addition, the absence of parties has made it more important for the congressional delegation to pay attention to local matters.

In other words, there is a connection between party weakness, a narrow economic base, and the attention that politicians must pay to issues of local importance. In a state without strong partisans and without a highly diverse economy, candidates must continually perform the kinds of services that will keep voters loyal. On the one hand, they are required to do careful constituent service because partisan coalitions are not clearly divided and mobilized by party cues. Support comes from many quarters. On the other hand, candidates are required to do careful constituent service because the entire population depends on two or three economic activities. However, these two variables— electoral homogeneity and a narrow economic base—are not necessarily unrelated. To the extent that there is consensus in Oregon about the importance of timber, tourism, and agriculture, the economy of the state unifies rather than divides the electorate. Oregon is similar to Arizona in this respect. An economic development platform with a component of constituent service will bring success to candidates from both parties. Homogeneity also makes the power of incumbency all the greater.

The history of Oregon's party leadership could hardly be called a carbon copy of national history. The roots of the independent Oregon electorate extend at least as far back as the New Deal, when many western Democrats split between progressives who followed President Roosevelt and "old guard" types whose chief object was attending to local issues for personal gain.[24] Republicans also split, and Senator Wayne Morse defected to the Democrats in 1952.

Mark Hatfield, then secretary of state, picked up the Republican mantle and went out on his own to form a personal organization and an unusual coalition of groups including labor, minorities, environmental groups, and consumers.[25] In the early 1950s, Oregon was a one-party Republican state, but the party was badly factionalized. Hatfield claimed that Oregon emerged as a two-party competitive state when conservative Republicans began to win more primary contests. In his opinion, national conservatism has hurt the party. He recounted the historical development of Oregon's party system:

> When I was starting, the Democrats were there. There were always Democrats registered. In the thirties, forties, and fifties, the Democratic rank-and-file was made up of a few radical lawyers, editors and professionals that identified with the New Deal. The party leadership abandoned these people for a while to avoid the radical label. By the 1950s, the New Deal types gained control to create a credible contrast to the Republicans.
>
> Meanwhile, Republicans became less progressive as a party. With the election of [Governor Tom] McCall and the more recent election of [Governor] Vic Atiyeh, the Republicans really became the party of the status quo. I have tried to reverse the trend the party is taking but haven't been entirely successful, and consequently Democrats have taken the state legislature and dominated in the House delegation.

In the late 1970s and throughout the 1980s, state political trends were moving opposite to what was occurring in national politics. Locally, the Republicans lost ground in general elections as they moved in the direction of the dominant conservative policies of the national party leadership. According to Hatfield, the vitality and strength of Oregon Republicanism lies in its independence and progressivism, not in its identification with the new right. When asked about the importance of dominant national cleavages, Hatfield said that Oregon's only natural tie to national politics "is in the area of natural resources, recreation, fisheries and public works. Only around 2 percent of our population is black."[26]

Still, the kind of independence valued by candidates in weak-party states is not necessarily an ideological independence of national partisanship. Certainly there are ideologically conservative voters. The conservative electorate is not always a strictly Republican one, however. Like Bob Stump's congressional district in northern and western Arizona, the conservative areas of Oregon are made up of some conventional Democratic constituencies where conservative candidates from either party can win. Independence is to be valued as an independence from organizations and other elite groups that might, at some point, become unpopular baggage in the eyes of a discriminating but activated electorate. The Republican elites in this state look very different from one another in many ideological respects. Recent examples from Oregon's gubernatorial politics will amplify the point.

Oregon Politics in the Post–New Deal Period

In 1962, everyone seemed to know that incumbent Mark Hatfield would defeat challenger Robert Thornton. The 1962 race has to be understood in the context of Hatfield's defeat of a Democratic incumbent in the Democratic year of 1958. Two years before, in the midst of Democratic victories in 1956, he had won the race for secretary of state. But Hatfield's rise as a political maverick was constructed in a field that was gradually tilting against Republican candidates. The registration edge that Republicans held through the 1930s and 1940s was wearing thin. By November 1958, Democrats accounted for 53 percent of the state's registered voters. Part of the problem in the 1950s was that the national Republican party took positions that were unpopular among Oregonians. The Eisenhower administration, for instance, discouraged public power, tightened credit, and decreased aid to farm families.[27] In a state so dependent upon public power, lumber, and farming, any successful Republican would have to take different positions on those issues. Hatfield won by adopting positions that won over many of his opposition's voters, while holding the Republicans in place by opposing a proposed state sales tax. Hatfield's victory in the face of economic recession is all the more remarkable. The lumber interests had been hurting due to high mortgage interest rates. Public power starts had slowed down, hampering the state's drive to attract new industry, and farmers who raised grain, potatoes, dairy products, fruit, and other commodities were facing an uncertain future.[28]

The "right-to-work" issue did not matter, because Hatfield's record in the legislature was favorably rated by labor interests.[29] Hatfield supported public control of utilities, taking that issue away from his opponent. Democrats simply could not tag him as a candidate of big business. When the Democrats would attempt to use the national economic recession against Republicans, Hatfield turned around and said that new jobs, industrial development, and overhaul of the tax structure were his primary goals. In the 1958 contest, Hatfield carried thirty-one of Oregon's thirty-six counties, including the Portland area. At age thirty-six, he became the youngest governor in Oregon history.

With this successful propensity to run against the tide, it was not surprising that in 1962, when the tide was in his party's favor, he would win by a landslide. Even the most liberal and Democratic papers favorably editorial-

ized. By the Portland *Oregonian,* he was labeled a "fresh, liberal and persua-
sive voice in the Republican party . . . his regime is noted for economy,
efficiency, and progressiveness."[30]

When the votes came in, Thornton had won 41.4 percent of the vote. The
Democrat ran strongest in the traditionally Democratic counties along the
coast, but many Democratic areas gave solid majorities to Hatfield. As one
might expect, party registration figures were not good predictors for either
the 1958 or 1962 contests. In 1958, only about 6 percent of the variation in the
county-level vote could be explained by local party registration figures. In
1962, the relationship was stronger, but much of the variation is unexplained
(figures not shown).

What explains Hatfield's success across the entire state in both elections,
even in Democratic areas? The traditional national cleavages account for
very little of the county-level vote (table 7.3). Republican candidates can win
otherwise Democratic areas in Oregon because the traditional Democratic
themes are not strongly reinforced by the issues of state politics. Where the
Democratic constituencies are present, though, there is a more familiar political pattern. Oregon politics displayed a consistent separation between industrial and nonindustrial areas through the 1960s. In this respect, the state
looked very much like Washington: manufacturing areas leaned Democratic
through the 1960s. There was also a slight tendency for urban areas to vote
Democratic. The data show, however, that no income cleavages divided the
state. Racial divisions appeared in the county-level data fairly infrequently,
cropping up in the 1970s, but disappearing again by the 1980s. In recent contests, then, customary national electoral divisions have not projected themselves very clearly in the state's politics. Oregon counties divide in unpredictable ways—sometimes a national political division emerges, only to be
submerged again by localism in the next election cycle.

The kind of candidate-centered voting present throughout Oregon history is visible elsewhere in the West. In 1958 and 1962, however, it is especially noteworthy because Hatfield was deliberately forming coalitions that
cut across national party lines. The absence of traditional electoral coalitions to cue voting behavior and the presence of an independent like Hatfield
played a role here. Hatfield ignored the party organization, not even men-
tioning his party on campaign advertisements. This trend continued through
the 1960s and 1970s. But Hatfield has repeatedly stated that the demise of
Republican prospects at the state level had been owing to the party's rightward drift—as if to say that local candidates' temptation to follow the national
Republican party has hurt them at the polls.

Table 7.3   Influences on the Republican Percentage of the Presidential and Gubernatorial Vote in Oregon, by County, 1960–1992

	Constant	Income	% Urban	Minority	% Mfg.	Adj. R²
President, 1960	58.8	.34	−.06	−.82	−.46*	.31
		(.47)	(.05)	(.43)	(.11)	
Governor, 1962	55.3	.60	−.12*	−.14	−.44*	.35
		(.44)	(.04)	(.40)	(.10)	
President, 1968	60.3	.03	.02	−3.01*	−.41*	.55
		(.25)	(.06)	(.63)	(.12)	
Governor, 1970	43.1	.50	.06	−1.32*	−.33*	.30
		(.26)	(.06)	(.64)	(.12)	
President, 1972	63.6	.10	−.05	−2.19*	−.38*	.53
		(.25)	(.06)	(.62)	(.12)	
President, 1980	65.6	−.20	−.17*	−.30	.14	.37
		(.34)	(.07)	(.41)	(.20)	
Governor, 1982	47.6	.72*	−.20*	.36	.03	.21
		(.31)	(.06)	(.39)	(.19)	
President, 1988	47.3	.43	−.26*	.09	.11	.30
		(.24)	(.08)	(.34)	(.27)	
Governor, 1990	47.8	−.04	−.12*	−.30	.20	.35
		(.19)	(.06)	(.26)	(.21)	
President, 1992	39.5	.14	−.16*	−.08	.03	.23
		(.21)	(.07)	(.30)	(.24)	

*p < .05   N=39

Source: Bureau of the Census, *County and City Databook* (Washington, D.C.: GPO, various years); Richard M. Scammon and Alice McGillivray, eds., *America Votes* (Washington, D.C.: Elections Research Center, various years); *County and City Extra* (Lanham, Md.: Bernan Press, 1992).

Note: Multiple linear regression, WLS estimation; unstandardized regression coefficients weighted for population; standard errors in parentheses; income is expressed in thousands of constant 1992 dollars.

Sustained Candidate-Centeredness in 1982 and 1990

Whereas Mark Hatfield's liberal positions in the 1958 and 1962 contests were indistinguishable from his opponent's positions, the low-key contest twenty years later would be more ideologically polarized. Incumbent Governor Vic Atiyeh, from Portland, was being challenged by liberal state senator Ted Kulongoski of Junction City. This was not a good year for Republicans nationwide, but Atiyeh resisted the national tide, winning with an over-whelming twenty-six-point margin, illustrating, again, the electoral insularity of the state from national trends.

What was lacking were credible charges that could tie the governor's record to the recession of the early Reagan years. Perhaps Atiyeh's incumbency would have been subject to more serious challenge had the recession of the early 1980s hit Oregon as it had hit the Midwest. Compared to Ohio and Pennsylvania, Oregon weathered the crisis well. In only one county, heavily Republican Grant, did the 1982 unemployment rate exceed 20 percent. In other words, while unemployment grew worse in most of Oregon's counties, Ted Kulongoski did not have the sick economy on his side. In two of the more liberal and Democratic counties, Benton and Polk, unemployment was slightly *lower* than in 1980. Unemployment rates were also lower in three counties in the east. Nowhere do we find the severe increases in unemployment that were evident in the Northeast and Midwest. The largest rise in unemployment took place in Tillamook County, along the coast, where it rose 6 percent in two years. Compared to other states, then, the impact of rising unemployment rates in Oregon was very ambiguous and had little impact on the voting for the party in power. While there was some talk in the newspapers about the detrimental effect of Reaganomics, and while the Democratic candidate tried to blame signs of economic downturn on the current administration, the economy was not sick enough to overcome Atiyeh's incumbency advantage.

As a matter of record, some common state-level concerns did divide the candidates: economic development, how to pay for basic state services, infrastructure, land-use planning, water, and the environment.[31] Kulongoski was a champion of labor. His background in the legislature and his platform underscored a solidly liberal record. He had sponsored a plant closure bill in the legislature, supported generous human services appropriations, and promoted the creation of a business development fund. In addition, Kulongoski criticized Atiyeh as the tool of the Portland business community.

The power of incumbency, however, gave the governor a sizable fund-raising advantage. He coasted to a surprisingly easy victory, winning 61.4 percent of the statewide vote. None of the elements of traditional party voting is present in the county-level data (table 7.3). The manufacturing cleavage, which often explains aggregate voting behavior in the Pacific Northwest, is not statistically significant. The race variable seems to slightly *increase* Republican prospects. The African-American population of the state is so small (1.6 percent in 1990) that it rarely influences elections except in very close races. National trends have probably had more influence on Oregon than

Oregon has had on the nation, but it is hardly justifiable to assume that national party alignments decide this state's elections.

The 1990 gubernatorial election would have given the state a Republican governor had the conservative wing of the party not abandoned their liberal nominee, Dave Frohnmayer. The year began with a surprise announcement by the incumbent governor, Neil Goldschmidt, that he would not seek a second term. Secretary of State Barbara Roberts, an unabashed liberal, then announced that she would run in Goldschmidt's place. Frohnmayer, the sitting attorney general, looked to be a shoo-in after an easy victory in a seven-candidate primary. The conservative Oregon Citizen's Alliance, a strong pro-life group, stepped in the way, however, claiming that Frohnmayer was no better than Roberts. Conservative pro-lifers then supported independent candidate Al Mobley. These same elements nearly succeeded in defeating Republican U.S. Senator Robert Packwood in the 1986 primary. This time, though, their efforts would ensure a Democratic victory. With Roberts solidifying her Democratic base by running to the left of Frohnmayer, and Al Mobley sapping conservative votes, the Republican nominee ultimately went down to a sound defeat.

Had Mobley's solid 13 percent of the vote gone to Frohnmayer, the Republicans would have won by a couple of percentage points. Mobley's third-party bid was unusually successful due to the two anti-abortion measures that were on the ballot that year. "Worried about his right flank," wrote the *Oregonian*, "Frohnmayer found it harder to go after moderate Democrats."[32] Mobley cut sharply into the Republican base in southern and eastern Oregon, taking 19 percent of statewide Republican party identifiers and 30 percent of self-identified conservatives. Roberts's plurality win was built upon the liberal-leaning urban areas around Portland and in other cities around the state.[33] As the data in table 7.3 indicate, Frohnmayer lost about 1.2 points for every 10 percent increase in the urban population of a county.

General election results in Oregon are governed by the accidents of nomination, not by political party control. Given the lack of persistent national cleavages in the Oregon electorate, it could hardly be otherwise. Organizations bind candidates when there is substantial agreement on the goals and purposes of a party. Strong party government assumes the existence of a distinct set of "ins" and a distinct set of "outs." With an electorate not divided into well-defined party coalitions, it is much more difficult to agree on party purposes. This leaves the system open to renegade candidacies like Mobley's and consensus reelection bids like that of Atiyeh.

National Divisions in the Oregon Electorate

One cannot rely on ecological data to paint a complete picture of a state's voting behavior. Fortunately, a limited number of exit polls are available to help us evaluate the presence of national coalitional divisions. Racial differences in party voting are present in most Oregon elections. As in the case of Washington State, however, the division between the white and minority communities is not nearly as pronounced in Oregon as it is in older eastern states (fig. 7.3). The cleavage between white and minority voters remained consistently low throughout the 1980s. Republicans are capable of winning as much as 40 percent of the minority vote and rarely tally less than 20 percent. Recall that in the case of New York, Republican candidates were lucky to win 20 percent. Labor union households tend to vote Democratic in Oregon politics, but Republicans do well in certain local contests. Mark Hatfield won a solid 60 percent of the labor vote in his 1984 reelection for U.S. Senate against

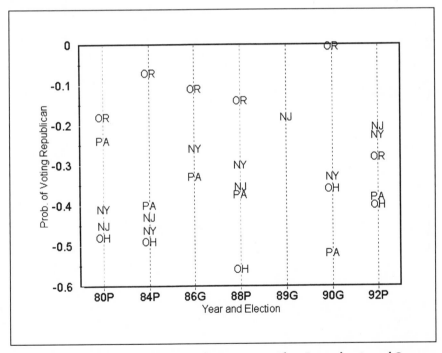

Figure 7.3   Racial Cleavages in New York, New Jersey, Ohio, Pennsylvania, and Oregon Elections

Source: Richard M. Scammon and Alice McGillivray, eds., *America Votes* (Washington, D.C.: Elections Research Center).

Table 7.4 Logit Analysis of the Influence of Race, Income, and Union Membership in Oregon Elections, 1980–1992

	Constant	Race	Income	Labor	No. of Cases	Predicted Null (%)
President, 1980	.97	−.72*	.25*	−.39*		60
		(.27)	(.05)	(.14)	1,141	60
Effect		−18.0	6.0	−10.0		
President, 1984	−.76	−.47*	.25*	−.47*		58
		(.24)	(.05)	(.12)	1,377	55
Effect		−7.0	4.0	−8.0		
Senate, 1984	.36	−1.05*	.34*	−.34*		59
		(.26)	(.05)	(.13)	1,325	67
Effect		−22.0	8.0	−8.0		
Senate, 1986	1.48	−.84*	.16*	−.41*		64
		(.01)	(.002)	(.006)	694	63
Effect		−22.0	4.0	−10.0		
Governor, 1986	.61	−.47*	−.05*	−.08*		51
		(.01)	(.002)	(.006)	703	52
Effect		−11.0	−1.0	−2.0		
President, 1988	1.59	−.19	.19*	−.77*		60
		(.35)	(.06)	(.18)	699	54
Effect		−14.0	4.0	−14.0		
Governor, 1990	−.99	−.01	.29*	−.36*		59
		(.01)	(.002)	(.007)	815	56
Effect		−.2	6.0	−8.0		
Senate, 1990	.27	−.72*	−.25	−.20*		58
		(.01)	(.002)	(.006)	942	54
Effect		−17.0	6.0	−5.0		
President, 1992	−.82	−.21	.15*	−.37*		68
		(.29)	(.07)	(.19)	768	67
Effect		−3.7	2.6	−6.6		
Senate, 1992	−.20	−.05	.09	−.27		54
		(.23)	(.05)	(.15)	1,025	52
Effect		−1.2	2.1	−6.4		

Source: CBS News/New York Times, *Election Day Surveys*, 1984, 1986. ABC News/Washington Post, *50 State Poll*, September–November 1988. Voter Research and Surveys, *General Election Exit Polls*, 1990, 1992.

Note: Dependent variable: 0 = Democrat, 1 = Republican; MLE coefficients; standard errors in parentheses; *p < .05; Effect = change in odds of voting Republican from moving x one unit at the means of the other variables.

a weak opponent. Robert Packwood similarly took 55 percent of the labor vote in the 1986 U.S. Senate contest. Labor was kind, however, to Democratic presidential nominee Michael Dukakis, favoring him by two to one over George Bush in 1988. Ronald Reagan roughly split the labor vote with his opponents in 1980 and 1984. Table 7.4 reflects these dramatic swings in labor's tendency to remain in the Democratic column. Presidential contests show a wider gulf between the labor and nonlabor communities.

Dominant national party cleavages do not strongly influence voting in recent gubernatorial contests. The 1986 contest was especially competitive. Neil Goldschmidt won by a narrow margin of two points. Goldschmidt managed to win 40 percent of the self-identified conservatives in the state and one-third of the Republicans, while holding onto 81 percent of the liberals and 80 percent of the Democrats. He also won majorities in nearly every income cohort. The success of maverick candidacies like Goldschmidt's explains why the customary divisions between low- income and high-income voters are reversed.

Summary: The Lessons of the Oregon and Washington Cases

In the 1950s, David Truman wrote that the basic political fact of federalism "is that it creates separate, self-sustaining centers of power, privilege, and profit which may be sought and defended as desirable in themselves."[34] Truman recognized that the federal structure of office decentralized the party system and encouraged the development of independent, hostile, and sectional groupings. The degree of local differentiation from national party interests determines the degree of factionalism within a state's parties. Some parts of the country are less likely to be factionalized than others. When a state or region has a set of interests that cut through rather than unify national party constituencies, a state's party system will remain weak and factionalized. In Oregon and Washington, the dominant national interests of peaceful race relations, peaceful class relations, and full employment may not be completely irrelevant, but there are other important interests such as resource distribution, regulation of resource use, nuclear power use, controlling growth through planning, and paying for schools with a narrow tax base.

In conclusion, it is sensible to suggest that states can be independent of the tides of national politics. In the Pacific Northwest, the federal system has created a state politics largely free from the encroachment of national parties and elections. Because the older and more populous states of the Northeast and Midwest were early contributors to the nation's political development, the political environment emerging in the distant Northwest was bound to look strange. At the time of admission to the Union, Oregon Democrats split into two rival factions, a "national Democrats" faction and a "local Democrats" faction. The national faction objected to the local faction's tendency to use local issues as party measures, preferring to base partisanship on national principles.[35] This shows that even from earliest times there was simply no natural linkage to national party politics. The western electorate's attitude toward politics grew largely out of its contact with state and local conditions. With a muddle of national issues and local issues interposing themselves haphazardly from election to election, voters have relied on candidates' qualities to cue their local balloting.[36] Political careers are based on forming coalitions independent of national party coalitions. To a considerable extent, this independence of national partisanship is evident in county- and voter-level divisions. Neither state has the predictably divided electoral foundation necessary to sustain party unity.

Is party unity necessary for good government? At the end of his book on state politics, V. O. Key wondered if it made any difference whether state parties were unified or promoted self-made, maverick candidacies.[37] Based on his earlier explorations of southern politics, he hypothesized that politicians would be restrained and moderated by others engaged in a joint enterprise of electioneering. In this manner, collective leadership promoted the public interest better than an atomized one. But the experience of Oregon and Washington forces us to acknowledge that many states do well with individualistic, candidate-centered systems. Unlike the South of Key's time, the western party systems are based on informed and active electorates. Hence, these states have been devoid of demagoguery of the type that worried Key. While personality rather than issue-oriented concerns figure prominently in state elections, a highly discriminating and independent-minded electorate ensures that politicians remain cautious in office. While not all elections are competitive, all elections are potentially competitive. There is still room for irresponsibility, which stronger parties could presumably control. Independent candidacies that garner small but significant percentages of the vote necessarily undermine the capacity of parties to represent broad coalitional bases. But the strong parties that could prevent a renegade candidacy are contingent upon an electorate that would not be attracted to such contestants. To reiterate a motif of this book, elites follow electors. It is the sectional uniqueness of the party in the electorate that most determines the paths state politicians will follow in their quest for office.

Sectionalism Disrupts the Party System: Idaho

Idaho: Electoral Background

IDAHO IS an electorally volatile state with a politically conservative tradition where Democrats have consistently run competitive races. Aside from famous potatoes, not much else is widely known about the state. Very little has been written about the history of Idaho political parties and electoral politics.[1] Because of its small population and isolation from national government, there has been little pressure from outside forces to nationalize its political system. Presidential contenders have rarely targeted the state as a campaign stop.

As in other Mountain states, Idaho's economy is simple and there is little sectional variation by occupation and economic interest. Except for isolated pockets of mining and lumbering and some emerging high-tech industry, the state is almost entirely agricultural. In 1960, about 20 percent of the state's population was classified as rural farm, compared with 7.5 percent for the nation, 1.9 percent for New York, and 5.4 percent for Ohio. Idaho has three distinctive geographical sections, although it is not clear that they are economically unique. The northern region, sometimes called the "panhandle" or "smokestack," consists of ten counties bordered by Montana on the east and Oregon and Washington on the west (see maps 8.1 and 8.2). This region closely resembles western Oregon and Washington in many respects. The farms are prosperous because there is adequate water and dominant products include wheat, fruit, livestock, and lumber.[2] The major cities of the region include Lewiston, Moscow, and Coeur d'Alene. Moscow is home of the University of Idaho and is considered to be a trade center for the area. Coeur

185

d'Alene, a tourist town near the lake of the same name, supports a large vacation and summer resort area.[3] Lewiston is the center of the wheat and lumber business on the Snake River. When the decline of the lumber business led to a substantial decline in employment in the 1950s and 1960s, many Idahoans migrated to Spokane and Boise where jobs were available.

Economically related political behavior is obvious in only three of Idaho's ten counties, each of which has a strong and consistent Democratic tradition rooted in the lumber and mining industries. These are Shoshone, Clearwater, and Latah. The rural lumbering precincts have an especially strong Democratic tradition. The remaining counties are competitive between the parties, sometimes swinging to the Republicans in state elections, other times to the

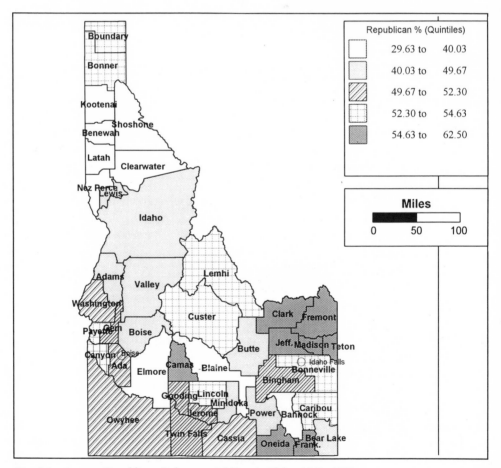

Map 8.1   Average Republican Gubernatorial Vote in Idaho, 1962–1970

Democrats. Except for the lumber and mining background of a few counties, however, voting patterns do not appear to be related to economic activity.

Boise and Nampa, the largest cities, are located in central Idaho. Boise is a trade center and state capital. Nampa was built on railroads and the sugar beet industry. Population growth has brought change to the area; Boise's population nearly tripled in size from 1960 to 1990. Politically, the central and southwestern counties have swung wildly between Republican and Democratic candidates over the last twenty years. Lemhi County, along the Montana border, was among the most Democratic of counties in the 1960s. By the 1980s, it was one of the most Republican.

The southeastern corner of the state is more akin to Utah than it is to the

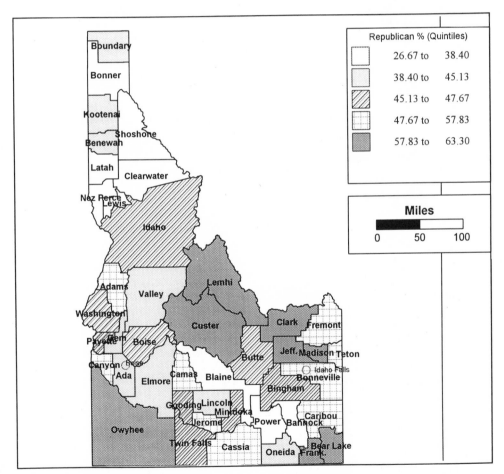

Map 8.2   Average Republican Gubernatorial Vote in Idaho, 1982–1990

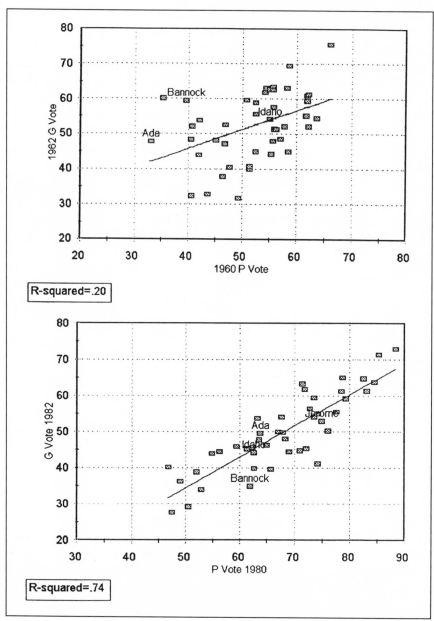

Figure 8.1 Relation Between Republican Percentage of the Presidential and Gubernatorial Votes of 1960–1962 and 1980–1982 in Idaho, by County

Source: Richard M. Scammon and Alice McGillivray, eds., *America Votes* (Washington, D.C.: Elections Research
  Center).

remainder of Idaho. The large Mormon population is very conservative and predominantly rural. The largest and most Democratic city in this region is Pocatello, home of Idaho State University. Pocatello's economy is dependent upon students, shipping, and food processing. The more Republican Idaho Falls has experienced an economic boom fueled by the highly educated population employed at Idaho National Engineering Laboratory (INEL). The four southeastern counties bordering Utah are the most conservative and Republican, due largely to their rural and mostly Mormon populations.

Because the state lacks the economic variation that sectionally segments voting in the Midwest and Northeast, its electoral behavior is not easily predicted with aggregate data. Figure 8.1 illustrates the incongruence of a state electorate that only occasionally follows its presidential voting patterns. The two scatterplots illustrate the relationship between the gubernatorial and presidential vote for 1962 and 1960 and 1982 and 1980. In the earlier contest, only 20 percent of the variation in the county-level gubernatorial vote could be explained by the 1960 presidential vote. The voting in the 1982 contest is closer to the 1980 race, but a large y-intercept indicates that there is an average 9 percent gap between the gubernatorial and presidential bases of support.

The state's volatile electoral setting may be attributable to the fact that economic interests do not vary enough to be a stable source of party conflict in state politics. Because the state's past has been so uniformly rooted in agriculture, class stratification is hard to find. There are several sectional and cultural cross-pressures that prevent the nationalization of the Idaho voter.

The New Deal did not have the impact on Idaho that it did elsewhere. The Depression's impact was less severe because the state had never been part of the nation's economic mainstream. Through the 1920s, "while the urban industrial states were thriving, agriculture was depressed and there was little attempt on the part of the federal administration to intervene. The deflated value of farm products was nothing new to Idaho farmers in 1930."[4] With this background in mind, it is not difficult to understand why the dominant New Deal cleavages did not surface. The state still lacks many of the core constituencies of the national party system. In 1990, only 11 percent of the labor force worked in manufacturing. Less than 1 percent of the state's population was African-American. Not only are national constituencies present in much smaller proportions, they are not regionally concentrated either. As in several other Mountain states, the population is evenly distributed. In 1960, the three most populous areas in the state (Boise, Nampa, and Pocatello) accounted for less than 30 percent of the population. At least two of these counties had strong Republican traditions. Finally, a greater homogeneity of income has not laid the foundation for strong class cleavages in the state's politics. Consequently, it is not surprising that Idaho's county-level voting patterns would not follow national voting patterns. This chapter will show that state elections are candidate operations and that voting in significant portions of the state is not determined by stable partisan cleavages.

Sources of Party Weakness in Idaho Politics

Parties have had trouble organizing in Idaho. Like V. O. Key's observation of Florida parties forty years ago, it is safe to say that Idaho's parties are both unbossed and unled.[5] There is no mechanism for recruitment of candidates. As former congressman and recent U.S. Senate candidate Richard Stallings put it: "I was never recruited by the party. The party is pretty much in disarray. Everyone knows that you don't need the party to get elected, so why work with the party? Frank Church was very popular in Idaho and he never ran with organization support." Stallings's career provides an example of the way Idahoans typically enter politics. Candidates are sometimes recruited by officeholders, but most of the time they simply file on their own, having recruited themselves. It doesn't make sense to speak of organizational involvement in a state where party organizations barely exist. The state's institutional machinery is similar to that of most other states. There is a direct primary and the usual hierarchy of chairpersons, right down to precinct-level committeemen and committeewomen. Candidates remain independent of the organization, however. One observer credits the weakness of organizations to the independence of the Idaho voter and the cost of statewide campaigns.[6]

In most northeastern or midwestern states, the bulk of the population often resides in two, three, or perhaps four large counties that support Democrats. The Republican vote is concentrated in a few suburban areas and in a reliable rural vote. Republican party machinery has been less tight and campaigns less organized because there is no urban basis to Republican voting. However, in the Idaho case, both the Republican and Democratic vote is spread evenly over a large land area dotted by many small towns of approximately equal size. Furthermore, there is no regional basis of Republican or Democratic strength. Southeastern Idaho tends to vote Republican, but Democrats have had success there. What this means is that a candidate must campaign across the entire state, sifting each county for votes. A party organization cannot afford to support an entire slate of candidates when its campaign must go everywhere.

Furthermore, the absence of party organization can be accounted for by the consistent emergence of crosscutting cleavages due to the religious and

Table 8.1   Influence of Mormon Tradition on the Republican Gubernatorial Vote in
Idaho, by County, 1962–1990

	Constant	Mormon County	Adj. R^2
Governor, 1962	49.7	10.5* (3.1)	.20
Governor, 1978	35.0	21.0* (3.3)	.49
Governor, 1982	46.1	14.9* (3.0)	.36
Governor, 1986	49.1	13.5* (3.8)	.21
Governor, 1990	33.0	13.5* (2.5)	.39

*p < .05   N=44

Source: Richard M. Scammon and Alice McGillivray, eds., *America Votes* (Washington, D.C.: Elections Research
   Center, various years).
Note: Linear regression, OLS estimation; unstandardized regression coefficients; standard errors in parentheses.

sectional character of the state. The kinds of appeals that work for a candidate
in Lewiston may not work in Idaho Falls. Richard Stallings said that what
mobilized most Idaho voters in his Second District were older, Populist issues:
"small farmers vs. refiners and processors, preventing the railroads from
eliminating service to small towns and issues that show you are for the 'little
guy.' "[7]
   Stallings's affiliation with the Mormon Church (the Church of Jesus
Christ of Latter-Day Saints) helped in the Mormon areas in his district where
Republican currents run strongest. The influence of Mormonism on the
Idaho vote is evident from the regression coefficients in table 8.1. According
to Lujan, fully one-fourth of Idaho's counties can be considered dominantly
Mormon: Lemhi, Jefferson, Teton, Fremont, Caribou, Bonneville, Oneida,
Madison, Cassia, Franklin, and Clark—all of which are part of the Second
Congressional District. Over time, as the table shows, the Mormon influence
on the gubernatorial vote remains strong.[8] In 1962, the Republican vote in
the Mormon counties ran about ten points ahead of the Republican margins
in the remaining counties. In 1978, 1982, 1986, and 1990, Republican voting
was even stronger in the Mormon counties, making Stallings's House victories even more remarkable.
   The Mormon tendency to vote Republican has historical roots. At the

time of statehood, an anti-Mormon party was formed in Oneida County near
the Utah border. Soon afterward, the anti-Mormon Test Oath Act was enacted at the state level, disenfranchising anyone who would not swear that he
was not a practicing polygamist. The Mormon Church eventually announced
in 1890 that plural marriage was no longer necessary and that Mormons
should abide by the laws of the state in which they lived. The Test Oath Act
was then repealed, and it appeared that Mormonism was a dead issue. At first,
Mormons voted Democratic because the national Republican party had favored the Test Oath Act. However, as Lujan points out, the Mormons were
betrayed by the Democrats who turned against them on repeal of the Test
Oath Act to embrace anti-Mormonism from 1902 to 1908.[9] Since then, Mormons have tended to vote Republican. The Republican predisposition of the
Mormon community has also been supported by the economic outlook of
church leaders. As Lujan explains,

> The Mormons have historically feared strong government, because
> in the past, the government has oppressed them. The Mormon
> Church, through judicious use of the tithe, has become a wealthy
> Church, with interests in private power companies, the Union Pacific
> Railroad and real estate developments involving the Utah Construc-
> tion Company. The Church has operated profitably in a free-market
> economy, and would view with suspicion government encroachment
> upon the control and regulation of the economy; . . . the Church has
> an extensive welfare program that provides for its needy members,
> and is less responsive to government sponsored welfare and social
> security programs. The Church has always opposed liquor and gam-
> bling and adversely views attempts by political parties to effect this
> type of legislation.[10]

Given this description of Mormon attitudes, it should come as no surprise
that the contemporary Republican party wins most of their votes. Politicians
like Stallings are strong Democratic candidates in this potentially hostile
environment. Democrats do best if they are conservative Mormons who
can appeal to the non-Mormons with a Populist platform. Candidates can
capably stand out as nonpartisan mavericks by taking advantage of the cross-
pressures in their region.

Party organizations, however, cannot take advantage of these district-
level cross-pressures. They must operate on a statewide basis while associat-
ing with the platform and ideology of their national party. In this sense, there
is an inflexibility constraining statewide party organization. The organization wears a national party label, which may not coincide with the relevant

issues and interests dividing the local community. If this incongruence persists over time, candidates may have no other choice but to go out on their own, separating themselves from organizational inflexibility to take advantage of local divisions in the community.

Finally, coherent party organization has been hampered by the population explosion in the state, which continues to displace the electorate. Just as in New Mexico, Arizona, and other Mountain states, Idaho's population is expanding due to the attraction of high-technology businesses to the area. A contrast between an old Idaho and a new Idaho is emerging, just as in the New Mexico case. Democratic leaders are hopeful that the attraction of upper-income constituents will benefit the party in the state because Republican party regulars are viewed as extremist and out of touch.[11]

There is a remarkable similarity between the developments in Idaho state politics and those of New Mexico and Arizona. In each case, the testimony is the same: a mobile population benefits the cities. People are leaving the rural areas and moving to where the jobs are. Employment gains are being made in well-educated areas in university towns. The challenge this poses to party organizers at the state level is to absorb the newcomers without alienating the old guard and the stable population base. In this manner, rapid electoral change generates conflict within the organization and encourages weak-party, candidate-centered politics. In an uncrystallized political setting, candidates are more likely to go out on their own by forming personal organizations and coalition groups.

In summary, the combination of Mormonism, population migration, and the uniformly agricultural character of the state—features that are not conducive to a hierarchical party politics—has created a political setting dominated by candidates and issues. The 1962 gubernatorial contest was not so much a contest of personalities as it was a contest over the morality of gambling. The 1982 gubernatorial election was a conflict over personalities. Richard Stallings is only one of a distinguished group of candidates who has stood alone in Idaho politics without organization support.

Idaho State Politics in the Post–New Deal Period

The substantial incongruence of state and national electoral cleavages is apparent in a review of the 1962 competition between the incumbent Republican governor, Robert Smylie, and Vernon K. Smith, a Boise attorney. The race was without reference to party organizational involvement, as Democratic party cohesion dissolved over the issue of gambling. Just as in California, Washington, New Mexico and Arizona, the biggest challenge facing a state executive in Idaho was how to provide basic state services when the population was growing so rapidly. Gambling was an issue in Idaho throughout the 1950s and was generally favored by the Democrats to increase revenues by "taxing" sources outside Idaho—that is, tourists and the convention trade, which gambling would presumably encourage.[12]

To the dismay of the Idaho Democratic state party organization, Smith had gone out on his own in the primary and won solely on a pro-gambling platform. In the platform convention in July, he clashed with party regulars on whether to incorporate a gambling plank. The convention was badly split and failed to take a position on gambling, deciding instead to leave it to the state legislature. Smith's views were universally supported only by Democrats in the "smokestack" northern counties where the lumber and mining industries were depressed. Conservative Democrats from the southern regions were strongly opposed to the gambling plan and many said they would not vote for governor rather than turn out and vote for a supporter of gambling or a Republican. As Lujan suggests, party support for Smith was all but withdrawn, and Smith announced that he preferred to be known as the "candidate for Governor, not as the *Democratic* candidate."[13]

There was more to the campaign than gambling, but not to the press and most voters. On November 4, two days before the election, Boise's *Idaho Statesman* (the only paper with statewide circulation), editorialized against gambling, calling it a "scourge" and a defiler of government. Smylie pointed out that Nevada's taxes are higher than Idaho's—in spite of gambling—and he forced Smith to admit that gambling would not bring tax relief.[14] Smylie pointed out that budget increases in state government were in the areas of education, public health, and public assistance—traditionally Democratic concerns—and asked rhetorically if these were the areas Smith intended to cut.

Considering that the 1962 election was a one-issue campaign, it is remarkable that Smith was able to poll 45.4 percent of the votes cast. More remarkably, he did this without party support or approval. Where did the support for gambling come from? The anti-gambling counties included the more urban areas and the Mormon areas. Pro-gambling areas included the mining areas and rural areas in central and northern Idaho, including the Coeur d'Alene tourist area. Where religion was a behavioral factor, for example, in conservative southeastern Idaho, Smylie ran strongest.

The cleavages separating gambling from non-gambling counties are partly economic and partly religious. No one can deny that, at the individual level, these ecological factors may carry less weight. Idaho's counties are heterogeneous, and the economic and demographic settlement patterns of the state may not reveal the true nature of individual-level voting behavior. However, it is safe to say that the national party divisions make little regional

Table 8.2 Influences on the Republican Presidential and Gubernatorial Vote in Idaho, by County, 1960–1992

	Constant	Income	% Urban	Minority	% Mfg.	Adj. R^2
President, 1960	82.5	−1.07*	.13*	−1.62*	−.46*	.29
		(.43)	(.05)	(.79)	(.18)	
Governor, 1962	52.9	−.19	.14*	.93	−.12	.07
		(.50)	(.06)	(.94)	(.21)	
President, 1968	79.4	−.51	.08	−5.12*	−.70*	.18
		(.38)	(.06)	(2.05)	(.21)	
Governor, 1970	93.1	−.98*	−.06	−4.25	−.78*	.21
		(.48)	(.08)	(2.25)	(.27)	
President, 1972	92.8	−1.00*	.05	−1.89	−.36*	.15
		(.30)	(.05)	(1.59)	(.17)	
President, 1980	90.9	−.84	.06	.36	−.23	.03
		(.60)	(.09)	(.57)	(.31)	
Governor, 1982	87.7	−1.27*	.09	−.26	−.25	.07
		(.58)	(.09)	(.55)	(.29)	
President, 1988	49.2	.40	−.02	.77	−.20	.02
		(.55)	(.09)	(.45)	(.29)	
Governor, 1990	51.7	−.40	−.11	.08	−.06	.24
		(.43)	(.07)	(.36)	(.23)	
President, 1992	35.2	−.008	.06	.81*	−.06	.12
		(.40)	(.06)	(.32)	(.21)	

*p < .05   N=44

Source: Bureau of the Census, *County and City Databook* (Washington, D.C.: GPO, various years); U.S. Department of Commerce, Bureau of the Census, *Summary Social, Economic and Housing Statistics*, Table 10 (Washington, D.C.: GPO, 1992). *County and City Extra* (Lanham, Md.: Bernan Press, 1992); Richard M. Scammon and Alice McGillivray, eds., *America Votes* (Washington, D.C.: Elections Research Center, various years).

Note: Multiple linear regression, WLS estimation; unstandardized regression coefficients weighted for population; standard errors in parentheses; income expressed in thousands of constant 1992 dollars.

sense of Idaho because two of the traditional cleavages are reversed. In the 1960 presidential contest, for example, counties with manufacturing employment and minority voters depressed Republican margins, but high-income areas did also (table 8.2). Republicans actually fared better in the more urban areas of the state. In recent elections, these variables have little explanatory power.

Elements of the electorate that are truly regular in their behavior are limited in size. The uncommitted precincts are in urban areas where voters are strongly cross-pressured and party influence is minimal. The transitional urban-rural precincts are also subject to strong cross-pressures. In these areas, "The marginally Republican lower-middle class voter is susceptible to influence from the strongly Democratic farm area, and a transfer of party support can take place."[15] But the sectional character of the state, rooted in religious conflicts, is probably the most influential source of crosscutting cleavage. Southern Idaho is substantially Mormon and is centered on Boise and Salt Lake City. Northern Idaho is anti-Mormon and Spokane-oriented. This split continued to be as strong in the 1970s and 1980s as in the 1960s. In 1980, Idahoans elected Ronald Reagan in a landslide, giving him 67.9 percent of the total vote. Even traditionally Democratic Shoshone and Clearwater Counties gave Reagan convincing victories. Two years later, while the rest of the country was in the midst of recession, Idaho was not faring as badly. Press accounts suggested that the state's economic woes were the worst since the Great Depression, but from 1980 to 1982 the employment situation had actually improved in one-fourth of the state's counties. Only three counties suffered unemployment exceeding 20 percent. Shoshone County, home of the mining industry, had suffered most—experiencing a precipitous 19 percent drop in employment from 1980 to 1982. Statewide, however, when compared to 1980, the state's downward economic trends had begun to level off, as severe job losses in some areas were balanced by modest job gains in others.

Sustained Candidate-Centeredness: 1982 and 1990

Against the backdrop of the Reagan landslide in 1980, Idaho's steady economy, and the national recession of 1982, the stage was set for the gubernatorial race between Lieutenant Governor Phil Batt and Democratic Governor John Evans, the incumbent. The economy was not the valence issue that it was elsewhere. Instead, the combat was over a classic position issue: right-to-work legislation.[16] Batt, an antiunion, conservative farmer, successfully made it the central issue that separated the two. He argued that a right-to-work law was needed to get Idaho's economy rolling again. The proposed legislation would prohibit the payment of union dues as a condition of employment. Idaho's economy, however, had not experienced the downward spiral seen in states like Ohio, Michigan, and Pennsylvania. As with California's Tom Bradley, Phil Batt's message may not have been completely true to the state's economic situation. Consequently, this contest was not a lopsided one, where the voters turn strongly against the president's party, as they did in Ohio. This was one of the closest races in Idaho's history with Democrat Evans pulling out a last-minute victory by a scant 4,208 votes, or about four votes for every precinct in the state.

Undoubtedly, Batt's emphasis on the right-to-work issue did strengthen his support in longtime Republican, antiunion areas. But it would not win him crossover voters in the Democratic counties. The threat of a right-to-work law mobilized organized labor into an aggressive voter registration and mobilization drive. While Batt ran up solid leads in several important counties, he lost by landslide margins in Nez Perce (Lewiston) and Bannock (Pocatello) Counties where the labor vote was strongest.

When the votes were tabulated, Evans carried twenty-four counties and Batt carried twenty. The sectional split in the state was even more pronounced than usual, and economics did not appear to play a crucial role in the aggregate data. Evans swept nine of the ten "smokestack" counties in the north. Predictably, Batt won solid victories in the Mormon areas in the southeast. As a postscript, a right-to-work law did eventually pass the legislature in 1986.

"Voters Shout: Andrus," read the bold, black headline of the *Idaho Statesman* the day after the 1990 gubernatorial election. Sitting governor Cecil Andrus went on to win his fourth term in a landslide. With the right-to-work issue settled and a popular incumbent prevailing over an economic boom, the 1990 contest against former state senator Roger Fairchild looked to be a mismatch from the start. The campaign was very low-key, as Andrus completely ignored his underdog opponent. He had the typical fund-raising advantage of a well-recognized incumbent, spending $1 million to Fairchild's $50,000. The victory meant that Democrats would remain in control of an office they had held since 1970. In spite of Andrus's two-to-one victory, the Republican candidate for the U.S. Senate, Larry Craig, coasted to a equally lopsided victory over his Democratic opponent. This simply underscores how candidate-centered Idaho elections can be. Highly visible personalities make each office separable from every other office.

Typical of Idaho's factionalism, Fairchild won the primary over two strong Boise candidates in May. He was not the party organization's choice, and he frequently complained throughout the general election campaign that the Republicans had abandoned him. At first, Fairchild appeared to have the strong support of pro-life forces who were angry at Andrus for vetoing a strict anti-abortion measure overwhelmingly passed by the state legislature. Among the 14 percent of the states' voters who claimed to be most against abortion, however, Andrus still wound up winning 46 percent. Andrus was

Table 8.3   Logit Regression Analysis of the Influence of Race and Income in Idaho
Elections, 1990–1992

	Constant	Race	Income	No. of Cases	Predicted Null (%)
Governor, 1990	−.81	.06*	−.01*		69
		(.004)	(.002)	1,465	68
Effect		1.3	−.2		
Senate, 1990	.41	−.15*	.10*		62
		(.003)	(.002)	1,440	62
Effect		−3.6	2.4		
President, 1992	.07	−.27	.17		57
		(.55)	(.09)	344	56
Effect		−6.7	4.2		
Senate, 1992	1.07	−1.09*	.08		55
		(.49)	(.08)	509	54
Effect		−25.8	2.0		

Source: Voter Research and Surveys, *General Election Exit Polls*, 1990, 1992.

Note: Dependent variable: 0 = Democrat, 1 = Republican; MLE coefficients; standard errors in parentheses;
   *$p < .05$; Effect = change in odds of voting Republican from moving x one interval at the means of the other
   variables.

able to take credit for the state's impressive economic growth during the
1980s. During the third quarter of 1990, sales of existing homes had risen 22
percent, the second fastest growth rate in the nation.[17] Recession, and the im-
minent anti-incumbency sentiment that followed, were at least a year away.

With the consensus reelection of Andrus, it is not surprising that the
traditional partisan cleavages do not appear in the aggregate-level figures
(table 8.2, above) and show up only weakly in the polling data (table 8.3).
Andrus won 68 percent of both the white and the minority vote. Party differences were not strong either: Andrus took 49 percent of the Republican vote
and 70 percent of the vote of independents. Even Mormons cast 57 percent of
their ballots for Andrus. This election shows that even typically reliable
coalition groups like the Mormons cannot always be depended upon to cast a
Republican ballot. Idahoans have conservative tastes in presidential elections,
but like voters in Oregon, Arizona, and Washington State, they are highly
discriminating. While all elections are potentially competitive, not all are
closely fought, since in Idaho individually popular Democrats have won consensus election victories while running independent of, and even against,
their national party.

National Divisions in the Idaho Electorate

I have argued on the basis of the weighted county-level figures that national coalitional patterns do not consistently emerge in Idaho politics and that this fact has inhibited party unity. Unfortunately, very little polling data are available from the usual archival sources on recent Idaho elections. General tendencies from the 1988 *ABC News/Washington Post* presidential exit poll can be noted in its undersized sample of 182 Idaho voters. Roughly 60 percent of the voters from labor union households voted for Dukakis. The union-nonunion cleavage is as well defined in Idaho's presidential politics as it is in eastern states, although a small percentage (less than 20 percent) of Idahoans live in labor union households.[18] The class cleavage dividing Bush voters from Dukakis voters is weak at best. The lowest income bracket that year was comprised of voters earning less than $12,000 per year. About 13 percent of Idaho voters fell in this category and they evenly divided their vote between the parties. Voters in all other income brackets cast overwhelmingly Republican ballots.

As for state elections, recent network exit polls expose Idaho's voting patterns. While no questions about labor union membership were asked, table 8.3 presents an analysis of the impact of income and race on the 1990 gubernatorial vote and the 1992 presidential contest. While both race and income had some significance in the race for governor, rising income *depressed* the Republican vote, while minority status *increased* it. In this instance, due to the poor performance of the Republican candidate, the usual New Deal cleavages were reversed in Idaho. Neither race nor class was important as divisions in the 1992 presidential contest.

Summary: Incongruent Party Politics and Candidate Responsiveness

In Idaho, not only do the statewide electoral bases of the presidential and gubernatorial parties appear dissimilar to those in older states, but they also differ among themselves. Due to a localism in the state's politics, national cleavages have been crosscut by the development of a fierce sectionalism centered only partly on economic interest. Idaho's sectional traditions have created a politics that unifies counties and precincts along lines that may not necessarily be economically rational.

Idaho elections are excellent examples of the competition *without* cohesion thesis—that a state can have competitive general elections without the presence of party organizations. Idaho is a weak-party state, where pressure groups sometimes decide the outcome of the election. Nevertheless, the absence of party organizations in this state has not necessarily impeded the development of a *responsible* system. Like California and the rest of the West, Idaho lacks organizations, but candidates can still be held responsible for their own programs and legislative record. Phil Batt's stiff challenge to the incumbent governor in 1982 was a programmatic challenge—calling up issues like the governor's unqualified support of labor.

To some extent, analysts' views of weak-partyism have been conditioned by Key's great book on southern politics. We often mistakenly think of all states with weak party organizations as noncompetitive and irresponsible. Responsiveness, however, depends primarily on the threat of retribution at the polls, not the presence of a certain party organizational form. Moreover, competition at the polls may or may not lead to party cohesion. In the West, the locus of competition is often different from that of the national parties. In response to the cross-pressures of state and national party systems, candidates go out on their own, creating their own coalitions. This every-person-for-himself tendency and the lopsided electoral margins it often produces are unrelated to whether a state's political system is responsive or responsible.

★

9

Competition and the Sources of Candidate-Centeredness in State Politics

OR YEARS, scholarship on political parties has been dominated by a particular view of the relationship between the electorate, party organization leaders, and political officeholders. This view holds that the "model" electoral party disciplines officeholders by using the instrument of electoral accountability provided by fierce interparty competition. In turn, this interparty competition provides the impetus for party elites to cooperate. Electoral competition is supposed to be a prerequisite for party unity. Candidates will be encouraged to band together into cohesive organized groupings when their electorate makes up a stable half of the two-party vote.

According to this established line of research, southern intraparty factionalism was explained away by the one-party system emerging from the Civil War. Western states were generally ignored as electorally inconsequential, or, alternatively, were accounted for by the progressive institutional reforms (that is, the direct primary, civil service systems) adopted early in the region. Of course, such explanations completely ignored how widespread these institutional reforms were and how little influence they had on political machines in so many eastern and midwestern states.[1]

The party competition explanation for party unity does not explain very much. Western states have often been two-party competitive.[2] Never has there been such a long history of one-party domination as in the South. Yet while there is steady competition in the West, there is none of the expected party unity. This does not mean that electoral behavior is completely unrelated to party organization strength. The electoral environment, and specifically the electoral cleavages defining partisanship, have much to do with the cohesion of party organizations. A history of independence from national party conflicts makes it harder for state and local parties to organize. When regional interests and ideologies differ from those at the national level, it is more difficult to mobilize voters around a slate of candidates that think and act alike. The party cannot encompass both local and national levels of thought and action when those levels of thought and action diverge sharply.

Chapter 1 suggested that in electoral settings where local and national cleavages differ it is difficult for a candidate to locate predictable pockets of electoral support. Cleavages differ because voters' partisanship is poorly defined. Faced with such voters, a candidate will be less likely to identify with other candidates or appeal to national party coalitions. Local elites often fare better by taking positions that are different from the positions taken by their national counterparts. The necessity of remaining independent of national party positions and platforms always threatens party cohesion in states where localism is strongest.

Gubernatorial primary divisiveness is one measure of state party cohesion. Primary divisiveness has risen in just about all states since the early 1960s. In the West, the legacy of primary divisiveness extends back as far as statehood. Crowded primaries are recent phenomena in the East and Midwest, but old-party states still show a stronger measure of control over their primaries than the states in the West (table 9.1).

Colorado and Utah, with the power to award convention endorsements, stand as exceptions to the generalization that western states are unable to control competition within their gubernatorial primaries. New Jersey, with its system of publicly supporting primary contenders, also has a recent history of fiercely contested primaries.

Party control over nominations has waned in older industrial states, as national and state party systems have grown further apart. Would-be party builders have been presented with challenges to unity that did not exist thirty years ago. The result is a rise in candidate-centered general elections and the power of incumbency. The patterns of party support and party strength found in the early 1980s in the four traditional-organization states suggest just such a drift from party cohesion. In Ohio and New York, the rightward movement of the national party left Republicans at the state level in disarray. Voters were confronted for the first time with choices between local and presidential politics. A conservative candidate, Ronald Reagan, had won widespread grassroots support, something Barry Goldwater was never able to do. Faced with the surge in popularity of conservative presidential candidates, moderate and liberal state party leaders had to decide whether to move with the national

Table 9.1   Index of Divisiveness in Gubernatorial Primaries, 1960–1992
(ranked lowest to highest)

Republican	Index	Democratic	Index
New York[a]	.04	**Colorado**[a]	.05
Rhode Island[a]	.07	Delaware[b]	.08
Delaware[b]	.07	Connecticut[a]	.09
Connecticut[a]	.13	Rhode Island[a]	.19
Colorado[a]	.26	Illinois	.21
Utah[a]	.29	**Utah**[a]	.23
Pennsylvania	.30	**Idaho**	.25
Illinois	.31	New York	.26
Montana	.36	Ohio	.40
Arizona	.38	**Wyoming**	.41
Oregon	.38	**Washington**	.41
Ohio	.40	**Arizona**	.42
Washington	.40	**Nevada**	.44
New Mexico	.42	**New Mexico**	.46
Idaho	.43	**Montana**	.47
California	.43	**Oregon**	.49
Nevada	.46	**California**	.50
Wyoming	.50	Pennsylvania	.51
New Jersey[c]	.50	New Jersey[c]	.57

Source: Author's calculations.

Note: Western states are in boldface. The formula for primary divisiveness is given by: $1 - \Sigma\, p_i^2$, where p_i is the proportion of the primary vote won by the ith candidate. For a demonstration of the use of this index in state legislative primaries, see David R. Mayhew, *Placing Parties in American Politics* (Princeton: Princeton University Press, 1986), Appendix A.

a. Convention states for part of the period.

b. Challenge primary state.

c. Public financing of gubernatorial primaries since 1981.

tide or chart their own course.[3] The intraparty disagreements over this choice inevitably resulted in the spread of independent candidacies and stronger primary competition.

The politics of Ohio, New York, Pennsylvania, and New Jersey are less and less connected to party organizations. Lew Lehrman's nearly successful gubernatorial candidacy in New York gave elites in old-party states a new sense of the possibility of success to be gained from moving outside party machinery. Candidates realized the powerlessness of traditional party machinery once a large bloc of voters abandoned established national party coalitions. In the West, voters have rarely relied upon party politicians to tell them how to vote. By contrast, in the old party states, candidates have only recently discovered their ability to run serious campaigns independent of party machinery.

In the West, party disunity arises from the electoral character of the region. There is no single major electoral interest behind each party in state elections for any length of time. In comparison to national political divisions in particular, in the West there is less class stratification, less racial polarization, less urbanization, and less union labor. V. O. Key was correct in writing that "the impact of national issues upon cleavages within state politics depends . . . on the socioeconomic composition of each state."[4] Furthermore, with a far-flung population, party organizations have been unable to dominate these states by concentrating their efforts in one or two metropolitan areas. Organizations must maintain a truly statewide focus—a difficult task when voters are geographically dispersed and their interests are as heterogeneous as California's.

The common element in the western states during the 1960s was the emphasis placed on candidate-managed, rather than party-sponsored grassroots mobilization efforts. Only New Mexico shows some semblance of old-fashioned party mobilization, although it occurs alongside highly personal electioneering. In Washington and Oregon, the dominant pattern is the high salience of issues relating to the environment, land-use planning, and growth control which do not divide electors in quite the same way they are divided along class lines. The Pacific Northwest leads a separate political existence from the rest of the country. In California, rapid population changes have made it difficult to maintain party regularity. California's even population distribution, spread among five major cities and two regions, has made it difficult to organize a geographically centralized party bureaucracy that could dominate in statewide politics. Finally, in Idaho, the population distribution is much like that of California. Candidates in western states must sift every county for votes, not rely on the concentrated effort of an urban organization. Given the sectional split in the state, and the absence of dominant national interests such as race relations and urban/rural conflict, candidates have substantial freedom to create heterodox coalitions.

Evidence from the 1990 gubernatorial elections serves to illustrate the point that the coalitions behind the parties in western states remain dissimilar to the national system. Table 9.2 shows the percentage of party support originating from each of several sociodemographic groups in 1990.[5] Nationally, minorities comprise about 4.5 percent of Republican party identifiers in off-year elections, while comprising about 11 percent of Republican identifiers in California, 10 percent in Arizona, and 17 percent in New Mexico. Nationally, only about 12 percent of Republicans reside in large cities (those with populations over 250,000). This compares to 20 percent for California, 52 percent for Arizona, and 27 percent in New Mexico.

Table 9.2 Party Support Provided by Selected Demographic Groups in Five Western States and Nationwide, 1990 (in percent)

	Republican	Independent	Democrat
United States			
Minority group	4.5	6.4	16.1
Union members	6.8	9.5	11.6
High income[a]	7.1	4.2	3.7
Low income[b]	8.4	9.8	15.6
Large city	12.4	16.2	20.4
Arizona			
Minority group	9.5	10.4	27.4
Union members	—	—	—
High income[a]	6.7	7.4	4.9
Low income[b]	6.2	11.1	17.6
Large city	51.5	61.6	57.1
California			
Minority group	10.5	15.8	37.1
Union members	9.0	9.8	16.5
High income[a]	15.4	9.4	8.1
Low income[b]	7.2	7.6	15.7
Large city	19.5	25.1	27.2
Idaho			
Minority group	2.1	3.3	5.4
Union members	—	—	—
High income[a]	4.7	1.5	0.7
Low income[b]	12.2	16.5	22.8
Large city	32.1	31.8	32.8
New Mexico			
Minority group	17.4	21.1	53.3
Union members	—	—	—
High income[a]	3.9	0.7	0.2
Low income[b]	14.8	19.9	26.5
Large city	27.1	26.5	29.8
Oregon			
Minority group	3.3	3.7	4.5
Union members	7.6	14.0	15.2
High income[a]	5.4	3.0	3.8
Low income[b]	9.6	11.4	16.6
Large city	27.6	28.2	35.7

Source: Voter Research and Surveys; *General Election Exit Polls: State and National Files*, 1990.

a. $100,000 and over.

b. Under $15,000.

States maintain their own unique political identities and react to national circumstances differently. When the national economy is performing poorly, pressure is exerted on the politics of many states, whether their economies are strong or not. That pressure, however, does not necessarily force states into some kind of national mold. Because the national economy is of universal concern—a valence rather than a position issue—it heightens the candidate-centeredness of elections. Rather than voting according to party, voters pay attention to who is in power, often casting ballots against the gubernatorial candidate of the president's party. In addition, when a national recession hits, states are not being governed by the same party or by the same people. Sometimes incumbent governors are hurt by a poor national economy (Pennsylvania's Thornburgh in 1982) while other times incumbents are helped (Arizona's Babbitt in 1982). In some places, economic hard times encourage candidates of the opposite party of the president to crowd primaries in hopes of winning the general election. Candidates who are of the president's party may face primary challenges from insurgent factions when the economy sours. Alternatively, candidates from the president's party may flee from the contest, leaving the seat to the opposition in a lopsided, candidate-focused race. So the effect of a poor national economy on state elections is far from uniform, and the presence of this issue in state races does not suggest that state politics is being nationalized. Furthermore, national economic conditions are not of concern in every election. This leaves considerable room for local politics to take over in years when the national economy is not an issue. In some states, like those of the Pacific Northwest, localism asserts itself quite strongly despite national economic forces.

Undoubtedly, there are influences on candidate-centered, weak-party politics besides incongruent electoral cleavages. I have just argued that the condition of the national economy focuses attention on candidates rather than parties. Institutions obviously play a role too: direct primaries, open or blanket primaries, the elimination of patronage, public financing of primaries, and other institutional reforms. So, too, the emergence of national network media as sources of political information has lessened the demand for local party cues. In various quarters of political science, these have all served as partial explanations for party disunity. In this analysis, the fundamental explanation for unified parties in state politics rests in political behavior and the calculations that prospective candidates make when deciding whether to run with party organizations or to run independently. The dependent variable—party unity (the extent to which candidates rely upon each other and upon party machinery)—has been described through a variety of sources designed to add depth and texture to the analysis. The independent variable has been described through a state-by-state analysis of cleavages between distinct, politically relevant groups. In establishing an association between incongruent cleavages and candidate-centeredness, I have presented the case that predictable electoral divisions greatly ease elite cooperation, lowering the cost of mobilizing voters behind party nominees.

Returning to the original question, state party systems can operate as independent and autonomous political entities. If the institutions of state and national government were to encourage it, the West would develop the strongest third-party systems. As it stands, the two political parties at the state level are not always merely shadows of their national counterparts. Moreover, these autonomous party systems have not produced unified party organizations. Yet party politics without party organizations is not necessarily irresponsible. Voters can, and do, hold candidates responsible for their performance, as they did in nearly recalling Governor Evan Mechem in Arizona in 1987. There is a great Madisonian irony to the politics in competitive weak-party states. Where political partisanship and behavior is the least predictable, institutional structures maintaining the two-party system are the most powerful. Some state electorates would sustain their commitment to national party issues and a two-party system even without single-member, winner-take-all districts and Australian ballots. Elsewhere, though, in states where national and state cleavages are askew, political resemblance to the national scene is maintained only by confining thousands of would-be third-party voters to a choice of two candidates for office running under national party labels.

As for the rest of the country, there are signs that state and local politics are increasingly separable from the trends of national politics, even in states with a history of party unity. Partisan identifiers more frequently split the ballot now than thirty years ago, and this suggests a reduced role for party in studies of state voting behavior.[6] Incumbency and the personal appeal of candidates to voters are increasing trends almost everywhere. There are few state parties that can depend upon the issue cleavages of national politics to mobilize a local electorate in an off-year race. In this sense, campaign activity is strongly influenced by electoral characteristics and movements. The candidate-centered systems of western state politics now provide a paradigm for understanding the changes coming to parties, nomination contests, and voting in other parts of the nation. As in the West, issues and incumbency will become even more important determinants of state elections elsewhere. Which issues will be salient is likely to be decided by local conditions and the independent sensibilities of the candidates themselves.

APPENDIX
NOTES
BIBLIOGRAPHY
INDEX

Appendix A

Table A.1 T-test of Difference in Means Between Presidential Voting and Voting for U.S. House, Governor, and U.S. Senate, 1928–1950[a]

	U.S. House		Governor		U.S. Senate	
	Mean	T	Mean	T	Mean	T
Illinois	−1.71	1.16	−.42	.37	.58	.23
Pennsylvania	−3.18	2.36**	−3.95	1.86*	−3.49	2.20*
New Jersey	−3.99	3.19**	−2.13	1.25	−2.74	1.71
Ohio	−1.88	.90	.90	.33	−1.39	.53
New York	−.27	.26	−2.29	1.01	−.08	.08
Connecticut	−1.13	1.37	−.14	.14	−1.70	1.52
Delaware	−2.65	1.31	1.18	.88	1.33	.75
Rhode Island	−1.54	1.22	−1.61	1.24	−1.65	2.27*
Nevada	−1.84	1.05	−2.80	1.14		.50
California[b]	−6.40	−3.35**	−14.20	5.22**		3.61*
New Mexico	.98	.53	−3.39	1.68		−.27
Colorado	.45	.28	2.93	.75		1.23
Arizona	11.98	2.76**	2.37	1.05		5.50*
Idaho	−3.97	3.39**	−3.45	1.13		3.40*
Oregon	−10.35	3.56**	−5.08	.76		2.86*
Washington	−5.07	3.52**	−1.77	.84		−.10
Montana	−2.38	.99	−6.08	1.69		.61
Wyoming	−3.53	1.89*	−2.01	.69		.92
Utah	−3.30	1.95*	−3.33	1.33		1.53

**p > .05 *p < .10

Source: Richard M. Scammon and Alice McGillivray, eds., *America Votes* (Washington, D.C.: Elections Research Center, various years), and author's calculations.

Note: Negative signs indicate offices that are more Republican than presidential contests for this time period. Significance tests are 2-tailed.

a. Values reported are average differences and t-statistics on the differences between presidential-gubernatorial, presidential-U.S. House and presidential-U.S. Senate voting.

b. California's near-unanimous victories by Earl Warren (1946 governorship) and Hiram Johnson (1934 U.S. Senate) have been eliminated from these calculations due to their cross-filed candidacies.

Table A.2   Summary of Regression Analyses: 1960–1962 Republican Presidential and
Gubernatorial Vote, by County[a]

	Constant	% Urban	Minority	Income	% Mfg.	Adj. R²	N
ARIZONA							
President, 1960	13.5	−.08	.13	6.39	.99	.44	14
Governor, 1962	−25.8	−.35	.27	16.89	.89	.15	14
CALIFORNIA							
President, 1960	64.2	.18*	−1.09*	−2.96*	−.05*	.52	58
Governor, 1962	61.5	.23*	−1.16*	−3.91*	.06	.48	58
OREGON							
President, 1960	58.8	−.06	−.82*	1.56	−.46*	.31	36
Governor, 1962	55.3	−.12*	−.14	2.85	−.45*	.35	36
WASHINGTON							
President, 1960	36.8	.12	−.52*	.60	.59*	.49	39
Governor, 1960	38.6	.11*	−.59*	.40	.50*	.41	39
COLORADO							
President, 1960	57.6	−.06	−1.08*	1.35	−.09	.32	63
Governor, 1962	47.0	−.04	−.81*	3.69*	−.58*	.36	63
IDAHO							
President, 1960	82.5	.13*	−1.62*	−5.08*	−.46*	.29	44
Governor, 1962	52.9	.14*	.93	−.92	−.12	.07	44
NEW MEXICO							
President, 1960	45.1	.10	−.04	−.10	−.17	.01	32
Governor, 1962	44.7	.04	−.11	−.23	.31	.00	32
MONTANA							
President, 1960	38.6	−.09	−.30	3.93	−.34*	.12	56
Governor, 1960	36.4	−.07	−.29*	5.00*	−.42*	.17	56
WYOMING							
President, 1960	44.4	−.20	−.30	4.29	−.41	.04	23
Governor, 1962	26.6	−.26*	−.50	8.55	−.93	.16	23
UTAH							
President, 1960	69.3	−.05	.31	−3.06	.45	.08	29
Governor, 1960	26.9	−.05	.26	3.38	.60*	.03	29
Mean slope P		−.007	−.53	.69	.01		
Mean slope G		−.013	−.21	3.57	−.01		
PENNSYLVANIA							
President, 1960	43.2	−.31*	−.50*	6.64*	−.18	.72	67
Governor, 1962	44.9	−.16*	−.46*	6.18*	−.29*	.72	67
NEW YORK							
President, 1960	39.3	−.48*	−.007	7.00*	.02	.87	62
Governor, 1962	42.2	−.43*	.07	8.00*	−.15	.82	62
OHIO							
President, 1960	72.2	−.07	−.96*	.20	−.23*	.56	88
Governor, 1962	70.0	−.15*	−.06	.70	−.11*	.35	88
NEW JERSEY							
President, 1960	49.9	−.26*	−.37	6.39*	−.37*	.73	21
Governor, 1961	39.6	−.15	−.20	6.64*	−.62*	.63	21
ILLINOIS							
President, 1960	49.5	−.12*	−.94*	4.42*	−.30*	.80	102
Governor, 1960	50.3	−.12*	−.58*	2.62*	−.25*	.76	102
Mean slope P		−.25	−.55	4.93	−.21		
Mean slope G		−.20	−.25	4.83	−.28		
*p < .05							

Sources: Bureau of the Census, *County and City Databook* (Washington, D.C.: GPO, various years); Richard M. Scammon and
  Alice McGillivray, eds., *America Votes* (Washington, D.C.: Elections Research Center, various years).
Note: Multiple linear regression, WLS estimation; unstandardized regression coefficients weighted for population; income
  expressed in thousands of constant 1992 dollars.
  a. Connecticut, Rhode Island, and Delaware have been deleted from this analysis because these states have so few counties.

Table A.3   Summary of Regression Analyses: 1980–1982 Republican Presidential and Gubernatorial Vote, by County

	Constant	% Urban	Minority	Income	% Mfg.	Adj. R²	N
ARIZONA							
President, 1980	85.9	−.05	−.09	−1.33	1.65*	.23	14
Governor, 1982	53.3	.02	−.07	−1.26	1.41*	.35	14
CALIFORNIA							
President, 1980	72.9	.20*	−.78*	−1.22*	.28*	.43	58
Governor, 1982	72.8	.11	−.69*	−.94*	.13	.49	58
OREGON							
President, 1980	65.6	−.17*	−.30	−.34	.14	.37	36
Governor, 1982	47.6	−.19*	.36	1.22*	.03	.21	36
WASHINGTON							
President, 1980	73.4	−.004	−.09	−.60	−.47*	.38	39
Governor, 1980	62.0	.007	−.04	.004	−.39*	.21	39
COLORADO							
President, 1980	73.3	.06	−.98*	−.25	−.61	.49	66
Governor, 1982	54.7	.01	−.65*	−.62*	−.39*	.37	66
IDAHO							
President, 1980	90.9	.06	.36	−1.44	−.23	.03	44
Governor, 1982	87.7	.09	−.26	−2.17*	−.25	.07	44
NEW MEXICO							
President, 1980	52.0	−.02	−.01	.19	.30	.12	32
Governor, 1982	30.0	.21	.08	−.18	.55	.10	32
MONTANA							
President, 1980	62.2	−.17*	−.23*	.39	−.31	.39	56
Governor, 1980	58.8	−.05	−.18*	−.64	.15	.16	56
WYOMING							
President, 1980	64.4	−.26*	−.15	.55	.77	.49	23
Governor, 1982	23.3	−.15*	−.74	1.10	.85	.36	23
UTAH							
President, 1980	113.8	−.001	−.17	−2.30*	.36	.32	29
Governor, 1980	69.4	−.03	.07	−1.52*	.47	.22	29
Mean slope P		−.04	−.24	−.64	.19		
Mean slope G		.003	−.21	−.50	.26		
PENNSYLVANIA							
President, 1980	42.2	−.13*	−.24*	1.07*	.05	.58	66
Governor, 1982	17.7	−.10*	−.10	2.57*	−.09	.62	66
NEW YORK							
President, 1980	48.9	−.04	−.33*	.70*	−.29*	.74	62
Governor, 1982	57.0	−.18*	−.49*	.40*	.26*	.93	62
OHIO							
President, 1980	58.6	−.06	−.44*	.40	−.19	.33	88
Governor, 1982	61.5	−.06	−.55*	.10	−.48*	.28	88
NEW JERSEY							
President, 1980	61.8	−.05	−.44*	.13	−.08	.74	21
Governor, 1981	42.1	−.27*	−.10	1.54*	−.12	.48	21
ILLINOIS							
President, 1980	50.7	.00001	−.71*	.59*	−.04	.88	102
Governor, 1982	32.0	−.00004	−.67*	1.54*	−.18	.82	102
Mean slope P		−.06	−.43	.578	−.11		
Mean slope G		−.12	−.38	1.23	−.12		
*p < .05							

Sources: Bureau of the Census, *County and City Databook* (Washington, D.C.: GPO, various years); Richard M. Scammon and Alice McGillivray, eds., *America Votes* (Washington, D.C.: Elections Research Center, various years).

Note: Multiple linear regression, WLS estimation; unstandardized regression coefficients weighted for population; income expressed in thousands of constant 1992 dollars.

Table A.4 Differences Between Strong-Party and Weak-Party States in the Extent of Split-Ticket Voting for State and Local Offices
(in percent)

	Competitive Strong-Party States (East)	Competitive Weak-Party States (West)	Noncompetitive Weak-Party States (South)
1952–1958			
Split	25.0	41.6	17.3
Straight	75.0	58.4	82.7
1960–1968			
Split	40.4	53.7	31.9
Straight	59.6	46.3	68.1
1970–1978			
Split	57.1	66.4	49.7
Straight	42.9	33.6	50.3
1980–1992			
Split	54.5	61.9	47.7
Straight	45.5	38.1	52.3

Source: ICPSR, *National Election Studies Cumulative Datafile,* 1952–1992.
Note: N = 10,331.

Table A.5 Logit Analysis of the Influence of Race, Income, and Union Membership on
Presidential Elections from 1952 to 1992

	Constant	Race	Income	Labor	No. of Cases	Predicted Null (%)
President, 1980	3.34	−2.71*	.30*	−.80*	790	65.3
Effect		(.38)	(.08)	(.18)		58.2
		−52.2	10.8	−19.8		
President, 1984	2.44	−2.04*	.45*	−1.03*	1,246	67.7
Effect		(.24)	(.06)	(.15)		56.3
		−44.4	5.2	−24.9		
Presudent, 1988	2.98	−2.48*	.22*	−.67*	1,099	64.5
Effect		(.28)	(.06)	(.16)		52.9
		−48.0	2.5	−16.0		
President, 1992	1.15	−1.65*	.30*	−.52*	1,243	63.2
Effect		(.23)	(.06)	(.16)		58.4
		−31.0	6.1	−11.7		
President, 1952–1992	2.60	−2.07*	.20*	−.71*	12,333	62.9
Effect		(.10)	(.02)	(.05)		53.2
		−42.1	4.9	−17.4		

*p < .05

Source: ICPSR, *National Election Studies Cumulative Datafile,* 1952–1992.
Note: Dependent variable: 0 = Democrat, 1 = Republican; MLE coefficients; standard errors in parentheses;
  *p < .05; Effect = change in odds of voting Republican from moving x one unit at the means of the other
  variables.
  a. Values reported are average differences and t-statistics on the differences between presidential-gubernatorial,
  presidential-U.S. House and presidential-U.S. Senate voting.
  b. Connecticut, Rhode Island, and Delaware have been deleted from this analysis because these states have so
  few counties.

Notes

Chapter 1. National Elections and the Autonomy of American State Party Systems

1. Edward W. Chester, *Issues and Responses in State Political Experience* (Totowa, N.J.: Littlefield, Adams, 1968), 154.

2. Robert S. Erikson, Gerald C. Wright, and John P. McIver, *Statehouse Democracy* (New York: Cambridge University Press, 1993), 209.

3. Malcolm Jewell and David M. Olson, *Political Parties and Elections in American States*, 3rd ed. (Chicago: Dorsey Press, 1988), 256–60. Frank Sorauf, *Party Politics in America*, 5th ed. (Boston: Little, Brown, 1984), 198–203.

4. "Electoral incongruence": others have used a similar term in describing the juxtaposition and/or conflict of political environments. See Thad Brown, *Migration and Politics* (Chapel Hill: University of North Carolina Press, 1988), 125; "Voting allegiances": Paul Kleppner, *The Cross of Culture* (New York: Free Press, 1970), 36, 101.

5. David R. Mayhew, *Placing Parties in American Politics* (Princeton, N.J.: Princeton University Press, 1986); Kenneth N. Owens, "Pattern and Structure in Western Territorial Politics," *Western Historical Quarterly* 1, no. 4 (Oct. 1970): 373–92. Paul Kleppner, "Voters and Parties in the Western States: 1876–1900," *Western Historical Quarterly* 13, no. 1 (Jan. 1982): 49–68; Walter C. Woodward, *Political Parties in Oregon, 1843–1868* (Portland, Oreg.: J. K. Gill, 1913); Robert W. Johannsen, "National Issues and Local Politics in Washington Territory, 1857–1861," *Pacific Northwest Quarterly* 42, no. 1 (Jan. 1951): 3–31; Howard R. Lamar, *The Far Southwest, 1846–1912: A Territorial History* (New Haven, Conn.: Yale University Press, 1966); Paul Kleppner, *The Cross of Culture* (New York: Free Press, 1970).

6. Xandra Kayden, "Party Structure in Massachusetts," in *New England Political Parties*, ed. Josephine Milburn and William Doyle (Cambridge, Mass.: Schenkman, 1983), 97–114 (also see other essays in this volume); John Kenneth White, "New York's Selective Majority," in *Party Realignment and State Politics*, ed. Maureen Moakley (Columbus: Ohio State University Press, 1992), 210–24.

7. "Prerequisites for political party organizations": Mayhew, *Placing Parties in American Politics*; "reliability of electorates": Sorauf, *Party Politics in America*, 131.

8. This reasoning is based on Chester Barnard's classic statement of the basis for formal organization, *The Functions of the Executive* (Cambridge, Mass.: Harvard University Press, 1938), 82–92.

9. V. O. Key, Jr., *Parties, Politics, and Pressure Groups* (New York: Thomas Crowell, 1956), 307–15.

10. V. O. Key, Jr., *American State Politics: An Introduction* (New York: Alfred A. Knopf, 1956), 217–54.

11. Duane Lockard, *The Politics of State and Local Government*, 2nd ed. (New York: Macmillan, 1969), 165.

12. This is the principal idea behind James L. Sundquist's two-stage theory in *Dynamics of the Party System* (Washington, D.C.: Brookings, 1983), chap. 11; "Voter feels psychological pressure," 228–29.

13. John R. Petrocik, *Party Coalitions: Realignments and the Decline of the New Deal Party System* (Chicago: University of Chicago Press, 1981); Paul Allen Beck, "Partisan Dealignment in the Postwar South," *American Political Science Review* 71 (1977): 477–96; Martin P. Wattenberg, "The Decline of Political Partisanship in the United States: Negativity or Neutrality," *American Political Science Review* 75 (1981): 941–50; Everett Carll Ladd, Jr., and Charles Hadley, *Transformations of the American Party System* (New York: W. W. Norton, 1975).

14. Petrocik, *Party Coalitions*, 16–17. Everett Carll Ladd, "Like Waiting for Godot," in *The End of Realignment?* ed. Byron E. Shafer (Madison: University of Wisconsin Press, 1991), 24–36.

15. The South put up the most stubborn resistance to the New Deal realignment but even southerners eventually converted. See Sundquist, *Dynamics of the Party System*, chaps. 11–12, 261.

16. Joseph Schlesinger, "On the Theory of Party Organization," *Journal of Politics* 46 (1984): 369–97; Sorauf, *Party Politics in America*, esp. chaps. 3–4; Mayhew, *Placing Parties in American Politics*.

17. Mayhew, *Placing Parties in American Politics*.

18. V. O. Key, *Southern Politics in State and Nation* (New York: Alfred A Knopf, 1949), 308; Sarah McCally Morehouse, *State Politics, Parties and Policy* (New York: Holt, Rinehart & Winston, 1981), chap. 2.

19. According to Grant McConnell, "a one-party politics is a no-party politics." See *Private Power and American Democracy* (New York: Alfred A. Knopf, 1966), chap. 6, 175.

20. Morehouse, *State Politics, Parties and Policy*, chaps. 2, 4, 45–94, 143–201.

21. Ibid.

22. Key, *Politics, Parties, and Pressure Groups*, 326.

23. For party competition indices, see Jewell and Olson, *Political Parties*, 26–27. For an earlier period, see Frank Munger, *American State Politics* (New York: Thomas Y. Crowell, 1966), 373–81.

24. "Party weakness in North direct result of progressive institutions": Key, *American State Politics*, chap. 6; "Use of primary and adoption of civil service reform": Key himself later recognized the inadequacy of the direct primary explanation in *Politics, Parties, and Pressure Groups*, chap. 14, 420; Daryl Fair, "Party Strength and Political Patronage," *Southwestern Social Science Quarterly* 45 (Dec. 1964): 264–71.

25. Paul Kleppner, "Politics Without Parties," in *The Twentieth-Century West: Historical Interpretations*, ed. Gerald D. Nash and Richard W. Etulain (Albuquerque: University of New Mexico Press, 1989), 295–338.

26. "Weaker commitments": Brown, *Migration and Politics*, 13; "New voters lack established patterns of behavior": Samuel P. Huntington, "Political Development and Political Decay," *World Politics* 27 (1965): 386–430; Courtney Brown, "Voter Mobilization and Party Competition in a Volatile Electorate," *American Sociological Review* 52 (1987): 59–72; Brown, *Migration and Politics*.

27. In 1960, for example, the distance between New York's poorest and wealthiest county was $4,004 (median family income), approximately twice that of the distance between Oregon's wealthiest and poorest county. By 1980, there was some convergence, but still a notable difference. Oregon's wealthiest county was separated from its poorest one by $11,000 (median family income). New York counties remained more stratified, with $15,000 separating the wealthiest from poorest areas.

28. Jerry Medler and Alvin Mushkatel, "Urban-Rural Class Conflict in Oregon Land-Use Planning," *Western Political Quarterly* 31, no. 3 (Sept. 1979): 338–49.

Chapter 2. The Variants of Two–Party Competition

1. Following Mayhew's scheme in *Placing Parties in American Politics*, I classify the following as cohesive, strong organization states: New York, Connecticut, New Jersey, Rhode Island, Delaware, Ohio, Pennsylvania, and Illinois. The nonorganization states are Montana, Wyoming, Oregon,

Washington, California, Nevada, Idaho, Utah, Colorado, New Mexico, and Arizona. Alaska and Hawaii also fit this latter category but are excluded from the analysis because of the brevity of their electoral history.

2. This time period was selected for three reasons: (1) much of the third–party activity associated with Populism and Progressivism had died out by 1914 and the two major parties were here to stay; (2) several of the western states that are subjects of this comparison were admitted to the Union early in the twentieth or shortly before (Arizona and New Mexico in 1912, Idaho in 1890, Utah in 1896, Wyoming in 1890, and Montana in 1889); and (3) the Senate was not universally elected by popular vote until 1914 following ratification of the Seventeenth Amendment.

3. Coefficient of variation = (standard deviation/Mean)*100.

4. When analyzing the total vote, a competitive election is defined here as one in which one of the two parties wins 45–55 percent of the total vote. When analyzing the two-party vote, a competitive election is one where one of the two parties falls within 47.5–52.5 percent of the vote.

5. David W. Brady, "A Reevaluation of Realignments in American Politics: Evidence from the House of Representatives," *American Political Science Review* 79 (Mar. 1985): 28–49.

6. The electoral returns have been paired by year. For example, a state's Republican percentage of the 1980 U.S. House vote is subtracted from that state's Republican percentage of the 1980 presidential vote. Election returns for off-year U.S. House, Senate, and gubernatorial races, have been subtracted from the previous presidential race. Also, the 1982 Republican percentage of a state's gubernatorial vote is subtracted from the 1980 Republican presidential election returns. These differences are then averaged and compared with the standard t-statistic. In constructing the comparisons in this manner, I intended to capture a state's off-year deviation from presidential patterns in addition to its deviation in on-years. This procedure also provided a larger number of cases to compare for purposes of constructing tables 2.4, and A.1. Special attention should be paid to the figures for Arizona, Illinois, Utah, Montana, and Washington which had on-year gubernatorial elections for all or part of this period.

7. Key, *American State Politics*, 33.

8. Eric R.A.N. Smith and Peverill Squire, "State and National Politics in the Mountain West," in *The Politics of Realignment: Party Change in the Mountain West*, ed. Peter F. Galderisi et al. (Boulder: Westview Press, 1987), 33–54.

9. Walter Dean Burnham, *Critical Elections and the Mainsprings of American Politics* (New York: W. W. Norton, 1970).

10. V. O. Key, *The Responsible Electorate* (Cambridge, Mass.: Harvard University Press, 1966), 1–28. Burnham, *Critical Elections*, chap. 5.

11. Paul Kleppner, "Politics Without Parties."

12. Burnham, *Critical Elections and the Mainsprings of American Politics* (New York: W. W. Norton, 1970), 135–74.

13. Burnham, *Critical Elections*; one interpretive hazard with county-level data is that in two western states, Arizona and Nevada, one or two counties contain vast percentages of the state's overall population. Much of the variation in the state's political behavior is obscured by the figures for a single, large county. For this reason, it will be important to analyze available individual-level data in coming chapters.

14. Duane Lockard emphasizes the importance of substate regionalism in the party politics of several New England states in *New England State Politics* (Princeton: Princeton University Press, 1959). Paul Kleppner specifically addresses the sources of western exceptionalism in "Politics Without Parties"; John Fenton emphasizes the role of urban-rural conflict in the midwestern states in *Midwest Politics* (New York: Holt, Rinehart & Winston, 1966).

15. Robert Axelrod describes the constituencies of both parties in the post-New Deal period in "Where the Votes Come From: An Analysis of Electoral Coalitions, 1952–1968," *American Political Science Review* 66 (Mar. 1972): 11–20; Ladd and Hadley, *Transformations of the American Party System;* Sundquist, *Dynamics of the Party System.*

16. These election years were selected because of their proximity to accurate census measures for counties. Elections occurring midway between decennial censuses are not likely to be estimated as precisely with data gathered in 1960 or 1980.

17. The other figures for unionization in 1982 are 18 percent in Colorado, 21.7 percent in Montana, 27.5 percent in Oregon, 15.6 percent in Wyoming, 22.1 percent in Nevada, and 16.1 percent in Idaho.

18. Mayhew, *Placing Parties in American Politics.*

Introduction to Part II

1. Sorauf, *Party Politics in America;* Jewell and Olson, *Political Parties;* Key, *American State Politics;* Key, *Politics, Parties, and Pressure Groups.*

2. In describing the importance of the electoral incentive for members of Congress, David Mayhew writes, winning "has to be the *proximate* goal of everyone, the goal that must be achieved over and over if other ends are to be entertained" *Congress: The Electoral Connection* (New Haven, Conn.: Yale University Press, 1974), 16.

3. Sorauf, *Party Politics in America.*

4. Key points out (*Southern Politics in State and Nation,* 498–500) that in the South separate offices had distinct electoral foundations. More people voted for governor than for senator and U.S. House. See also Jeffrey Stonecash, "Political Cleavage in Gubernatorial and Legislative Elections: Party Competition in New York, 1970–1982," *Western Political Quarterly* 42, no. 1 (Mar. 1989): 69–81.

5. Several smaller states (Delaware, Rhode Island, Connecticut) also fit in this category, but with so few counties, ecological analysis of voting cleavages in these states is impossible.

6. To restate a point made in chapter 2, the goal of the data analysis is to present an approximate picture of cleavages and the distance between groups with distinct politically relevant traits. The goal is not to predict the vote precisely. The logistic regression analysis and the ecological data analysis are designed only to give a reduced form approximation of how these communities divide.

7. John Kingdon, "Politicians' Beliefs About Voters," *American Political Science Review* 61, no.1 (Mar. 1967): 137–45.

8. Thomas Mann and Norman Ornstein, eds. *The American Election of 1982* (Washington, D.C.: American Enterprise Institute, 1983).

9. Mayhew notes that the traditional party states of the Northeast and Midwest are largely devoid of demagoguery. *Placing Parties in American Politics,* 248–53.

Chapter 3. The Once Firm Foundation: New York and New Jersey

1. Michael Barone and Grant Ujifusa, *The Almanac of American Politics, 1988* (Washington, D.C.: National Journal, 1988), 782–83.

2. Interview with Congressman Ray McGrath, July 29, 1992.

3. Interview with Congressman George Hochbrueckner, July 29, 1992.

4. Donald Bogue and Calvin Beale, *Economic Areas of the United States* (Glencoe, Ill.: Free Press, 1961), 882–83. By 1980, New York City's manufacturing sector employed 17 percent of its work force, compared to 25 percent in 1960.

5. Key, *Politics, Parties, and Pressure Groups,* 326; Howard A. Scarrow, *Parties, Elections and Representation in the State of New York* (New York: New York University Press, 1983), 20.

6. Stonecash, "Political Cleavage," 69–84.

7. Interview with Congressman John LaFalce, July 29, 1992; Jeffrey Stonecash, "Observations from New York: The Limits of 50-State Studies and the Case for Case Studies," *Comparative State Politics* 12, no. 4 (August 1991): 1–9.

8. My discussion of New York state party organizations draws from Stuart Witt, "The Legislative-Local Party Linkage in New York State," Ph.D. diss., Syracuse University, 1967. Chapter 3 is especially pertinent. I also draw from Scarrow, *Parties, Elections and Representation*.

9. Scarrow, *Parties, Elections and Representation*, 23–25.

10. Interview with Congressman Ray McGrath (R-N.Y., 5th), July 29, 1992.

11. Interview with Congressman George Hochbrueckner (D-N.Y., 1st), July 29, 1992.

12. Witt, "Party Linkage in New York State," 52.

13. Interview with Congressman Sherwood Boehlert (R-N.Y., 25th), June 24, 1992; Witt, "Party Linkage in New York State," 72.

14. Robert H. Connery and Gerald Benjamin, *Rockefeller of New York* (Ithaca, N.Y.: Cornell University Press, 1979), 44.

15. Peter D. McClelland and Alan Magdovitz, *Crisis in the Making* (Cambridge: Cambridge University Press, 1981), 209.

16. "Ethnic and racial cleavage": White, "New York's Selective Majority"; Frank J. Munger, "New York," in *Explaining the Vote: Presidential Choices in the Nation and the States, 1968* ed. David Kovenock et al. (Chapel Hill: Institute for Research in the Social Sciences, University of North Carolina, 1973); Robert H. Connery and Gerald Benjamin, *Rockefeller of New York* (Ithaca, N.Y.: Cornell University Press, 1979); "voting weakly determined by class status," Malcolm Jewell, *Parties and Primaries* (New York: Praeger, 1984), 113–14.

17. "Gubernatorial voting decisions": John E. Chubb, "Institutions, the Economy and the Dynamics of State Elections," *American Political Science Review* 82, no. 1 (Mar. 1988): 133–51; Dennis M. Simon, "Presidents, Governors and Electoral Accountability," *Journal of Politics* 51, no. 2 (May 1989): 286–304; "the 1982 election in New York": on the difference between position and valence issues, see Donald Stokes, "Spatial Models of Party Competition," in *Elections and the Political Order*, ed. Angus Campbell et al. (New York: John Wiley, 1966), 161–79.

18. *CBS News/New York Times Election Day Surveys*, 1982; For details of the race, I rely on the *New York Times, Rochester Democrat and Chronicle*, and *Buffalo News*.

19. From the first debate between Lehrman and Cuomo, as quoted in "Lew's Labors Lost," *New Republic* 187, no. 18 (Nov. 8, 1982), 11–12.

20. "London and Rinfret in a Dead Heat": *New York Times*, Nov. 5, 1990, 1; "London's challenge": *New York Times*, Nov. 4, 1990.

21. James A. Reidel, "New York: Costly, Close Governor's Race," *Comparative State Politics Newsletter* 3, no. 6 (Dec. 1982): 8–9.

22. Class is measured by income on a five-point scale. Race is coded 0 for white, 1 for nonwhite. Unionization is coded 0 for nonunion household, 1 for labor union member in household. Urbanization is not included in the individual-level analysis for three reasons: (1) while it makes good theoretical sense in ecological regressions, it is not clear that urbanization is theoretically relevant as an *individual-level* influence on voting; (2) questions designed to elicit the voter's description of his or her current living environment are often missing from exit polls; and (3) questions designed to elicit the voter's description of where they grew up are uniformly absent from exit polls. Modeling the state's cleavages with this reduced-form model also permits me to compare the results with similar national figures in appendix table A.5.; For comparison to a *national* model of race, class, and labor-nonlabor cleavages, see appendix table A.5, which is the same model appearing in table 3.2 (and

similar subsequent tables for other states) applied to the pooled American National Election Study presidential election surveys from 1960 to 1992.

23. Mayhew, *Placing Parties in American Politics,* 35–37.

24. *CBS News/New York Times Election Day Surveys,* 1982.

25. Mayhew, *Placing Parties in American Politics,* 34.

26. White, "New York's Selective Majority," 221.

27. Interview with Congressman William Hughes (D-N.J., 2nd), July 22, 1992.

28. Maureen Moakley, "Political Parties," in *The Political State of New Jersey,* ed. Gerald Pomper (New Brunswick, N.J.: Rutgers University Press, 1986), 45–65.

29. Congressman William Hughes (D-N.J., 2nd) in an interview, July 22, 1992, reported that in his district the strongest Democratic organization was in Gloucester County, corresponding to the presence of blue-collar workers.

30. Gerald Pomper, "Electoral Trends," in *Politics in New Jersey,* ed. Alan Rosenthal and John Blydenburgh (New Brunswick, N. J.: Rutgers University Press, 1975), 31–58.

31. Blydenburgh, "Party Organizations," in *Politics in New Jersey,* ed. Rosenthal and Blydenburgh, 130–32.

32. I rely on journalistic accounts from the *New York Times, Newark Star-Ledger,* and the *Trenton Times.*

33. *New York Times,* Oct. 18, 1961, 24.

34. *New York Times,* Oct. 28, 1961, 4.

35. Moakley, "Political Parties, 49.

36. Blydenburgh, "Party Organizations."

37. For accounts of the race, I rely on the *New York Times,* various issues and dates in 1981.

38. "Legacy of Kean": *New York Times,* Nov. 8, 1989, B9; "Courter message of continued deregulation": *Philadelphia Inquirer* and *New York Times,* various dates in 1989.

39. On the causes of gubernatorial primary divisiveness, see William D. Berry and Bradley C. Canon, "Explaining the Competitiveness of Gubernatorial Primaries," *Journal of Politics* 55, no. 2 (May 1993), 454–71.

Chapter 4. Deindustrialization and the Erosion of Party Unity:
Ohio and Pennsylvania

1. Interview with Congressman Louis Stokes (D-Ohio, 21st), Sept. 15, 1992.

2. Interview with Congressman Mike Oxley (R-Ohio, 4th), Aug. 5, 1992.

3. Interview with Senator Howard Metzenbaum (D-Ohio), July 22, 1992.

4. "Celebreeze Wasn't Cleveland Enough": Cleveland *Plain-Dealer,* Nov. 7, 1990, 11, 5c; "prolabor features of New Deal": Fenton, *Midwest Politics,* 130.

5. "Democratic party's base in Ohio": Robert Axelrod, "Where the Votes Come From: An Analysis of Electoral Coalitions," *American Political Science Review* 66, no. 2 (June 1972): 11–20; "Republican tradition": Fenton, *Midwest Politics.*

6. Fenton, *Midwest Politics,* 125.

7. "Available evidence from Mayhew's survey": Mayhew, *Placing Parties in American Politics;* "Cincinnati's reform government": Fenton, *Midwest Politics,* 135–37.

8. Fenton, *Midwest Politics,* 151.

9. Interview with Congressman Mike Oxley (R-Ohio, 4th), Aug. 5, 1992.

10. Interview with Senator Howard Metzenbaum (D-Ohio), July 22, 1992.

11. *Columbus Dispatch,* Nov. 3, 1962, 8.

12. Ibid.

13. Theodore Eismeier, "Votes and Taxes: The Political Economy of the American Governorship," *Polity* 15, no. 3 (Spring 1983): 368–79.

14. Chubb, "Institutions, the Economy, and the Dynamics of State Elections."

15. Cleveland *Plain-Dealer*, Nov. 2, 1990, 12a.

16. Interview with Congressman Bob Borski (D-Pa., 3rd), June 24, 1992.

17. Interview with Congressman Robert Walker (R-Pa., 16th), Aug. 5, 1992.

18. Interview with Congressman Bob Borski (D-Pa., 3rd.), June 24, 1992.

19. "Pennsylvania did not resist New Deal": Burnham, *Critical Elections*, 34–70; "state's electoral movements": Burnham, *Critical Elections*, 65.

20. Mayhew, *Placing Parties in American Politics*, 55–64.

21. *Pittsburgh Press*, Nov. 4, 1962, A1, A5.

22. Interview with Congressman Bob Borski (D-Pa., 3rd.), June 24, 1992.

23. Frank Sorauf, *Party and Representation: Legislative Politics in Pennsylvania* (New York: Atherton Press, 1963), 15.

24. Interview with Congressman Robert Walker (R-Pa., 16th), Aug. 5, 1992.

25. "Ertel worked hard to connect Thornburgh" and "Ertel offered economic redevelopment strategy": *Pittsburgh Press*, Nov. 3, 1982, A1, A16; "[Ertel's] other tactics": *Philadelphia Inquirer*, Nov. 2, 1982, B8.

26. *Philadelphia Inquirer*, Nov. 4, 1990, 1B, 4B.

27. Ibid. See quote from political scientist Michael Young, 4B.

28. "One conservative Lancaster County activist wrote": ibid., 4B; "Republican officials removed [Hafer's] name": *Philadelphia Inquirer*, Nov. 7, 1990, 1A, 15A.

29. James Eisenstein and Michael King, "Pennsylvania: A Close Two-Party Balance," *Comparative State Politics Newsletter* 3, no. 6 (Dec. 1982): 3–6.

30. Axelrod, "Where the Votes Come From."

31. Bernard R. Berelson, Paul F. Lazarsfeld, and William N. McPhee, *Voting: A Study of Opinion Formation in a Presidential Campaign* (Chicago: University of Chicago Press, 1954), 126.

Introduction to Part III

1. John F. Bibby, "State House Elections at Midterm," in *The American Election of 1982*, ed. Thomas Mann and Norman Ornstein (Washington, D.C.: American Enterprise Institute, 1983), 117.

2. Key, *Southern Politics in State and Nation*.

Chapter 5. Candidate-Centered Politics in the Desert Southwest: New Mexico and Arizona

1. A recent New Mexico survey asked, "If people like them 'have any say in New Mexico politics,' an overwhelming 73% thought they did." Still, the same research report concluded that "complexity of political issues addressed in New Mexico—including groundwater contamination, WIPP [Waste Isolation Pilot Plant], economic development and other issues seems occasionally to make New Mexicans unsure about what they want to do with their political clout" (University of New Mexico Institute for Public Policy, *Quarterly Profile of New Mexico Citizens*, Fall–Winter 1988).

2. University of New Mexico Institute for Public Policy, *Quarterly Profile of New Mexico Citizens*, Summer–Fall 1991.

3. Jack Holmes, *Politics in New Mexico* (Albuquerque: University of New Mexico Press, 1967), 118–30.

4. Clive S. Thomas, ed. *Politics and Public Policy in the Contemporary American West* (Albuquerque: University of New Mexico Press, 1991), 501.

5. Holmes, *Politics in New Mexico*, 119.

6. Interview with Congressman Steve Schiff (R-N.M., 1st), Feb. 8, 1990.

7. Mario Barrera, *Race and Class in the Southwest: A Theory of Racial Inequality* (South Bend, Ind.: University of Notre Dame Press, 1979).

8. University of New Mexico Institute for Public Policy, *Quarterly Profile of New Mexico Citizens,* Winter 1989–90.

9. "Parties did not do good job": University of New Mexico Institute for Public Policy, *Quarterly Profile of New Mexico Citizens* 4 (Summer 1992): "regulatory and redistributive nature": Peter Galderisi et al., eds., *The Politics of Realignment: Party Change in the Mountain West* (Boulder: Westview Press, 1987).

10. Interview with Congressman Joe Skeen (R-N.M., 2nd), Feb. 6, 1990.

11. Interview with Congressman Steve Schiff (R-N.M., 1st), Feb. 8, 1990.

12. Ibid.

13. Mayhew, *Placing Parties in American Politics,* 181.

14. I rely on accounts of the campaigns from the *Albuquerque Journal* and the Santa Fe *New Mexican,* various dates and years.

15. Frank Jonas, "The 1962 Elections in the West," *Western Political Quarterly* 16 (June 1963): 375–85.

16. As in chapter 3, income is measured by county-level median family income figures from the 1960, 1970, 1980, and 1990 U.S. censuses. Race is measured as the percentage of the county population that is non-Caucasian. Manufacturing is measured as the percentage of the county work force employed in manufacturing. Urbanization is measured as the percentage of the county population residing in an urban area.

17. *New Mexican,* Nov. 3, 1982, A1, A7.

18. Ibid.

19. *CBS News/New York Times Election Day Surveys,* 1982.

20. *Albuquerque Journal,* Nov. 4, 1990, A1, A8; ibid., Nov. 7, 1990, A1.

21. Tom Sharpe, "King's Loyal Following," *Hispanic,* June 1991, 44–46.

22. As in chapters 3 and 4, class is measured on a six-point scale. Race is coded 1 for black or Hispanic, 0 for Caucasian. Labor is coded 0 for nonunion household, 1 for union household.

23. Interview with Congressman Bob Stump (R-Ariz., 3rd), and Lisa Jackson, Stump's administrative assistant and state director, Aug. 8, 1989.

24. "Arizonans are independent": interview with Congressman Bob Stump (R-Ariz., 3rd), and Lisa Jackson, Stump's administrative assistant and state director, Aug. 8, 1989; "Peyser's switch a 'metamorphosis'": John Mark Hansen, *Gaining Access: Congress and the Farm Lobby, 1919–1981* (Chicago: University of Chicago Press, 1991), 196–200.

25. Key, *American State Politics.*

26. Bruce Babbitt, as quoted by David Berman, "The Arizona Pattern," in *Party Realignment in State Politics* ed. Maureen Moakley (Columbus: Ohio State University Press, 1992), 52; "Jackson emphasized Stump's conservativism": interview with Congressman Bob Stump (R-Ariz., 3rd), and Lisa Jackson, Stump's administrative assistant and state director, Aug. 8, 1989.

27. Elmer R. Rusco, "Voting Behavior in Arizona" (Reno: Bureau of Governmental Research, University of Nevada, 1967).

28. Interview with Bob Stump (R-Ariz., 3rd), and Lisa Jackson, Stump's administrative assistant and state director, Aug. 8, 1989.

29. Ross R. Rice, "Recent Legislative Politics in Arizona," *Western Political Quarterly* 17 (Sept. 1964), 69–70.

30. Mayhew, *Placing Parties in American Politics.*

31. "United party organizations": Ross R. Rice, "Arizona: Politics in Transition," in *Politics in the American West*, ed. Frank Jonas (Salt Lake City: University of Utah Press, 1969), 41–72; "patronage is dispensed by individuals": David Berman, "The Arizona Pattern," in *Party Realignment and State Politics*, ed. Moakley, 53.

32. "Presence of large numbers of Indians:" Elmer R. Rusco, "Voting Behavior in Arizona" (Reno: Bureau of Governmental Research, University of Nevada: 1967), 27; Conrad Joyner, "The 1962 Election in Arizona," *Western Political Quarterly* 16 (June 1963), 390–95.

33. For Arizona's divisive state issues, I rely on newspaper accounts of the election from Phoenix's *Arizona Republic* and the Tucson papers, *Arizona Daily Citizen* and *Arizona Daily Star*; "school aid has been an issue," Rice, "Recent Legislative Politics in Arizona," in *Western Political Quarterly*.

34. David Berman, "The Arizona Pattern," in *Party Realignment and State Politics*, ed. Moakley, 35–55.

35. "[Goddard] lacked complete support of his party": Joyner, "The 1962 Election in Arizona." Republicans did not campaign together either. Barry Goldwater was one of many to rely on campaign management that, while being Republican, came from outside the state's political party machinery. "Goddard put Hayden and Udall's name on his advertising": Joyner, "The 1962 Election in Arizona."

36. Rice, "Arizona: Politics in Transition."

37. For the classic statement on the difference between position issues and valence issues, see Stokes, "Voting and the Party System," 161–79.

38. Ruth S. Jones, "Arizona Gubernatorial Politics: 1982," in *Re-electing the Governor: the 1982 Elections*, ed. Thad L. Beyle (Lanham, Md.: University Press of America, 1986), 33–50.

39. Ibid., 37.

40. *Los Angeles Times*, Apr. 24, 1990, A24.

41. "To get [Goddard's] name out to strong Democrat areas": Glen Craney, "Mechem Comeback Attempt Enlivens Primary Scene," *Congressional Quarterly Weekly Report*, Sept. 1, 1990, 2795; "Goddard and Symington had swapped some blocs of support": *Arizona Republic*, Nov. 7, 1990, A13.

42. *Los Angeles Times*, Nov. 18, 1990, C14.

43. Ibid.

44. David Berman, "The Arizona Pattern," 53–54.

45. *Arizona Republic*, Nov. 4, 1982, A8.

46. Key, *American State Politics*, 179.

47. Brown, *Migration and Politics*, 151–52.

48. Martin P. Wattenberg, *The Rise of Candidate-Centered Politics* (Cambridge, Mass.: Harvard University Press, 1991), 30.

Chapter 6. Panning for Partisans in a Turbulent Environment: California

1. Earl Warren as told to Frank J. Taylor, "California's Biggest Headache," *Saturday Evening Post*, Aug. 14, 1948, 20–21, 72, 74. Also quoted in *The Politics of California*, ed. David Farrelly and Ivan Hinderaker (New York: Ronald Press, 1951).

2. Interview with Congressman Vic Fazio (D-Calif., 4th), Oct. 6, 1992.

3. Spencer C. Olin, "Globalization and the Politics of Locality," *Western Historical Quarterly* 22, no. 2 (May 1991): 143–59.

4. Allen J. Scott, *Metropolis: From the Division of Labor to Urban Form* (Berkeley: University of California Press, 1988), 189. Also, Spencer C. Olin, "Globalization and the Politics of Locality: Orange County, California, in the Cold War Era," *Western Historical Quarterly* 22, no. 2 (May 1991): 143–61.

5. "Employment in manufacturing": statistics on employment and earnings are drawn from the

U.S. Department of Commerce, Bureau of the Census, *Summary of Economic Statistics,* Table 10 (Washington, D.C.: U.S. Government Printing Office, 1992) and *County and City Extra* (Lanham, Md.: Bernan Press, 1992); interview with Congressman Vic Fazio (D-Calif., 4th), Oct. 6, 1992.

6. Dean R. Cresap, *Party Politics in the Golden State* (Los Angeles: The Haynes Foundation, 1954).

7. Interview with Congressman Vic Fazio (D-Calif., 4th), Oct. 6, 1992.

8. Bud Lembke, "The Growing Grey Market in Political Slate Mailers," *California Journal* 14, no. 1 (January 1983): 13–16.

9. James Fay and Kay Lawson, "Is California Going Republican?" in *Party Realignment and State Politics,* ed. Moakley, 17–34. Also, John C. Syer and John H. Culver, *Power and Politics in California,* 4th ed. (New York: Macmillan, 1992), 122.

10. Fenton, *Midwest Politics;* on the extent to which machine cities adopted reforms, see James Gimpel, "Reform-Resistant and Reform Adopting Machines: The Electoral Foundations of Urban Politics, 1910–1930," *Political Research Quarterly* 46, no. 2 (June 1993): 371–82. Also, John Buenker, *Urban Liberalism and Progressive Reform* (New York: Scribner's, 1973).

11. Interview with Congressman Vic Fazio (D-Calif., 4th), Oct. 6, 1992.

12. Don M. Muchmore, "Party and Candidate in California," in *The Politics of California,* ed. Farrelly and Hinderaker.

13. Several of the mountain and western states exceeded this 13 percent in-migration rate. None of the middle Atlantic or midwestern states approached this figure.

14. Brown, *Migration and Politics.*

15. Spencer C. Olin, "Globalization and the Politics of Locality," *Western Historical Quarterly* 22, no. 2 (May 1991): 143–61.

16. See James Q. Wilson, *The Amateur Democrat* (Chicago: University of Chicago Press, 1962).

17. Interview with Senator Alan Cranston (D-Calif.), Aug. 5, 1989.

18. Much of this discussion is drawn from several sources including Leonard Rowe, *Preprimary Endorsements in California Politics* (Berkeley: University of California: Bureau of Public Administration, 1961); Francis Carney, *The Rise of the Democratic Clubs in California* (New York: Henry Holt, 1958); Hugh A. Bone, "New Party Associations in the West" *American Political Science Review* 45 (Dec. 1951): 1115–25; Currin V. Shields, "A Note on Party Organization: The Democrats of California," *Western Political Quarterly* 7 (June 1954): 673–83.

19. Rowe, *Preprimary Endorsements in California,* 45.

20. "Clubs populated mainly by younger voters": Carney, *The Rise of the Democratic Clubs;* "movement was distinct from the national Democratic party": Carney, *The Rise of the Democratic Clubs.*

21. T. G. Harris, "California's New Politics: Big Daddy's Big Drive," *Look* 26, no. 19 (Sept. 25, 1962): 78–81.

22. Ibid.

23. Carney, *The Rise of the Democratic Clubs.*

24. Interview with Senator Alan Cranston (D-Calif.), Aug. 5, 1989.

25. Ibid.

26. Interview with Congressman Vic Fazio (D-Calif., 4th), Oct. 6, 1992.

27. "Issues in the campaign": for accounts of the race, I rely on press reports from the *Los Angeles Times, Fresno Bee, Sacramento Bee,* and *San Francisco Chronicle,* various dates in 1962; "Brown advocated a conservation program": *San Francisco Chronicle,* Nov. 3, 1962, 7.

28. "Nixon charged that Brown forces had falsely accused him": *San Francisco Chronicle,* Nov. 6, 1962, 1, 18; "Haldeman filed suit": ibid., Nov. 3, 1962, 7.

29. "Will It Be Brown or Nixon?" *Newsweek,* Oct. 29, 1962, 19–23.

30. James N. Gregory, *American Exodus* (New York: Oxford University Press, 1989).

31. In 1960, the Democratic registration edge was 18.3 percent. Registration figures, however, are a questionable guide to actual partisan voting, since changes in the state's electoral codes during the 1970s now prevent the purging of "deadwood" from the registration rolls. See John H. Culver, "The Transformation of the California Electorate," paper presented at the 1992 annual meeting of the Western Political Science Association, San Franicisco, March 19–21, 1992.

32. *Fresno Bee,* Nov. 1, 1982, A1, A20.

33. For accounts on the issues of the race, I rely on press reports from the *San Francisco Chronicle, Los Angeles Times, Fresno Bee,* and *Sacramento Bee,* various dates in 1982.

34. *Los Angeles Times,* Oct. 18, 1982, 1, 3, 18–20; ibid., Oct. 19, 1982, 2–3, 16.

35. *San Francisco Chronicle,* Oct. 30, 1982, 16, 24.

36. See press coverage on the 1990 gubernatorial race between Pete Wilson and Dianne Feinstein in the *Los Angeles Times,* Oct. 7, 1970, D1.

37. *San Francisco Chronicle,* Oct. 30, 1982, 16, 24.

38. "Booker editorialized": Simeon Booker, "Washington Notebook," *Ebony* 37, no. 7 (May 5, 1982): 26; "Bradley understood": *Los Angeles Times,* Oct. 21, 1982, 2–3, 24–26.

39. *Fresno Bee,* Nov. 3, 1982, A10.

40. *Los Angeles Times,* Nov. 1, 1990, A1.

41. *CBS News/New York Times Election Day Exit Polls,* 1990.

42. James N. Gregory, *American Exodus* (New York: Oxford University Press, 1989).

43. Brown, *Migration and Politics;* Wattenberg, *The Rise of Candidate-Centered Politics.*

Chapter 7. Where Federalism Is a Solvent of Party: The Pacific Northwest

1. See Daniel M. Ogden, "The 1954 Elections in Washington," *Western Political Quarterly* 7 (Dec. 1954): 629–32; Hugh A. Bone, "Washington State: Free Style Politics," in *Politics in the American West,* ed. Jonas.

2. Bogue and Beale, *Economic Areas of the United States,* 1092–93.

3. Recent press accounts from the 1992 Washington State Republican convention suggested that right-wing abortion opponents had concentrated on dominating the power positions in the state Republican party. These same reports also indicated a dearth of qualified anti-abortion candidates. See Bellvue *Journal American,* June 19, 1992, A1, A5; ibid., June 24, 1992, 1.

4. Interview with Congressman Sid Morrison (R-Wash., 4th) and Gretchen White, Morrison's administrative assistant and state director, Nov. 20, 1989.

5. Interview with Congressman John Miller (R-Wash., 1st), Feb. 1, 1990.

6. Interview with Congressman Sid Morrison (R-Wash., 4th) and Gretchen White, Morrison's administrative assistant and state director, Nov. 20, 1989.

7. "Brett Bader claimed": Tacoma *News Tribune,* June 20, 1992, A12; "'off-base' and reckless": Spokane *Spokesman-Review,* June 21, 1992, 1; "Chandler denounced right-wing takeover": Bellvue *Journal American,* June 24, 1992, A1, A6.

8. Interview with Congressman John Miller (R-Wash., 1st), Feb. 1, 1990.

9. Ibid.

10. I rely on press accounts on the races from the Seattle *Post-Intelligencer,* Olympia *Olympian,* and Spokane *Spokesman-Review,* various issues and dates in 1960.

11. Seattle *Post-Intelligencer,* Nov. 3, 1960, 3.

12. Bone, "Washington State: Free Style Politics," 381–416.

13. I rely on news accounts of the race from the Seattle *Post-Intelligencer,* Spokane *Spokesman Review,* and Olympia *Olympian,* various dates in 1980.

14. *Seattle Post-Intelligencer,* Nov. 2, 1980, A20.

15. Paul Hagner and William F. Mullen, "Washington: More Republican, Yes; More Conservative, No," *Social Science Journal* 8, no. 3 (October 1981), 115–29.

16. Hugh A. Bone, "Washington State: Electoral Upsets," *Comparative State Politics Newsletter* 3, no. 6 (Dec. 1982): 44–45.

17. Interview with Senator Mark O. Hatfield (R-Oreg.), July 28, 1989.

18. "Oregon's economy is neither as strong nor as diverse": Lester Seligman, "A Prefatory Study of Leadership Selection in Oregon," *Western Political Quarterly* 12 (March 1959): 153–67; "one-third of Oregon's manufacturing jobs": Barbara Roberts, *Oregon Bluebook,* 1989–1990 (Salem: State of Oregon, 1989), 258–59. Also cited is Sheldon Kamieniecki, Matthew A. Cahn, and Eugene R. Goss, "Western Governments and Environmental Policy," in *Politics and Public Policy in the Contemporary American West,* ed. Clive S. Thomas (Albuquerque: University of New Mexico Press, 1991), 479–97.

19. Bogue and Beale, *Economic Areas of the United States,* 964.

20. Interview with David Henderson, state director for Congressman Denny Smith (R-Oreg., 5th), July 26, 1989.

21. "Goldschmidt won the governorship": interview with David Henderson, July 26, 1989; "Goldschmidt's politics": Barone and Ujifusa, *The Almanac of American Politics, 1990,* 1002.

22. Seligman, "A Prefatory Study of Leadership Selection in Oregon."

23. Ibid., 153–67.

24. Maure L. Goldschmidt, "The 1952 Elections in Oregon," *Western Political Quarterly* 12 (March 1953): 123–26. See also Robert E. Burton, *The Democrats of Oregon: The Pattern of Minority Politics, 1900–1956* (Eugene: University of Oregon Press, 1970).

25. Interview with Senator Mark O. Hatfield (R-Oreg.), July 28, 1989.

26. Ibid.

27. John M. Swarthout, "The 1958 Election in Oregon," *Western Political Quarterly* 12 (March 1959): 328–44.

28. Ibid.

29. Travis Cross, "The 1958 Hatfield Campaign in Oregon," *Western Political Quarterly* 12 (June 1959), 568–71.

30. Portland *Oregonian,* Nov. 4, 1962, 46.

31. I rely on newspaper accounts from the Eugene *Register-Guard,* Salem *Statesman,* and Portland *Oregonian,* various dates in 1982.

32. *Oregonian,* Nov. 4, 1990, B3.

33. *Oregonian,* Nov. 7, 1990, A9.

34. David B. Truman, "Federalism and the Party System," in *Federalism: Mature and Emergent,* ed. Arthur W. MacMahon (Garden City, N.Y.: Doubleday, 1955), 115–36.

35. Owens, "Pattern and Structure," 373–92.

36. Bone, "Washington State: Free Style Politics."

37. Key, *American State Politics,* 272.

Chapter 8. Sectionalism Disrupts the Party System: Idaho

1. For a thorough analysis specifically addressing the state's electoral parties at midcentury, see Herman J. Lujan, "Voting Behavior in Idaho 1950–1962: A Study of Party Predisposition at the Precinct Level," Ph.D. diss., University of Idaho, 1964. Also, Robert H. Blank, *Regional Diversity of Political Values: Idaho Political Cultures* (Washington, D.C.: University Press of America, 1978). On political cleavages in the Idaho legislature, see Stephanie L. Witt and Gary Moncrief, "Religion and Roll Call Voting in Idaho," *American Politics Quarterly* 21, no. 1 (Jan. 1993): 140–49.

2. Bogue and Beale, *Economic Areas of the United States,* 625.

3. Ibid.

4. Robert H. Blank, *Individualism in Idaho* (Pullman: Washington State University Press, 1988), 73.

5. Key, *Southern Politics in State and Nation.*

6. Boyd A. Martin, "Idaho: The Sectional State," in *Politics in the American West,* ed. Jonas, 181–200.

7. Interview with Congressman Richard Stallings (D-Idaho, 2nd), Feb. 20, 1990.

8. Since exact Mormon population figures are unavailable, I used a dummy variable in the equation coding the presence of Mormon influence *1* and the absence *0*; "Mormon influence on gubernatorial vote": Lujan, "Voting Behavior in Idaho."

9. Ibid., 103–04.

10. Ibid., 104.

11. Interview with Congressman Richard Stallings (D-Idaho, 2nd), Feb. 20, 1990.

12. Lujan, "Voting Behavior in Idaho," 123.

13. "Conservative Democrats from southern regions": for accounts of the race, I rely on press coverage from Boise's *Idaho Statesman;* "party support for Smith": Lujan, "Voting Behavior in Idaho," 124.

14. *Idaho Statesman,* Nov. 4, 1962, 2, 4.

15. Lujan, "Voting Behavior in Idaho," 175.

16. I rely on press accounts for descriptions of the issues in the race.

17. *Idaho Statesman,* Nov. 6, 1990, 1A.

18. A 1986 poll of Idaho voters showed that Democratic state legislative candidates led Republican candidates by eleven points among labor union households (University of Idaho, Bureau of Public Affairs Research, Decision Making Information, *Telephone Survey of Registered Voters in the State of Idaho,* Jan. 1986).

Chapter 9. Conclusions: Competition and the Sources of
Party Unity in State Politics

1. John Buenker, *Urban Liberalism and Progressive Reform* (New York: Charles Scribner's Sons, 1973); James Gimpel, "Reform-Resistant and Reform-Adopting Machines: The Electoral Foundations of Urban Politics 1910–1930," *Political Research Quarterly* 46, no. 2 (June 1993): 371–82.

2. Frank Munger, "Comparative State Politics," in *American State Politics,* ed. Munger (New York: Thomas Y. Crowell, 1966), 373–82. Among the two-party states with systemwide party competition, Munger lists California, Nevada, Montana, Utah, Idaho, Oregon, and Washington; John F. Bibby et al., "Parties in State Politics," in *Politics in the American States,* 4th ed., ed. Virginia Gray, Herbert Jacob and Kenneth N. Vines (Boston: Little, Brown, 1983), 59–96. These authors classify Colorado, Wyoming, Washington, Arizona, and Idaho as two-party competitive states for 1974–1980; California, Oregon, Arizona, Nevada, Washington, Montana, Idaho, Colorado, and Wyoming are all listed as two-party competitive for the 1965–1988 period (Jewell and Olson, *Political Parties*).

3. Jewell and Olson, *Political Parties,* 256–60.

4. Key, *American State Politics,* 24–25.

5. Washington State is excluded because it does not hold elections in off years.

6. Paul Allen Beck, "Party Realignment in America: A View from the States," in *Party Realignment and State Politics,* ed. Moakley, 259–78.

Bibliography

Arrington, Leonard. "The New Deal in the West: A Preliminary Statistical Inquiry." *Pacific Historical Review* 38 (August 1969): 311–16.

Axelrod, Robert. "Where the Votes Come From: An Analysis of Electoral Coalitions, 1952–1968." *American Political Science Review* 66 (1972): 11–20.

Barone, Michael, and Ujifusa, Grant. *The Almanac of American Politics*. Washington, D.C.: National Journal, 1988.

Barnard, Chester. *The Functions of the Executive*. Cambridge: Harvard University Press, 1938.

Barrera, Mario. *Race and Class in the Southwest: A Theory of Racial Inequality*. Notre Dame: University of Notre Dame Press, 1979.

Beck, Paul Allen. "Partisan Dealignment in the Post–War South," *American Political Science Review* 71 (1977): 477–96.

Bensel, Richard. *Sectionalism and American Political Development 1880–1980*. Madison: University of Wisconsin Press, 1984.

Berelson, Bernard, et al. *Voting*. Chicago: University of Chicago Press, 1954.

Bibby, John F. "State House Elections at Midterm." In *The Elections of 1982*, ed. Thomas E. Mann and Norman Ornstein. Washington, D.C.: American Enterprise Institute for Public Policy Research, 1982: 111–32.

Blank, Robert H. *Regional Diversity of Political Values: Idaho Political Cultures*. Washington, D.C.: University Press of America, 1979.

Blank, Robert H. *Individualism in Idaho*. Pullman: Washington State University Press, 1988.

Blydenburgh, John. "Party Organizations." In *Politics in New Jersey*, ed. Alan Rosenthal and John Bludenburgh. New Brunswick: Rutgers University, 1975.

Booker, Simeon. "Washington Notebook." *Ebony* 37, no.7 (May 5, 1982): 26.

Bogue, Donald and Calvin Beale. *Economic Areas of the United States*. Glencoe, Ill.: The Free Press, 1961.

Bone, Hugh A. "New Party Associations in the West." *American Political Science Review* 45 (Dec. 1951): 1115–25.

——. "Political Parties in New York City." *American Political Science Review* 40 (Apr. 1946): 272–82.

Brown, Courtney. "Voter Mobilization and Party Competition in a Volatile Electorate." *American Sociological Review* 52 (1987): 59–72.

Brown, Thad A. *Migration and Politics*. Chapel Hill: The University of North Carolina Press, 1988.

Burnham, Walter Dean. *Critical Elections and the Mainsprings of American Politics*. New York: W. W. Norton, 1970.

Burton, Robert E. *Democrats of Oregon: The Pattern of Minority Politics, 1900–1956*. Eugene: University of Oregon Press, 1970.

Campbell, Angus, et al., eds. *Elections and the Political Order*. New York: John Wiley, 1966.

Carney, Francis. *The Rise of the Democratic Clubs in California*. New York: Henry Holt, 1958.

Chambers, William Nisbet, and Walter Dean Burnham. *The American Party Systems: Stages of Political Development*. New York: Oxford University Press, 1967.

Chester, Edward W. *Issues and Responses in State Political Experience*. Totowa, N.J.: Littlefield, Adams, 1968.

Chubb, John E. "Institutions, the Economy and the Dynamics of State Elections." *American Political Science Review* 82 (Mar. 1988): 133–52.

Clubb, Jerome, and Howard Allen. *Electoral Change and Stability in American Political History*. New York: The Free Press, 1971.

Connery, Robert H., and Gerald Benjamin. *Rockefeller of New York*. Ithaca: Cornell University Press, 1979.

Cotter, Cornelius, et al. *Party Organizations in American Politics*. New York: Praeger, 1984.

Cresap, Dean R. *Party Politics in the Golden State*. Los Angeles: The Haynes Foundation, 1954.

Culver, John H. "The Transformation of the California Electorate"Paper delivered at the 1992 annual meeting of the Western Political Science Association, San Francisco, March 19–20, 1992.

Daley, Michael. "Lew's Labors Lost." *New Republic* 187, no. 18 (Nov. 8, 1982): 11–12.

David, Paul T. *Party Strength in the United States*. Charlottesville: University Press of Virginia, 1972.

Downs, Anthony. *An Economic Theory of Democracy*. New York: Harper, 1957.

Eisenstein, James, and Michael King. "Pennsylvania: A Close Two-Party Balance." *Comparative State Politics Newsletter* 3 (Dec. 1992): 3–6.

Eismeier, Theodore. "Votes and Taxes: The Political Economy of the American Governorship." *Polity* 15 (Spring 1983): 368–79.

Fenton, John. *Midwest Politics*. New York: Holt, Rinehart, Winston, 1965.

Foster, Mark S. "Frank Hague of Jersey City: The Boss as Reformer." *New Jersey History* 86 (Summer 1968): 106–16.

Galderisi, Peter, et al., eds. *The Politics of Realignment: Party Change in the Mountain West*. Boulder: Westview Press, 1987.

Greenstone, J. David. *Labor in American Politics*. New York: Vintage Books, 1970.

Gregory, James N. *American Exodus*. New York: Oxford University Press, 1989.

Hagner, Paul, and William F. Mullen. "Washington: More Republican, Yes; More Conservative, No." *Social Science Journal* 18, no. 3 (Oct. 1981): 115–29.

Hansen, John Mark. *Gaining Access: Congress and the Farm Lobby, 1919–1981.* Chicago: University of Chicago Press, 1991.

Harris, T. G. "California's New Politics: Big Daddy's Big Drive." *Look* 26, no. 19 (Sept. 25, 1962): 78–81.

Hichborn, Franklin. "The Party, the Machine and the Vote: The Story of Crossfiling in California Politics, Part I." *California Historical Society Quarterly* 28 (Dec. 1959): 349–57.

——. "The Party, the Machine and the Vote: The Story of Crossfiling in California Politics, Part II." *California Historical Society Quarterly* 29 (Mar. 1960): 19–34.

Hill, G. H. "Do-or-Die for Nixon," *Saturday Evening Post,* May 12, 1962, 17–25.

Huckshorn, Robert, et al.,"Party Integration and Party Organization Strength." *Journal of Politics* 48 (1986): 976–91.

Huntington, Samuel P. "Political Development and Political Decay," *World Politics* 27 (1965): 386–430.

Ingram, Helen, et al. *A Policy Approach to Political Representation.* Baltimore: Johns Hopkins University Press, 1980.

Jewell, Malcolm, and David M. Olson. *Political Parties and Elections in American States,* 3rd ed. Chicago: Dorsey Press, 1988.

Johnson, Allen. "The Nationalizing Influence of Party." *The Yale Review* 15 (November 1906): 283–92.

Jonas, Frank, ed. *Politics in the American West.* Salt Lake City: University of Utah Press, 1969.

——. "The 1962 Elections in the West." *Western Political Quarterly* 16 (June 1963): 375–85.

Joyner, Conrad. "The 1962 Election in Arizona." *Western Political Quarterly* 16 (June 1963): 390–95.

Kayden, Xandra, and Eddie Mahe, Jr. *The Party Goes On.* New York: Basic Books, 1985.

Keith, Bruce E., et al. *The Myth of the Independent Voter.* Berkeley: University of California Press, 1992.

Key, V. O. *American State Politics: An Introduction.* New York: Alfred A. Knopf, 1956.

——. *Parties, Politics and Pressure Groups.* New York: Thomas Crowell, 1956.

——. *Southern Politics in State and Nation.* New York: Alfred A. Knopf, 1949.

Kingdon, John. "Politicians' Beliefs About Voters," *American Political Science Review* 61 (1967): 137–45.

Kleppner, Paul. *The Cross of Culture.* New York: Free Press, 1970.

Kleppner, Paul. "Politics Without Parties." In *The Twentieth–Century West: Historical Interpretations,* ed. Gerald D. Nash and Richard W. Etulain. Albuquerque: University of New Mexico Press, 1989.

——. "Voters and Parties in the Western States: 1876–1900." *Western Historical Quarterly* 13 (Jan. 1982): 49–68.

Kousser, J. Morgan. "Ecological Regression and the Analysis of Past Politics." *Journal of Interdisciplinary History* 4 (Autumn 1973): 237–62.

Kramer, Michael. "Who Is This Guy Lew Lehrman?" *New York,* Apr. 5, 1982, 24–27.

Lembke, Bud. "The Growing Grey Market in Political Slate Mailers." *California Journal* 14 (Jan. 1983): 13–16.

Ladd, Everett Carl, and Charles Hadley. *Transformations of the American Party System.* New York: W. W. Norton, 1975.

Lockard, Duane. *New England State Politics.* Princeton: Princeton University Press, 1959.

Lujan, Herman. "Voting Behavior in Idaho, 1950–1962: A Study of Party Predisposition at the Precinct Level." Ph.D. diss., University of Idaho, 1964.

Mann, Thomas E., and Norman Ornstein, eds. *The Elections of 1982.* Washington, D.C.: American Enterprise Institute for Public Policy Research, 1982.

Mayhew, David R. *Congress: The Electoral Connection.* New Haven: Yale University Press, 1974.

——. *Party Loyalty Among Congressmen.* Cambridge: Harvard University Press, 1966.

——. *Placing Parties in American Politics.* Princeton: Princeton University Press, 1986.

McConnell, Grant. *Private Power and American Democracy.* New York: Knopf, 1966.

Medler, Jerry, and Alvin Mushkatel. "Urban-Rural Class Conflict in Oregon Land–Use Planning," *Western Political Quarterly* 31, no. 3 (1979): 338–49.

Merriam, Charles, and Harold Gosnell. *The American Party System.* New York: Macmillan, 1929.

Michels, Robert. *Political Parties.* New York: Free Press, 1966.

Milburn, Josephine, and William Doyle, eds. *New England Political Parties.* Cambridge, Mass.: Schenkman, 1983.

Milbrath, Lester. "Political Participation in the States." In *Politics in the American States: A Comparative Analysis,* ed. Herbert Jacob and Kenneth Vines. Boston: Little, Brown, 1965.

Moakley, Maureen, ed., *Party Realignment and State Politics.* Columbus: Ohio State University Press, 1992.

Morehouse, Sarah McCally. *State Politics, Parties and Policy.* New York: Holt, Rinehart & Winston, 1981.

Muchmore, Don M. "Party and Candidate in California." In *The Politics of California,* ed. David Farrelly and Ivan Hinderaker. New York: Ronald Press, 1951.

Munger, Frank, ed. *American State Politics.* New York: Thomas Y. Crowell, 1966.

Mushkat, Jerome. *Tammany.* Syracuse: Syracuse University Press, 1971.

Nash, Gerald D., and Richard W. Etulain, eds. *The Twentieth–Century West: Historical Interpretations.* Albuquerque: University of New Mexico Press, 1989.

Olin, Spencer C. "Globalization and the Politics of Locality: Orange County, California, in the Cold War Era." *Western Historical Quarterly* 22 (May 1991): 143–61.

Owens, Kenneth N. "Pattern and Structure in Western Territorial Politics." *Western Historical Quarterly* 1 (Oct. 1970): 373–92.

Patterson, James. *The New Deal and the States: Federalism in Transition.* Princeton: Princeton University Press, 1969.

——. "The New Deal in the West." *Pacific Historical Review* 38 (Aug. 1969): 317–27.

Peel, Roy V. "The Political Machine of New York City." *American Political Science Review* 27 (Aug. 1933): 611–19.

Petrocik, John R. *Party Coaltiions: Realignments and the Decline of the New Deal Party System*. Chicago: University of Chicago Press, 1981.

Polsby, Nelson. "The Institutionalization of the U.S. House of Representatives." *American Political Science Review* 62 (Mar. 1968): 145.

Pomeroy, Earl. *The Pacific Slope*. New York: Alfred A. Knopf, 1965.

——. "What Remains of the West?" *Utah Historical Quarterly* 35 (Winter 1967): 37–55.

Pomper, Gerald. "Electoral Trends." In *Politics in New Jersey*, ed. Alan Rosenthal and John Blydenburgh, 31–58. New Brunswick, N.J.: Rutgers University Press, 1975.

Pomper, Gerald M., ed. *The Political State of New Jersey*. New Brunswick, N.J.: Rutgers University Press, 1986.

Rae, Douglas, and Michael Taylor. *The Analysis of Political Cleavages*. New Haven: Yale University Press, 1970.

Reidel, James A. "New York: Costly, Close Governor's Race," *Comparative State Politics Newsletter* 3 (Dec. 1982): 8–9.

Rice, Ross R. "Recent Legislative Politics in Arizona." *Western Political Quarterly* 17 (Sept. 1964): 69–70.

——. "Arizona: Politics in Transition." In *Politics in the American West*, ed. Frank Jonas, 41–72. Salt Lake City: University of Utah Press, 1969.

Rosenthal, Alan, and John Blydenburgh, eds. *Politics in New Jersey*. New Brunswick, N.J.: Rutgers University Press, 1975.

Rowe, Leonard. *Preprimary Endorsements in California Politics*. Berkeley: University of California: Bureau of Public Administration, 1961.

Rusco, Elmer R. "Voting Behavior in Arizona." Reno: University of Nevada Bureau of Governmental Research, 1966.

Scarrow, Howard. *Parties, Elections and Representation in the State of New York*. New York: New York University Press, 1983.

Schlesinger, Joseph. "On the Theory of Party Organization." *Journal of Politics* 46 (1984): 369–97.

Scott, Allen J. *Metropolis: From the Division of Labor to Urban Form*. Berkeley: University of California Press, 1988.

Scott, James. "Corruption, Machine Politics and Political Change." *American Political Science Review* 75 (December 1969): 1142–58.

Shefter, Martin. "The Emergence of a Political Machine: An Alternative View." In *Theoretical Perspectives on Urban Politics*, ed. J. David Greenstone and Paul Peterson. Englewood Cliffs, N.J.: Prentice Hall, Inc., 1975.

——. "Regional Receptivity to Reform: The Legacy of the Progressive Era." *Political Science Quarterly* 98 (Fall 1983): 459–83.

Shields, Currin V. "A Note on Party Organization: The Democrats of California." *Western Political Quarterly* 7 (June 1954): 673–83.

Simon, Dennis M. "Presidents, Governors and Electoral Accountability," *Journal of Politics* 51 (May 1989): 286–304.

Sorauf, Frank. *Party Politics in America*. 5th ed. Boston: Little, Brown, 1984.

———. *Party and Representation: Legislative Politics in Pennsylvania.* New York: Atherton Press, 1963.

Stein, Robert M. "Economic Voting for Governor and U.S. Senator: The Electoral Consequences of Federalism." *Journal of Politics* 52 (February 1990): 29–53.

Stonecash, Jeffrey. "Political Cleavage in Gubernatorial and Legislative Elections: Party Competition in New York, 1970–1982." *Western Political Quarterly* (Mar. 1989): 69–81.

———. "Observations from New York: The Limits of 50-State Studies and the Case for Case Studies." *Comparative State Politics* 12 (Aug. 1991): 1–9.

Sundquist, James. *Dynamics of the Party System.* Washington, D.C.: Brookings Institution, 1983.

Syer, John C., and John H. Culver. *Power and Politics in California,* 4th ed. New York: Macmillan, 1992.

Taylor, Frank J. "California's Biggest Headache." *Saturday Evening Post* (August 14, 1948): 20–21, 72, 74.

Thomas, Clive S., ed. *Politics and Public Policy in the Contemporary American West.* Albuquerque: University of New Mexico Press, 1991.

U.S. Department of Commerce. Bureau of the Census. *County and City Databook.* Washington, D.C.: U.S. Government Printing Office, 1960, 1962, 1972, 1983, 1988.

Wattenberg, Martin P. "The Decline of Political Partisanship in the United States: Negativity or Neutrality." *American Political Science Review* 75 (1981): 941–50.

Witt, Stephanie L., and Gary Moncrief. "Religion and Roll Call Voting in Idaho." *American Politics Quarterly* 21 (Jan. 1993): 140–49.

"Will It Be Brown or Nixon?" *Newsweek,* Oct. 29, 1962, 19–23.

Wilson, James Q. *The Amateur Democrat.* Chicago: University of Chicago Press, 1962.

Witt, Stuart. "The Legislative–Local Party Linkage in New York State." Ph.D. diss., Syracuse University, 1967.

Index